ALSO BY BART D. EHRMAN

Jesus Before the Gospels

How Jesus Became God

The Other Gospels

The Bible: A Historical and Literary Introduction

Forgery and Counterforgery

Did Jesus Exist?

The Apocryphal Gospels

Forged

Jesus, Interrupted

God's Problem

The Lost Gospel of Judas Iscariot

Peter, Paul, and Mary Magdalene

Studies in the Textual Criticism of the New Testament

Misquoting Jesus

The Apostolic Fathers

Truth and Fiction in The Da Vinci Code

A Brief Introduction to the New Testament

The New Testament:
A Historical Introduction to the Early Christian Writings

Christianity in Late Antiquity

Lost Christianities

Lost Scriptures

Jesus: Apocalyptic Prophet of the New Millennium

The Orthodox Corruption of Scripture

The Text of the Fourth Gospel in the Writings of Origen

Didymus the Blind and the Text of the Gospels

How a

Forbidden

Religion

Swept

the World

The
TRIUMPH
of
CHRIS † IANITY

Bart D. Ehrman

SIMON & SCHUSTER

New York London Toronto Sydney New Delhi

Simon & Schuster
1230 Avenue of the Americas
New York, NY 10020

First Simon & Schuster hardcover edition February 2018

SIMON & SCHUSTER and colophon are registered trademarks
of Simon & Schuster, Inc.

For information about special discounts for bulk purchases,
please contact Simon & Schuster Special Sales at 1-866-506-1949
or business@simonandschuster.com.

The Simon & Schuster Speakers Bureau can bring authors to
your live event. For more information or to book an event,
contact the Simon & Schuster Speakers Bureau at 1-866-248-3049
or visit our website at www.simonspeakers.com.

Interior design by Lewelin Polanco

Manufactured in the United States of America

10 9 8 7 6 5 4 3 2 1

Library of Congress Cataloging-in-Publication Data

Names: Ehrman, Bart D., author.
Title: The triumph of Christianity / Bart D. Ehrman.
Description: First Simon & Schuster hardcover edition. | New York : Simon &
  Schuster, 2018. | Includes bibliographical references.
Identifiers: LCCN 2016056895 | ISBN 9781501136702 (hardcover)
Subjects: LCSH: Constantine I, Emperor of Rome, –337—Influence. | Church
  history—Primitive and early church, ca. 30–600.
Classification: LCC BR180 .E47 2017 | DDC 270.1—dc23 LC record available
  at https://lccn.loc.gov/2016056895

ISBN 978-1-5011-3670-2
ISBN 978-1-5011-3672-6 (ebook)

Contents

Chapter 7   178
   Christians Under Assault: Persecution, Martyrdom, and Self-Defense

Chapter 8   217
   The First Christian Emperor

Chapter 9   243
   Conversion and Coercion: The Beginnings of a Christian Empire

Afterword   279
   Gains and Losses

Acknowledgments

I am deeply grateful to everyone who has helped me write this book. First and foremost is my brilliant and insightful wife, Sarah Beckwith, not only a partner for life but also an extraordinarily helpful reader, who has provided numerous pointers and perceptive observations. Four other scholars with deep expertise read the entire manuscript and made insightful comments: Elizabeth Clark, John Carlisle Kilgo Professor, emerita, Department of Religion, Duke University; Harold Drake, Professor of History, emeritus, University of California at Santa Barbara; Andrew Jacobs, Mary W. and J. Stanley Johnson Professor of Humanities, Scripps College; and James Rives, Kenan Eminent Professor of Classics, University of North Carolina at Chapel Hill. These are among the top scholars in the world in the fields I cover in the book. Their comments and suggestions have been invaluable to me, and they saved me from several serious faux pas. For those that remain, the fault, alas, lies with me.

I also chose to have several non-scholars read the book, and in doing so I have done something rather unusual. This will take a bit of explaining.

I started the Bart Ehrman Blog just over five years ago. The blog covers all the areas of my academic interest: the New Testament, the historical Jesus, the writings of Paul, the early Christian apocrypha, the Apostolic Fathers, the manuscript tradition of the early Christian writings, the history of Christianity during the first four centuries, and so on. I post about a thousand words a day on the blog, five to six times a week. The only hitch is that to read my posts, a person has to join the blog, and to join costs money (but not much).

I do the blog, and charge the money, in order to raise funds for those in need. Every penny goes to charities—two local to me, two international—that deal with poverty, hunger, and homelessness. The blog keeps growing, as do the moneys that we raise through it. Last year we raised $120,000. I hope to do even better this year. For those interested in joining, go to www.ehrmanblog.org.

As I have done previously, I decided to offer members of the blog a chance to read the book and make comments on it, prior to publication, in exchange for a donation of a set amount. Several members took me up on the offer. I provided them with the manuscript; they read it and made remarks; and I took their comments seriously in making my final revisions. I am deeply thankful to them all: Randy Corbet, Patty Floyd, Paul Jacobs, Jon Sedmak, Steve Sutter, Trevor Wiskus, and my two friends Gabriela Laranjeira and Bill Sutherland. I am grateful as well to blog member Jim Stevenson, for helping me think about the rates of Christian growth in the first four centuries, and especially James Bell, who provided extraordinary assistance in showing how such calculations of growth must work.

I have also had the benefit of assistance from several graduate students in the Program of Ancient Mediterranean Religions at UNC, all of them already experts in early Christian studies: Luke Drake, Andrew Hagstrom, and Shaily Patel. These are fine scholars and I am lucky to have them in my world. Special thanks go to my recently graduated PhD student Travis Proctor, now teaching at Northland College, who read the entire manuscript and made incisive comments.

This book would not have seen the light of published day if it were not for the guidance and vision of my literary agent Roger Freet, who helped me envision the project, develop it, and produce it. Roger excels at his work and enjoys a good martini and an occasional cigar. We are perfectly matched.

I also would like to thank Megan Hogan, assistant editor at Simon & Schuster, for numerous helpful comments on the manuscript. Most especially, I am grateful to my new editor, Priscilla Painton. Her passion for books and the intellectual life broadly, and for this project in particular, have been both gratifying and inspiring. Throughout the process she has given me the benefit of her keen insights, high standards, and remarkable editing talents, and I am deeply in her debt.

In the book I have cited many ancient texts and have benefited from modern translations, always acknowledged. Quotations from the Old Testament are taken from the New Revised Standard Version (slightly revised, in some instances). Translations of the New Testament are my own.

Time Line

29 BCE–14 CE—Reign of Caesar Augustus, the first Roman emperor

4 BCE—Birth of Jesus

27–30 CE—Public ministry of Jesus

30 CE—Crucifixion of Jesus

33 CE—Conversion of Paul

50–60 CE—Letters of Paul

64 CE—Fire in Rome; deaths of Peter and Paul under Emperor Nero

112 CE—Pliny's persecution of Christians; letter of Pliny to Trajan

150–60 CE—Apologies of Justin Martyr

177 CE—Apology of Athenagoras

195–225 CE—Writings of Tertullian

215–54 CE—Writings of Origen

249–51 CE—Persecutions under Emperor Decius

250–58 CE—Letters of Cyprian

257–60 CE—Persecutions under Emperor Valerian

284–305 CE—Reign of Emperor Diocletian

293 CE—Diocletian institutes the Tetrarchy

303–13 CE—The Great Persecution

311 CE—Lactantius writes *Divine Institutes*

312 CE—Conversion of Emperor Constantine

312 CE—Battle at the Milvian Bridge

313 CE—The "Edict of Milan" (cessation of persecution and full religious tolerance)

314 CE—Council of Arles (dealing with the Donatist controversy)

317 CE—Lactantius writes *Death of the Persecutors*

324 CE—Constantine defeats Licinius to become sole ruler of the empire

324 CE—Final publication of Eusebius's *Church History*

325 CE—Council of Nicaea (dealing with the Arian controversy)

330 CE—Minucius Felix writes *Octavius*

337 CE—Death of Constantine

339 CE—Eusebius writes *Life of Constantine*

341 CE—Beginning of anti-pagan legislation under Constantius II

345 CE—Firmicus Maternus writes *The Error of the Pagan Religions*

361–63 CE—Reign of Julian "the Apostate"

379–95 CE—Reign of Theodosius I

380 CE—Gregory of Nyssa writes *On the Life and Wonders of Gregory the Wonderworker*

381–92 CE—Anti-pagan legislation of Theodosius I

396 CE—Sulpicius Severus writes *Life of Saint Martin of Tours*

422 CE—Augustine writes *The City of God*

Introduction

In my junior year of college I took a course in English literature that made me understand for the first time how painful it can be to question your faith. The course introduced me to poets of the nineteenth century who were struggling with religion. Even though I was a deeply committed Christian at the time, I became obsessed with the work of the great Victorian poet of doubt, Matthew Arnold. Nowhere is Arnold's struggle expressed more succinctly and movingly than in that most famous of nineteenth-century poems, "Dover Beach." The poem recalls a brief moment from Arnold's honeymoon in 1851. While standing by an open window, overlooking the cliffs of Dover, Arnold takes in the shoreline below, mesmerized by the sights and sounds of the sea as the tide goes out:

> The sea is calm to-night.
> The tide is full, the moon lies fair
> Upon the straits;—on the French coast the light
> Gleams and is gone; the cliffs of England stand,
> Glimmering and vast, out in the tranquil bay.

He asks his bride to join him at the window to enjoy the sweet night air and to look down where the waves break upon the beach:

> Listen! You hear the grating roar
> Of pebbles which the waves draw back, and fling,
> At their return, up the high strand,
> Begin, and cease, and then again begin,
> With tremulous cadence slow, and bring
> The eternal note of sadness in.

This is the sound, he notes, that Sophocles described many centuries before, in his play *Antigone*—a sound that made the Greek dramatist think of the "turbid ebb and flow / Of human misery." The sound gives Arnold a thought as well, but one quite different and particularly attuned to his age. For Arnold the retreating sea is a sad metaphor for the Christian faith, ebbing from his world and leaving a naked shoreline in its wake.

There was a time, he wistfully recalls, when the world was comfortably filled to the full with faith:

> The Sea of Faith
> Was once, too, at the full, and round earth's shore
> Lay like the folds of a bright girdle furl'd.

But that sea too is now retreating, and one can hear the sucking sound as it pulls back from the shore:

> But now I only hear
> Its melancholy, long, withdrawing roar,
> Retreating, to the breath
> Of the night-wind, down the vast edges drear
> And naked shingles of the world.

For Arnold, the modern, educated person no longer has the comforts of religion, the presence of an all-powerful and loving divinity, or the redemption provided by a Son of God who has come into the world to save those who are lost. In the void left by the withdrawal of the Christian faith, all that remains is a confusing and chaotic emptiness, filled only in part by the presence of others, the people we love and cherish who can join us through the uncertainties, pains, and anxieties of life. And so he concludes his poem:

> Ah, love, let us be true
> To one another! For the world, which seems
> To lie before us like a land of dreams,
> So various, so beautiful, so new,
> Hath really neither joy, nor love, nor light,
> Nor certitude, nor peace, nor help for pain.
> And we are here as on a darkling plain
> Swept with confused alarms of struggle and flight,
> Where ignorant armies clash by night.

Here is a world of profound and disastrous mayhem and confusion—a struggle of armies fighting to the death, in the dark, with no joy, peace, or certainty. In this void we have only are our friends, companions, and loves: "Ah, love, let us be true to one another."

"Dover Beach," and other poems of its era, resonated with me as a young college student because I was beginning to move through my own nineteenth century. In my liberal arts education I had begun learning about the geological and biological sciences, philosophy, critical thinking, and intellectual history—all of which posed problems for my faith, much as they had for the intellectuals of Arnold's era. And I too found my emerging doubts deeply disturbing.

Now, forty years later, I have a different perspective on these nineteenth-century struggles. Rather than experiencing them personally as a Christian, I look on them as a historian specializing in the study of religion. Even though I myself am no long at sea, I can empathize with those who have been racked with doubt and uncertainty, forced to reconsider and even abandon their faith, not simply since the rise of modernity but throughout history.

THE CHRISTIAN REVOLUTION

In the first four Christian centuries, the religions of the Roman Empire came under assault by those proposing a new faith, declaring that only the worship of the god of Jesus could be considered true religion. As Christianity spread, it destroyed the other religions in its wake, religions that had been practiced for millennia and that were simply assumed, everywhere and by everyone, to be good and true. But Christians insisted they were evil and false. For those reluctant to accept these claims—or even those unsure of what to believe—this transition was no less agonizing than that of Victorians living centuries later.

The Christian revolution proved far more massive and its triumph far more enduring than the skepticism that emerged as a counterforce in the nineteenth century. Even though many Victorians experienced radical doubt, or left the faith altogether, the Christian tradition did not disappear. There are still two billion Christians in the world. By way of contrast, in antiquity, when Christianity succeeded in taking over the Roman Empire, any pagan religions left in its wake were merely isolated and scattered vestiges of ancient "superstition."

The ancient triumph of Christianity proved to be the single greatest cultural transformation our world has ever seen. Without it the entire history of Late Antiquity would not have happened as it did. We would never have had the Middle Ages, the Reformation, the Renaissance, or modernity as we know it. There could never have been a Matthew Arnold. Or any of the Victorian poets. Or any of the other authors of our canon: no Milton, no Shakespeare, no Chaucer. We would have had none of our revered artists: Michelangelo, Leonardo da Vinci, or Rembrandt. And none of our brilliant composers: Mozart, Handel, or Bach. To be sure, we would have had other Miltons, Michelangelos, and Mozarts in their places, and it is impossible to know whether these would have been better or worse. But they would have been incalculably different.

By conquering the Roman world, and then the entire West,

Christianity not only gave rise to a vast and awe-inspiring set of cultural artifacts; it also changed the way people look at the world and choose to live in it. Modern sensitivities, values, and ethics have all been radically affected by the Christian tradition. This is true for almost all who live in the West, whether they claim allegiance to Christianity, to some other religious tradition, or to none at all. Before the triumph of Christianity, the Roman Empire was phenomenally diverse, but its inhabitants shared a number of cultural and ethical assumptions. If one word could encapsulate the common social, political, and personal ethic of the time, it would be "dominance."

In a culture of dominance, those with power are expected to assert their will over those who are weaker. Rulers are to dominate their subjects, patrons their clients, masters their slaves, men their women. This ideology was not merely a cynical grab for power or a conscious mode of oppression. It was the commonsense, millennia-old view that virtually everyone accepted and shared, including the weak and marginalized.

This ideology affected both social relations and governmental policy. It made slavery a virtually unquestioned institution promoting the good of society; it made the male head of the household a sovereign despot over all those under him; it made wars of conquest, and the slaughter they entailed, natural and sensible for the well-being of the valued part of the human race (that is, those invested with power).

With such an ideology one would not expect to find governmental welfare programs to assist weaker members of society: the poor, homeless, hungry, or oppressed. One would not expect to find hospitals to assist the sick, injured, or dying. One would not expect to find private institutions of charity designed to help those in need.

The Roman world did not have such things. Christians, however, advocated a different ideology. Leaders of the Christian church preached and urged an ethic of love and service. One person was not more important than another. All were on the same footing before God: the master was no more significant than the slave, the patron than the client, the husband than the wife, the powerful than the weak, or the robust than the diseased. Whether those Christian ideals worked themselves out in practice is another question. Christians sometimes—indeed, many times—spectacularly failed to match their pious sentiments with concrete actions, or, even more, acted in ways contrary to their stated ideals. But the ideals were nonetheless ensconced in their tradition—widely and publicly proclaimed by the leaders of the movement—in ways not extensively found elsewhere in Roman society.

As Christians came to occupy positions of power, these ideals made their way into people's social lives, into private institutions meant to encapsulate them, and into governmental policy. The very idea that society should serve the poor, the sick, and the marginalized became a distinctively Christian concern. Without the conquest of Christianity, we may well never have had institutionalized welfare for the poor or organized health care for the sick. Billions of people may never have embraced the idea that society should serve the marginalized or be concerned with the well-being of the needy, values that most of us in the West have simply assumed are "human" values.

This is not to say that Judaism, the religion from which Christianity emerged, was any less concerned with the obligations to "love your neighbor as yourself" and "do unto others as you would have them do unto you." But neither Judaism nor, needless to say, any of the other great religions of the world took over the empire and became the dominant religion of the West. It was Christianity that became dominant and, once dominant, advocated an ideology not of dominance but of love and service. This affected the history of the West in ways that simply cannot be calculated.

EXPLAINING THE TRIUMPH OF CHRISTIANITY

But there was no reason this cultural shift had to happen, no historical necessity that Christianity would, in effect, destroy the pagan religions of the Roman Empire and establish itself as the supreme religion and ascendant political and cultural power of its world. That is why the question I address in this book is so important. Why did this new faith take over the Roman world, leading to the Christianization of the West? It is obviously not a matter of purely antiquarian interest, relevant only to academic historians. What question could be more important for anyone interested in history, culture, or society?

To be more specific: How did a small handful of the followers of Jesus come to convert an unwilling empire? According to the New Testament, some days after Jesus's crucifixion, eleven of his male followers and several women came to believe he had been raised from the dead. Before four centuries had passed, these twenty or so lower-class, illiterate Jews from rural Galilee had become a church of some thirty million. How does a religion gain thirty million adherents in three hundred years?

As I give lectures around the country on a variety of topics related to early Christianity, this is the question I hear more than any other. The answers people suggest are wide-ranging. Many committed Christians appeal directly to divine providence. God did it. God guided history so the world would become Christian. I respect those who have this opinion, but I have one very big problem with it. If God wanted the world to become Christian, why hasn't the world become Christian? If God wanted the masses to convert, why are most of the masses still not converted? Moreover, just in historical terms, if God made the Roman Empire Christian, why did it take so long? And why was the job never completed? Why did non-Christian religions continue to exist at all? Why are they still in the majority today?

By far the most common secular answer I hear is that the Roman Empire became Christian because the emperor Constantine converted to the faith. Constantine was the sole ruler of the empire in the first part of the fourth century. Early in his reign he turned from traditional "pagan" religions to become a follower of Christ. After that, masses of people began to convert as Christianity went from being a persecuted minority to being the religion of most-favored status, and eventually the religion of Rome. So it was all about Constantine, right?

Until recently, that is what I myself thought. But I no longer think so. On the contrary: I think Christianity may well have succeeded even if Constantine had not converted. That will be one of the theses of this book.

Still, it cannot be disputed that, after Constantine's conversion, masses of people came to embrace the Christian faith. Not absolutely everyone. And not immediately after Constantine did so. Indeed, not even a century after Constantine's death. But eventually Christianity became the religion of the multitudes, and the Roman pagan religions they had formerly practiced more or less disappeared or, in a few instances, went underground. For those supporting the Christian cause, this has always been considered a real triumph.

I will not, however, be writing this book in a triumphalist vein. That is to say, I will not be celebrating the rise and eventual domination of Christianity, claiming it was inherently superior or even necessarily a very good thing. On the other hand, I do not want to claim it was bad either. Ultimately good or ultimately bad: as a historian I will remain neutral on these kinds of value judgments—in part, this is because the triumph of Christianity also entailed losses, especially for the devoted followers of other religious practices. Whenever one group wins a struggle, others lose. Those of us with historical interests need to consider both winners and losers.

WINNERS AND LOSERS

And so, before detailing the remarkable events that led to the triumph of Christianity, I want to pause to reflect on loss.

Nowhere in modern times have the losses occasioned by clashes of religions and cultures crystallized more dramatically than in the city of Palmyra, Syria, where, in 2015, representatives of ISIS captured the city, executed a number of its inhabitants, destroyed archaeological remains, and ravaged its antiquities, torturing and beheading their chief conservator. Nothing of equal savagery has ever affected the site. But this is not the first time Palmyra endured an assault by religious fanatics who found its sacred temples and the holy objects they contained objectionable. For that we need to turn the clock back seventeen hundred years.

The ancient city of Palmyra lay to the northeast of Damascus, almost exactly midway between the Mediterranean in the west and the Euphrates in the east. Originally a caravan oasis, it became a center of transport and commerce, an obvious stopping point at the crossroads between Rome and Persia.

As it grew in size and economic importance, Palmyra attracted the attention of Mediterranean powers from the Greeks in the fourth century BCE to the Romans later on. Assaulted by Mark Antony in 41 BCE, it was eventually incorporated into the empire under Tiberius (emperor 14–37 CE). Two and half centuries later it established its independence as a breakaway state, ruled most famously by Queen Zenobia until its reconquest by the Roman emperor Aurelian in 272 CE. Taking Zenobia captive for his triumph back in Rome, Aurelian eventually ordered the city's destruction. Although partially rebuilt, it was never again to return to its former glory. Its magnificent private and public structures stood for centuries, isolated in the Syrian desert.

The first recorded instance of specifically religious intolerance leading to the destruction of Palmyra's antiquities occurred at the end of the fourth century. The Roman imperial throne was occupied at the time by Theodosius I (ruled 379–95 CE), a passionately committed Christian determined to establish Christianity as the official religion of the empire. Theodosius was not the first Christian emperor. That, as I have indicated, was Constantine (ruled 306–37 CE). And Theodosius was not the first Christian emperor to order the destruction of pagan temples. That was Constantine's son Constantius II (ruled 337–61). But Theodosius was the first to legislate Christianity as the one legitimate religion and to order a general cessation of pagan practices. The enforcement of Theodosius's policies was spotty at best, but it did affect Palmyra and at least one of its most glorious sacred shrines, the temple of Allat, the Syrian pagan goddess.[1]

Allat was worshiped by nomads throughout the region and eventually came to be identified as the Greek goddess Athena. An archaeological team from Poland excavated the ruins of her temple in the spring seasons of 1975 and 1976. Inscriptions discovered at the site, along with coins, pottery, and a severely mutilated statue of the divinity, allowed these experts to write the history of the sanctuary. Built in the middle of the second century CE, the sanctuary stood for over two hundred years, until being destroyed sometime in the 380s. It did not perish from natural causes, such as an earthquake or storm. That much is clear from the remains of the cult statue, whose facial figures had been intentionally mutilated. As the archaeological report notes, this kind of mutilation "suggests that it was done by a man of set purpose rather than by brute forces of nature."[2]

We know of numerous other statue mutilations around the empire from about the same time. They were not perpetrated by thoughtless, godless hordes but by committed Christians with clear intentions. Statues of pagan deities often had their eyes, noses, ears, mouths, hands, and genitals removed. This was a religious statement. The gods of the pagans were nothing but stone or wood. They could not see, smell, hear, speak, or act. They were useless, lifeless, and dead. The Christians were out to prove it.[3]

The date established for the destruction of the temple of Allat is particularly telling. It coincides with some of the most virulent antireligious legislation the ancient world had ever seen. From 381 to 392 CE Theodosius issued laws forbidding pagan sacrifice and ordering the closing of pagan temples. This legislation—like most legislation throughout the history of the Roman Empire—was inefficiently administered. The Roman state simply had no apparatus for empire-wide enforcement of the imperial will. But the legislation that did issue forth was taken seriously in some places, leading to regional destructions of temples and pagan cult objects, including some of the great gold, bronze, and stone statuary of the empire.

The best-known acts of enforcement involved one of the highest-ranking officials in Theodosius's administration, the praetorian prefect

Maternus Cynegius. Like Theodosius, Cynegius was a deeply commit-ted and zealous Christian. In 385 CE he undertook a tour of the eastern provinces to carry out Theodosius's anti-pagan policies. In the words of one modern archaeologist, this tour led to an "unprecedented dev-astation of the most admired objects of pagan sacred architecture and art."[4] Cynegius spent considerable time in Syria, and with the backing of local Christian leaders, destroyed the important Temple of Zeus in the city of Apamea.

There is nothing to suggest that Cynegius was personally active in Palmyra. But his presence in the region motivated local Christians to send in wrecking crews of their own. That is what happened with the temple of Allat. It was a local job, inspired, rather than carried out, by imperial authorization. It is impossible to say whether the de-struction was sponsored by the leaders of the Christian communities in the city or was instead the work of a marauding mob of fervent Christians. We do know that, several decades later, Christian leaders converted other pagan temples into Christian churches, including the oldest and finest pagan sanctuary of the city, the famous temple of Bel whose remains were destroyed by ISIS in 2015.

We grieve over such senseless—or, rather, highly intentional—destruction of antiquities in part because we see in remnants of an-cient culture the treasured history of our own past. And so we are dismayed, or even incensed, to hear a recent archaeologist declare: "There can be no doubt on the basis of the written and archaeolog-ical evidence that the Christianization of the Roman Empire and early medieval Europe involved the destruction of works of art on a scale never before seen in human history."[5]

The ancient world did not share our modern passion for the ma-terial remains of earlier millennia. The agony of that era's destruc-tion was even more profound, since these temples and statues were still then part of a living, vibrant culture. The very core of people's personal and spiritual lives was under assault, mocked, mutilated, and destroyed before their very eyes.

I do not want to undervalue the enormous benefits derived from the triumph of Christianity. Christians and non-Christians can surely agree that the cultural glories we have inherited from the Christian tradition—the art, music, literature, and philosophy—justify our gratitude and awe. But I begin with the temple of Allat in Palmyra to emphasize my point: every triumph is also a defeat, and the ecstasies of those who prevail are matched by the agonies of those who lose.[6]

Chapter 1

The Beginning of the End:
The Conversion of Constantine

F ew events in the history of civilization have proved more transformative than the conversion of the emperor Constantine to Christianity in the year 312 CE. Later historians would sometimes question whether the conversion was genuine. But to Constantine himself and to spiritual advisors close to him, there appears to have been no doubt. He had shifted from one set of religious beliefs and practices to another. At one point in his life he was a polytheist who worshiped a variety of pagan gods—gods of his hometown Naissus in the Balkans, gods of his family, gods connected with the armies he served, and the gods of Rome itself. At another point he was a monotheist, worshiping the Christian god alone. His change may not have been sudden and immediate. It may have involved a longer set of transitions than he later remembered, or at least said. There may have been numerous conversations, debates with others, and reflections within himself. But he dated the event to October 28, 312. At that point he began to consider himself a Christian.[1]

The results were tremendous, but not for the reasons often claimed. It is not that Constantine eventually made Christianity the state religion. Christianity would not become the official religion of

Rome until nearly eight decades later, under the reign of Emperor Theodosius I. And it is not that Constantine's conversion was the single decisive turning point in the spread and success of the Christian religion, the one moment that changed all history and made the Christian conquest a success. At the rate it was growing at the time, Christianity may well have succeeded otherwise. If Constantine had not converted, possibly a later emperor would have done so—say, one of his sons. Instead, what made Constantine's conversion revolutionary was that the imperial apparatus that before then had been officially opposed to Christianity and worked hard, in some regions of the empire, to extirpate it completely suddenly came to support it, promoting Christianity instead of persecuting it. Constantine did not make Christianity the one official and viable religion. He made it a licit religion, and one that enjoyed particular, even unique imperial privileges and funding. This support did indeed advance the Christian cause. The recognition that this faith was now favored from on high appears to have contributed to the already impressive numbers adding to the growth of Christianity, including the conversion of increasing numbers of imperial and local elites whose resources had until then funded (and thus made possible) the religious practices of their pagan world.

As important as Constantine's conversion was to the welfare of the Christian movement, it is surprisingly difficult to describe what he converted *from*. Modern historians of religion who speak of conversion can mean a variety of things by it.[2] Possibly it is simplest to keep the meaning broad and use the term to refer to a decided shift away from one set of religious practices and beliefs to another. That certainly happened with Constantine. At a moment that seemed, at least later in hindsight, to be clear and well-defined, he stopped being a pagan and became a Christian.

Conversion was not a widely known phenomenon in antiquity. Pagan religions had almost nothing like it.[3] They were polytheistic, and anyone who decided, as a pagan, to worship a new or different god was never required to relinquish any former gods or their previous patterns of worship. Pagan religions were additive, not restrictive.

Christians, on the other hand, did require a choice. Converts were expected to forgo the worship of all the other gods and revere the Christian god alone. Only Judaism had similar expectations and demands. Among pagans—that is, among the 93 percent or so of the world that by custom, habit, and inclination worshiped multiple gods—worshiping a range of divine beings was not a religion that anyone chose. It was simply what people did. Being a pagan meant participating in the various religious activities associated with the official state gods, local municipal gods, personal family gods, and any other gods that were known to be involved with human experience. For everyone except Jews, and then Christians, this was more a way of life than a conscious decision. It was a matter of doing what everyone had always done, very much like participating in the life of the local community, with the exception that most people were involved with only one community but could be engaged in the worship of a virtually incalculable number of gods.

For that reason paganism should not be thought of as a solitary "thing" but as hundreds—thousands—of things.[4] Those who practiced traditional religions—in other words, just about everyone—would never have recognized themselves as participating in something called "paganism" or, indeed, any kind of "ism." There was not a thing there, nothing that could be named so as to sum up the totality of all the non-Jewish religious observances or beliefs or cultic practices of prayer and sacrifice ubiquitous in the culture. No pagan would have understood what it would mean to call themselves pagan. They were simply acting in time-honored ways of worshiping the gods.

Constantine, like everyone else who was not raised Jewish or Christian, participated in this worship. But he gave it up to follow the one god of the Christians. The narrative of how Constantine became a Christian is both intriguing and complex. It involves issues that we today would consider strictly social and political and other issues that we would consider strictly religious. But in the early fourth century—as in all the centuries of human history before that time—these two realms, the sociopolitical and the religious, were not seen as distinct. They were tightly and inextricably interwoven. On just the linguistic level, there were no Greek or Latin terms that neatly differentiated between what we today mean by "politics" and "religion." On the practical level, the gods were understood to be closely connected with every aspect of the social and political life of a community, from the election of officials, to the setting of the annual calendar, to the laws and practices that governed social relations, such as marriage and divorce, to the administration of civil justice, to the decisions and actions of war, to all the other major decisions of state. The gods were active in every part of social and political life, and the decisions made and actions taken were done in relation to them.

On the imperial level this meant that it was widely known—and genuinely believed by most—that it was the gods who had made the empire great. The empire responded by sponsoring and encouraging the worship of the gods. Doing so would promote the commonweal. There was no sense that there was, should be, or could be a separation of church and state.

Starting in the mid-third century, the emperors themselves sensed this full well and acted accordingly. That is why, some years before Constantine converted, the Christian religion had been persecuted by order of the state. The Christians refused to worship or even acknowledge the gods of the empire, claiming in fact that these were evil, demonic beings, not beneficent deities that promoted the just cause of the greatest empire the world had ever known. The refusal to worship was seen by others to be dangerous to the well-being of the empire and thus to the security of the state. And so the decision to persecute—which seems to us, perhaps, to be a strictly religious affair—was at the time inherently sociopolitical as well. The Christians were to be removed like a cancer from the body politic. No emperor came to believe this more firmly—in no small part because of the alarming growth of this cancer—than Constantine's predecessor on the throne, Diocletian, who instigated the most vicious empirewide persecution ever seen. Constantine himself was later to rescind the demands of this persecution. But while it was still in process, he converted.

This conversion proved to be a linchpin of imperial history, not just for the fate of the Christian religion but also for the workings of the Roman state. We will look at the persecution of Diocletian in a later chapter, and at the broader biography of Constantine in another. For now, we are interested specifically in his conversion and how it radically changed the balance of power, both for the persecuted Christians and for the running of the Roman government. To make sense of the conversion we need to understand some of the political and religious backdrop to the story.

CONSTANTINE'S RISE TO POWER

By the end of the third century CE, the empire was too vast and complex to be ruled by one emperor. It reached from Britain to Iraq and entailed virtually all areas connected to the Mediterranean, north into modern Europe, south into North Africa and Egypt, and east into Palestine and Syria, all the way to Persia. For many years it had been riven by internal disputes and foreign invasions. The year 284 CE is usually cited as the end of the major upheavals collectively known as the "Crisis of the Third Century," a half century filled, internally, with imperial assassinations and usurpations involving some twenty-one legitimate emperors and thirty-eight usurpers. In addition, the empire had, for a time, been fractured by two breakaway states, one in the far west and one in the east. These had literally fragmented the empire and made the actual "Roman" state a slice of its former self. That is not to mention the incursions on the northern borders by barbarian hordes.[5]

The brilliant emperor-general Aurelian (ruled 270–75 CE) had defeated and reintegrated the breakaway states, but it was not until the reign of Diocletian that a fuller sense of order was restored internally, and with it a relatively secure border on the frontier. Diocletian was one of the truly great political administrators of Roman antiquity. His predecessors, including Aurelian, had never managed to bring any semblance of stability: Diocletian's eight immediate predecessors had all been murdered, some of them within weeks or even days of taking the throne. He himself was to enjoy a reign of over twenty years. Diocletian was the first emperor of Rome to abdicate voluntarily.

Diocletian is best known to casual readers of Roman history as the great persecutor of Christians. This he certainly was, as we will see more fully in chapter 7. But, even more, he was an insightful and creative leader and administrator. Among other things, he devised the first sensible system for the transfer of power from one emperor to the next. Despite its theoretical virtues, however, the system broke down just over a year after the first transfer occurred, and Constantine himself played a definitive role in that collapse, leading to his own assumption of imperial power in a reign that was second only to that of the great Caesar Augustus himself in both length and historical consequence.

From the time of Augustus, the first of the Roman emperors, the major political problem at the pinnacle of power had always been the succession. Once an emperor died, who was to succeed him? Augustus himself—unlike many of those who came in his wake—certainly had plans, and they always involved heirs who actually shared his bloodline. But one by one these potential successors died—or, if we believe the rumors, were assassinated—until virtually the last man standing was Augustus's stepson Tiberius. As emperor, Tiberius too had no legitimate heirs to the throne, and so the world inherited Gaius, otherwise known as the infamous Caligula. The succession went from there, not always happily.

Diocletian decided that there had to be a better way. He himself reigned with an iron fist for nearly a decade before carrying out his design. He devised a system of succession based not on dynastic ties but on merit. It was a plan to keep the empire completely unified, but ruled through a college of four emperors, an administrative unit known as the Tetrarchy ("rule of four"). There would be two senior emperors, each labeled an Augustus. Beneath each of them would be a junior emperor called a Caesar. The Caesars would be chosen based on their experience and qualifications. They would not be blood relatives of the Augusti.

And so it happened. Diocletian became the senior emperor of the East, with a military man named Galerius as Caesar; another military officer, Maximian, became senior emperor of the West, with Constantius—the father of Constantine—as his Caesar. Even though each emperor had principal responsibility for a distinct set of provinces, the empire was not technically divided into four units. Instead, the four were construed as co-rulers of a unified empire. The decisions of one were affirmed by the four; the conquests and victories of one were credited to the others. There were four emperors, but the empire was one.

Most important was the rule of succession that Diocletian devised. When an Augustus died or abdicated, his Caesar would then "move up" and assume his vacated position, and a new Caesar would be chosen by the most senior of the two Augusti.[6] This new junior emperor would not be the natural son of the newly elevated Augustus but a figure uniquely qualified for the position. And so, in theory, the system could continue indefinitely, since successors would always be chosen—well in advance—for their abilities to perform the tasks of office, not because of the accidents of birth. It was a completely novel and rather ingenious conception.

It was also doomed to failure. The children of current rulers could hardly be expected to accept the new system passively, and they didn't.

Because of health issues, after a long and successful reign of over two decades, Diocletian decided to retire from office on May 1, 305. For the sake of a smooth succession, he compelled his rather unwilling co-Augustus, Maximian, to do the same, to make way for the two Caesars, Galerius and Constantius, to rise to the senior offices. For their replacements, according to the principles that Diocletian had devised, two Caesars were chosen as junior emperors: Maximin Daia (not to be confused with the outgoing Augustus Maximian) to serve with Galerius in the East, and Severus to serve with Constantius in the West. There was now a "Second Tetrarchy."

At the time it may have seemed like a smooth and unproblematic transition, and in a sense it was—until one of the new Augusti died.

Then the plan of succession based on qualifications ran afoul of both the dynastic principle and the army.

The background to the story involves the new Augustus of the West, Constantius, and his son Constantine.[7] Constantine had risen through the ranks of military and political service over the years, as was natural for a scion of such a high-ranking official. He had served as a junior military officer in the court of Diocletian and then, for a brief time, under Galerius. When Galerius was promoted to be the new Augustus of the East, he realized the potential problem with Constantine, who could well expect an appointment to the level of Caesar in accordance with the traditional dynastic principle. But Constantine was not named to the position and almost certainly harbored some resentment and, possibly, some hope of remedy. If later reports are to be believed, Galerius's solution to this potential problem was to remove Constantine from the scene by regularly putting him in harm's way during various military endeavors. One later account, probably apocryphal, claims that Galerius, for his own amusement, once assigned Constantine to fight a lion one-on-one.

Constantine emerged from these attempts unscathed. Soon after Constantius was elevated to the level of Augustus, he requested his son's transfer to his own service. Whether out of relief or in a moment of weakness, Galerius ceded to the request. In later propaganda we are told that Constantine fled as quickly as he could—before Galerius could change his mind—and, taking the fastest and only state-sponsored imperial route on horseback, hamstrung the horses left behind at each way station to prevent Galerius from fetching him back on second thought.

Constantine, in any event, made it to Gaul, where his father was stationed, and joined him in his military campaigns on the borders, accompanying him to Britain to beat back incursions coming across Hadrian's Wall. It was there that Constantius took ill and died on July 25, 306.

That is when the dominoes began to fall. In designating his

successor in the Tetrarchy, Constantius did not choose one of his great military commanders based on personal merit but instead selected his son Constantine—returning precisely to the rule of dynastic succession that Diocletian had wanted to avoid. The problem is that Maximian, the rather reluctantly retired Augustus of the East, also had an adult son, named Maxentius, who had, along with Constantine, felt slighted by being bypassed for a place in the imperial college at his father's abdication. Once Maxentius saw that Constantine's army had invoked the dynastic principle by acclaiming him ruler, he pushed to receive the same privilege. With his urging, the Praetorian Guard in the city of Rome proclaimed him emperor. He assumed control of Rome and Italy, and now the "Rule of Four" had become five. To complicate matters further, Maxentius brought his father Maximian out of retirement to assist him, so that now the five were six. But not for long.

CIVIL WAR WITH MAXENTIUS

The emperors Galerius, Severus, and Constantine all—rightly—considered Maxentius a usurper, and knew they needed to dispose of him. There was no choice but civil war. It was not easy or swift. Galerius, the senior of the two Augusti, directed Severus to take his army into Italy and, if necessary, lay siege to Rome. Severus did so, but many of his soldiers defected to the opposing side and he was soundly defeated in battle, personally captured, and soon thereafter forced to commit suicide.[8] Galerius then decided to take matters into his own hands and attacked Maxentius from the East. He too failed to complete the mission. Finding himself unable to enforce a viable siege on the city, and experiencing numerous defections of troops, he fled Rome and barely managed to escape alive.[9]

During all this time, Constantine stayed away from the fray, conducting campaigns on his northern border against barbarian threats and allowing the other leaders of the empire to fight it out among themselves. He proceeded to do nothing about the situation for six years. Over that time he learned of problems that Maxentius was experiencing in Rome—famine and food shortages resulting in riots; rampaging soldiers; unjust imprisonments and executions—and reports of Maxentius's own profligate activities. In 312 CE he decided the time was right. In retrospect he claimed he simply could no longer allow tyranny in the capital. What he did not point out in public was that overthrowing the alleged tyrant would give him possession of Rome, all of Italy, and North Africa.

What especially matters for our narrative here is that, in addition to the enormous political and military consequences of a Constantinian victory, there was a highly unexpected religious outcome. This was to prove even more significant for the subsequent history of the Roman world. It was during his march on Rome, Constantine claimed later, that he experienced his conversion to Christianity.

The march itself was a thing of military beauty. Constantine demonstrated his enormous military prowess, acting boldly and swiftly, accompanying his army over the Alps and destroying all resistance en route. After several victories over Maxentius's forces in northern Italy, along with the surrender of other strongholds that could see the writing on the wall, Constantine moved his army south within striking distance of Rome itself, in preparation for an ultimate battle with the usurper, after which he would take control of the entire Italian peninsula. That is when Constantine had a vision.

At least, that is when Constantine later *claimed* he had his vision. One of the thorniest issues that biographers of Constantine contend with is the question of his vision—or, rather, his visions. As it turns out, we have several contemporary reports of several visions, all of them recorded by writers who personally knew Constantine and appear to be relating what they heard from him and/or his companions directly. As a result, it is very hard to know whether Constantine had one vision or two or three, whether the vision or visions came while he was awake or asleep, whether they came while he was still campaigning in Gaul, or en route to Rome, or stationed just north of Rome on the night before his battle.

To make sense of the reports that have come down to us, we have to put them in the context of Constantine's personal religious life, and that will require some further background.

THE VISIONS OF CONSTANTINE

We have comparatively excellent sources for Constantine's adult life, including his own writings, laws he enacted, a biography written about him by the fourth-century Christian bishop of Caesarea Maritima and "father of church history" Eusebius, and other contemporary reports.[10] But we are handicapped when it comes to his life prior to his accession to the throne, including his religious life. For this we have very slim records. We do know he was born in the northern Balkans, and we can assume that he originally participated in local indigenous religions that would have included such deities as the Thracian rider gods, divine beings astride horses. As was true of all citizens in the empire, he would also have participated in civic religious festivals, including the cults worshiping deceased Roman emperors. The Roman army too had its deities of choice; as a soldier and then commander Constantine would have worshiped these as well.[11]

What we do not know is how well informed he was of Christianity in the years before his conversion. His mother, Helena, was later in life—well into Constantine's reign—a very committed Christian, and some have suspected that she had Christian leanings even in his youth. But we simply have no compelling evidence. We have a bit more information about his father, Constantius, and some observers have claimed him too for the Christian cause, none more famously than Constantine's biographer, the Christian Eusebius.[12] It is indeed worth noting that during the original Tetrarchy, when Diocletian declared an empire-wide persecution (see chapter 7), Constantius paid the policy little more than lip service, shutting down some churches but not arresting, torturing, or martyring any Christians. Was he a sympathizer or even a devotee himself? Some historians have also been struck by the fact that one of Constantius's daughters (with a later wife) was called Anastasia, a Greek name that means resurrection—a highly appropriate name had her father been a Christian.

It is not likely, however, that he was. More plausibly Constantius, like the emperor Aurelian some years earlier, was a "henotheist," revering one god as superior to all others without denying the divinity of the others. In particular, he may have worshiped above all else the god of the sun, Sol Invictus ("Unconquered Sun"). That would make sense both of the fact that Constantine himself remained a pagan prior to his march on Rome in 312 CE and of Constantine's later ruminations about what led him to the god of the Christians.

We have three principal sources of information for the vision(s) of Constantine that led to his conversion. The first comes to us in a flattering speech—known as a panegyric—delivered by an anonymous orator in 310 CE, before Constantine had initiated his final actions against Maxentius. The speech was occasioned by a military victory in a skirmish with Maximian, Maxentius's father, who had been brought out of retirement. As was always the case with panegyrics, the speaker himself wrote his address and made it entirely sycophantic. Such speeches were designed to praise the recipient as one of the greatest human beings the universe had ever seen, as revealed by the subject's activities and experiences. It was in the context of celebrating Constantine's marvelous character that the panegyrist of 310 CE described a vision the emperor had recently had of the god Apollo, who is often associated in ancient thought with the sun and considered, then, the sun god.[13]

In the speech we are told that, after winning his battle, Constantine decided to visit a magnificent temple of Apollo, probably at Grand, Vosges (northeastern Gaul, modern France). There, outside the temple, Constantine had a vision of the god himself, who offered him several laurel wreaths, each of which symbolically represented thirty years of life, thus indicating that Constantine would be allotted a preternaturally long mortal existence. More than that, the god indicated that Constantine was the one who would rule the entire world. The panegyrist did not stop there, however. He went on to indicate that Constantine was a kind of human manifestation of Apollo himself: among other things, like the god he was young, handsome, and a bringer of health.

If any such vision did occur—or if Constantine thought it occurred, or even simply said it did—this may well be the time at which he began to revere Sol Invictus. Possibly he became a henotheist. This would not have required him to stop being pagan, as we will see more fully in chapter 3. He still could have acknowledged the divinity of other gods and recognized the right and even obligation of other people to worship them. But he may have turned his own entire focus onto the god he considered to be above all gods, choosing—as the emperor who aspired to be the greatest and most powerful human on earth—to worship only the greatest and most powerful divinity in heaven.

The fullest version of Constantine's vision, or visions, appears in a record produced nearly three decades later. It is also the most important source for Constantine's conversion. The report appears in the *Life of Constantine*, a biography of the emperor by Eusebius, who had firsthand information from the emperor himself and claims that his account of Constantine's conversion was what the emperor himself revealed and swore to be true.[14]

Eusebius indicates that Constantine decided, for the good of the empire, to overthrow the tyrant of Rome, Maxentius. He knew that he would need divine help in his endeavor. To the regret of many a later historian, Eusebius does not tell us when exactly Constantine's appeal for heavenly assistance occurred; all he says is that it was "on a military campaign he was conducting somewhere." Whenever it was, it happened before Constantine engaged Maxentius in the final battle for Rome. Constantine reflected on his religious options and realized that, without help from above, his cause could not be won:

> Knowing well that he would need more powerful aid than an army could supply because of the mischievous magical devices practiced by the tyrant, he sought a god to aid him. He regarded the resources of soldiers and military numbers as secondary, for he thought that without the aid of a god these could achieve

nothing, and he said that what comes from a god's assistance is irresistible and invincible. He therefore considered what kind of god he should adopt to aid him (*Life* 1.27).

Clearly Constantine was still at this stage operating within a pagan context, trying to decide where to appeal for divine help. As he reflected he came to regard a polytheistic position as politically and militarily untenable, for a remarkably empirical reason. All of his predecessors on the throne had "attached their personal hopes to many gods" and so worshiped them in expectation of success. But all failed miserably and "met an unwelcome end." (This of course was not true, but it is how Eusebius quotes the process of Constantine's thought.) The one exception was his father, Constantius, who died peaceably after having turned to the worship of only one god: "Only his own father had taken the opposite course to theirs by condemning their error, while he himself had throughout his life honored the God who transcends the universe, and found him a Savior and guardian of his Empire and a provider of everything good" (*Life* 1.27).

Constantine—or more likely Eusebius himself—was now claiming that Constantius was not just a henotheist but a worshiper of the Christian god. The historical record suggests otherwise, but at this stage we are more interested in Constantine's thought process, at least as it is laid out in Eusebius's account. Constantine went on to realize that the two previous rulers who had attacked Maxentius—Severus and Galerius—"had assembled their forces with a multitude of gods and had come to a dismal end." Clearly the polytheistic option was not working in the battle for Rome. And so Constantine came to a decision, concluding "that it was folly to go on with the vanity of the gods which do not exist, and to persist in error in the face of so much evidence, and he decided he should venerate his father's God alone" (*Life*, 1.27).

Constantine turned to this one god in prayer, and he was rewarded with a vision. And not just he alone: he and his entire army.

About the time of the midday sun, when day was just turning, he said he saw with his own eyes, up in the sky and resting over the sun, a cross-shaped trophy formed from light, and a text attached to it that said, "By this conquer." He and the whole company of soldiers that was then accompanying him witnessed the miracle and were gripped by amazement (*Life* 1.28).

Constantine could not understand the meaning of the vision, and he pondered the matter until nightfall. Then, in a dream, Christ appeared to him with the same sign Constantine had seen in the sky, directing him to make a copy of it as protection from the attacks of his enemies.

Constantine apparently did not fathom what it was he had seen in either experience. In his confusion he summoned several religion experts for an explanation. This is the clearest evidence that Constantine was not, at this point, desiring to become a Christian. He evidently did not fully realize who the Christian god was or what he stood for. He needed instruction. His advisors explained who Christ was as the "only begotten Son of the one and only God," who could bring "victory over death." They told him that the sign of the cross was a "token of immortality." They proceeded to explain why Christ had come to earth and to unfold for him the meaning of the incarnation. Constantine marveled as he listened—indicating, yet again, that it was news to him—and decided to explore "the divinely inspired writings" for himself. He did so, and with the help of his advisors "deemed it right to honor the God who had appeared to him" by worshiping him alone. Constantine then summoned his goldsmiths and jewelers and explained that he wanted a physical representation of the sign he had seen in his vision and dream, and they made it for him.

At this point in his account, Eusebius injects a personal note, claiming that after the emperor had described to him the object, he brought it out to show him.[15] It was a tall pole plated with gold, with a crossbeam that gave it the shape of a cross. At the very top was a jeweled and gilded wreath on which were superimposed the two Greek letters chi and rho—which are the first two letters of the Greek word for "Christ." Below the crossbeam was a suspended cloth. Eusebius indicates that "this saving sign was always used by the Emperor for protection against every opposing and hostile force, and he commanded replicas of it to lead all his armies" (*Life* 1. 31). In other words, Constantine took this object—known as the labarum—into battle with him, and it ensured victory. It apparently worked every time.

We also have a third account of Constantine's conversion, which is, to say the least, difficult to reconcile with the previous two. This other version comes to us in the writings of a Christian historian and theologian named Lactantius. Lactantius is a particularly important source of information. For one thing, he was personally acquainted with Constantine: in fact, he was appointed by the emperor to be the personal tutor of his eldest son Crispus. For another thing, his account was written not decades later (as was the case with Eusebius) but just a few years after the event. Is it the same event? Most historians have thought so, even though the differences are striking.

The account appears in a small book—a pamphlet, really—that is particularly notable for its unabashed Schadenfreude, called *Deaths of the Persecutors*. In this work Lactantius recounts with barely disguised glee the horrible and excruciating deaths experienced by the Roman officials responsible for the persecutions of the Christians. The book comprises not merely grisly deathbed scenes, however, but also a good deal of other historical information. Chapter 44 gives an account of Constantine's conversion that is terse and direct. According to this version, the epiphany came to Constantine the night before the decisive battle with Maxentius for the control of Rome. In a dream Constantine was instructed—we are not told by whom—to place the "heavenly sign of God" on the shields of his soldiers before going into battle. The next day he did so, instructing the soldiers to have their shields decorated with a letter *X* crossed through the middle by the letter *I*, the top of which was to be rounded. This (here is a parallel with Eusebius) would have looked then like a Chi-Rho (the letter chi looks like an *X* and the rho looks like a capital *P*—i.e., a straight *I* with the top rounded). Armed with these shields, Constantine's troops went into battle and, as it turns out, routed the opposition.

Various scholars have suggested different ways of reconciling the different versions of Constantine's vision or visions. Some think he had just one vision, two years before the Battle at the Milvian Bridge (just before the panegyric of 310 CE), which at the time he took to be of Sol Invictus but later came to interpret as being instead a vision of Christ. In this view, at a still later date Constantine came to think he had always understood it to be Christ and that, since the vision was so closely connected with his ultimate victory, he came to "remember" that it occurred the night before the battle. At the other extreme of interpretation, some have argued that Constantine was simply a visionary who had lots of visions and dreams, sometimes muddling them all up. It is striking that Eusebius himself, in a speech praising Constantine near the end of his life, indicates that Constantine was a famous visionary and that he had "thousands" of visions along with "thousands" of dreams in which Christ appeared to him.[16]

The accounts do share some striking features. For one thing, in each case the vision involved a solitary god whom Constantine decided was the only one to be worshiped: he chose no longer to engage in polytheistic practices. Moreover, the account from the panegyrist in 310 and, more striking still, the account of Eusebius many years later both agree that Constantine did not become a Christian immediately after the dream. The panegyrist says nothing about him becoming a Christian at all, which may suggest the conversion had not happened yet, or that Constantine had not yet made it public, or that the pagan orator decided not to delve into that little detail. Eusebius admits that the emperor needed to do considerable consultation, reading, and reflecting before working out the implications of what he saw. Who knows how long that would have taken?

One reason we have difficulty working out what the vision or dream was and when exactly it occurred is that modern research on conversion has demonstrated that, long after such an experience, a convert tends to confuse what actually happened in light of everything that occurs in its aftermath.[17] That is to say, years later, the accounts people tell, to both themselves and others, have been slanted by all they have learned, thought, and experienced in the interim. Surely that was true of Constantine as well.

No one will ever solve the problem of what actually happened, or when, to the satisfaction of all interested parties.[18] But here is one plausible reconstruction. Whether actual or imagined, the vision experience contributed to Constantine's religious meditations as he was reflecting on the problem of the gods and how to find much-needed divine support for his assault on Maxentius. He became convinced that his vision was a sign from the one true and ultimate god, and he decided to worship him.

My best guess is that the vision occurred just before it was first reported, in 310 CE, and at that point Constantine became a henotheist, one who revered the sun god, Sol Invictus, above and in lieu of all others. This would be two years before he launched his assault on Maxentius, and in that time he had plenty of opportunities to reflect on his new religious commitments. Among other things, he became increasingly cognizant of the growing Christian movement. (In chapter 6 we will be discussing just how rapidly it was growing at the time.) Soon before the battle for Rome, he had another vision, or a dream, or both, and came to a decision. This decision was not that he would switch loyalties from Sol Invictus to the god of the Christians. Instead, he decided that Sol Invictus *was* the god of the Christians.[19]

Constantine became a Christian convert. Possibly the most important point to make about the conversion is that Constantine—as is true of all converts—did not and could not understand everything there was to know about the Christian faith at the time. His faith and his knowledge may have been very rudimentary indeed. He may not have known that he needed to be baptized at some point. He may not have known that Christians not only refused to worship other gods but believed the pagan gods were demons and not gods at all. He may not have known that there were ethical requirements that went along with being Christian. He may not have known that there were refined theological views and serious debates among the Christians about the nature of God, the identity of Christ, and the relationship of Christ and God. He may not have known lots of things.

What he apparently did know was that he wanted to worship the

Christian god and that god only. He went into battle with that conviction. And he emerged victorious.

THE BATTLE AT THE MILVIAN BRIDGE

The battle itself reads almost as an anticlimax to the story and is quickly told. In the wake of the failed attempts by both Severus and Galerius, one can see why Constantine would be anxious about the campaign. But he had several advantages his predecessors lacked, and Maxentius, in this instance, made a disastrous decision. Constantine was aided by the fact that Maxentius's father, Maximian, a brilliant military commander, was no longer part of the equation: he had committed suicide under duress (from Constantine) two years earlier. Even more, Maxentius's situation in Rome had grown dire. When he had started his reign, the city had welcomed him with open arms. But the problems mentioned above had taken their toll.

In anticipation of the assault from the north, Maxentius made one rather sensible move. He destroyed all the bridges that crossed the Tiber River. That would make engagement more difficult for an attacking army. But then, almost as an afterthought, he made a second decision that was disastrous. He chose not to steel the city against a coming siege but to come out in force and face the opposition in the field.

With the bridges out, however, there was no way to cross the Tiber heading north onto favorable battlegrounds. So Maxentius had a temporary pontoon bridge built next to the recently destroyed Milvian Bridge, and he and his army crossed it. With their backs up against the river and soon outmaneuvered, they were routed. Troops desperately tried to recross the pontoons in a beeline for the city, but under the crushing weight, the bridge collapsed. Many of the soldiers, and Maxentius himself, drowned in the Tiber.[20]

Constantine entered Rome the next day as its new ruler and the emperor of the entire western half of the empire. As we will see in chapter 8, it was another twelve years before he became sole ruler of the empire as a whole. But he was very good at biding his time. In the meanwhile he came to see the wisdom of his religious decision. He had committed his life and worship to the god of the Christians and then he had won his victory. The Christian god was greater than the other gods of Rome. He alone would be Constantine's god. Constantine had become a Christian.

Or had he?

THE "SINCERITY" OF CONSTANTINE'S CONVERSION

For long (and somewhat dreary) years scholars debated the sincerity of Constantine's conversion. Many experts today regard the debate as a wasted effort, even if more casual observers continue to consider it a live question. The debate started in 1853 with a Swiss scholar named Jacob Burckhardt, who argued in his book *Die Zeit Konstantins des Grossen* (*The Age of Constantine the Great*) that Constantine was ultimately driven not by religious zeal but by a "consuming lust for power." There is a lot that can be said for this argument in and of itself, but in addition Burckhart drew a corollary: Constantine recognized that the burgeoning Christian church could assist him in reaching his megalomaniacal goals, and so he forged an alliance with it out of personal ambition. Constantine in fact could not have cared less about the church and its truth claims.

Over the course of the debate, historians cited numerous pieces of evidence in support of this basic thesis. To begin with, Constantine continued to embrace pagan views in the public eye. No medium in Roman antiquity better propagandized an emperor's personal agenda than the issuance of coins. The imperial mints selected imagery and inscriptions that would embody the views, ideologies, and imaginations of the ultimate ruler. With that in mind, it is no doubt significant that, beginning in 310, Constantine's coins began to show images of Sol Invictus, the sun god. As we have seen, one can plausibly date his professed henotheism to that time. Yet more striking for those who have wanted to argue against the sincerity of his Christian conversion: this imagery continued for years after the battle at the

Milvian Bridge. If Constantine had genuinely become Christian, why did he keep issuing coins with pagan imagery?

Moreover, it was argued, after his alleged conversion, Constantine and those closely connected to him were highly circumspect in their references to God. A case in point is the Arch of Constantine still preserved today near the Colosseum in Rome. This was the triumphal arch the senate had constructed to celebrate Constantine's great victory over Maxentius, dedicated on Constantine's second visit to Rome in 315 CE. On the arch is an inscription describing the great event, including the divine assistance that Constantine had invoked going into battle. Yet there is no explicit reference to the Christian god. On the contrary, the inscription refers in rather bland and noncommittal terms to guidance provided by the "inspiration of divinity." If Constantine had been a true convert, would he be reluctant to declare outright that it was specifically the Christian god who had helped him?

Moreover, advocates for Constantine's insincerity pointed out that, well after the decisive battle for Rome, Constantine certainly did not *act* like a Christian. Soon after his victory Constantine ordered the execution of his ten-year-old nephew, son of Galerius. Would a Christian kill a ten-year-old child? Later in his career he ordered the execution of his own eldest son, Crispus, who was next in line to succeed him, and then his own wife, Fausta. These seem to be actions not of a true believer but of a despot. Finally, it was noted that Constantine refused to be baptized as a Christian until on his deathbed, some twenty-five years after his supposed conversion. Was it then that he finally "saw the light"?

For all these reasons, scholars of the late nineteenth and twentieth centuries disputed whether Constantine was actually committed to the Christian cause. Historians today, however, tend to read the evidence differently.

It is absolutely true that Constantine continued to use the imagery of Sol Invictus in his personal propaganda after the events of 312 CE, sometimes even having himself portrayed alongside the sun god in twin profile. That is not evidence that he worshiped divinities other than the Christian god, however. Christians before Constantine's day had sometimes identified the Christian god as the god of the sun, and as I argued earlier, Constantine appears not to have chosen the god of the Christians *over* Sol Invictus but rather to have identified him *with* Sol Invictus.

The fact that Constantine did not always identify his god as the god of the Christians—for example, on the triumphal arch in Rome or on his coins—could well be for other reasons. For one thing it needs to be emphasized that Constantine himself did not write the inscription that appeared on the arch. This was a monument made for him, not by him.

Even more important, Constantine himself may have had solid reasons not to want to flaunt his new religious commitment. As one modern Constantine scholar, Harold Drake, has argued, Constantine was self-consciously a ruler not only of Christians but of all people in his empire, Christian, pagan, and Jew alike. As such he chose to affirm his monotheistic faith without offending the sensitivities of any of his constituencies. Constantine was far too politic to make a public display of his distinctive Christian beliefs. At the same time he was unwilling to compromise his monotheistic commitments. In order to balance and accommodate both competing agendas, imperial and Christian, Constantine tactfully chose public language that could embody his commitments without alienating those who held other views.[21]

As for Constantine not always acting as a Christian and doing things that Christian ethicists strongly insist one should not do, we need always to remember that his conversion was not an instantaneous adoption of traditional Christian beliefs and practices—or ethics. Moreover, historians must resist the urge to define "Christian" according to certain preconceived notions and then judge Constantine accordingly. Are we to imagine that someone is not a Christian if they behave badly? It is true, some of Constantine's actions were highly transgressive of traditional Christian morality. On the other hand, he did have an empire to run. He would not have lasted a month if he had styled his rule on the Sermon on the Mount.

What about Constantine's decision to delay baptism until the last minute? This is probably the least convincing of the arguments, since it was not an unusual practice. This was especially true among Christians who took seriously theological claims that sins committed after baptism could not be forgiven but would lead to eternal punishment. We see such claims already in the New Testament: "For if we willingly sin after receiving the knowledge of the truth, there is no longer left to us a sacrifice for sins but a fearful expectation of judgment and a furious fire that will consume the enemies" (Hebrews 10:26–27; see also Hebrews 6:4–6). Anyone who believed this can hardly be excused for delaying baptism until the very end. Many did so.

There is in fact overwhelming and public evidence that Constantine was a very real Christian during his reign, even if he only gradually came to understand fully what that meant. Some of the most striking policies he enacted after his victory at the Milvian Bridge involved favors poured out on the Christian churches. Within months of assuming control of Rome he came to an agreement with his co-emperor Licinius, now ruling the East with the passing in 311 of Galerius, that brought a complete cessation of the persecution begun ten years earlier under Diocletian. This so-called Edict of Milan (which was not an edict and was not from Milan) gave complete freedom of religious expression to all inhabitants of the empire, ending once and for all the prosecution of Christians.[22]

Christianity, however, was not only decriminalized; it went from being a persecuted faith to being the religion of most-favored status. Constantine commissioned and financed the building of numerous Christian churches both in Rome and abroad, most notably the Lateran Basilica, which was to play such an instrumental role in the history of Christianity as the official cathedral of the Roman bishop (i.e., the pope). He showered beneficences on Christian clergy. He instructed the leading administrator of Africa to restore all the property that had been confiscated from the Christian churches during the persecutions.

One might argue that Constantine was simply siding with the church for reasons of his own without being personally committed to

Christian truth claims. In theory that could be so, but it is completely discredited by two other kinds of evidence: the first is Constantine's almost immediate involvement with Christian practical and theological disputes, and the second are words that issued from his own pen in which he spelled out with clarity his religious views.

In terms of his active participation in church affairs, already in 313 and then more vigorously in 314 Constantine inserted himself into the rancorous Donatist controversy of Northern Africa. This was an intense debate over what should be considered the legitimate Christian church community and who should be considered its legitimately appointed leaders. Constantine threw himself into the fray not particularly caring at first which side was right, but over time he came to a very clear opinion on the matter, siding (to no one's great surprise) with the view supported by the great majority of church leaders, especially those in Rome.[23]

Yet more striking was the Arian controversy, which came to a head some thirteen years later. Now the issues did not involve church polity but hard-core theology, specifically the hot and detailed question of the identity of Christ and his relationship with God the Father (Are they equal? Or is the Father greater? Are they co-eternal? Or did the Father exist first?). Constantine, like most Christians to this day, did not follow, or even much appreciate, all the nuances of the debate. But he was deeply invested in it and called the famous Council of Nicaea in 325 CE in order to resolve it. He not only called the council; he actively participated in the discussions and enforced the final decision. It is a remarkable moment of history. Here was a hardened, experienced, and seriously bloodied military commander and iron-fisted ruler of the Roman state debating the philosophical meaning of words of Scripture with Christian bishops. It is hard to say he was not committed to the cause.

Above all we have words that Constantine wrote and publicly spoke, which show beyond any doubt his deep Christian sensibilities. Nowhere can this be seen more clearly than in his address widely known as the *Oration to the Saints*.[24] In written form the speech spans twenty-six chapters. It would have taken two hours to deliver orally. We know it was given around the time of Easter, but we don't know which year, with scholars proposing dates ranging from 315 to (somewhat more plausibly) 325 CE. The speech is principally a defense of the Christian belief over the views of paganism. It expresses Constantine's philosophical and theological views, even though no theologian then or now would consider it overwhelmingly deep or perspicacious. Constantine was highly educated, but he was no professional thinker. Still, the speech gives us his religious perspectives and shows clearly how deeply he felt committed to them—and how closely they aligned with his political objectives. It is always important to remember the point made at the beginning of this chapter. Ancient people, whether pagans, Jews, or Christians, did not neatly differentiate between the religious and the political. They would have had a hard time understanding the difference.

There certainly is not a clear difference in this speech. Early on, Constantine makes an impassioned plea that there is and must be only one ultimate divine ruler, one god over all. If there were many divinities, then people would commit a sacrilege anytime they chose to worship any one of them. But, even more significant, if there were many divine rulers, there would be divisiveness rather than unity. What the world needs is unity. Constantine is quite openly not thinking only of the unity of heaven. He is equally, if not more, concerned about life on earth.

The divine situation, then, reflects the human. Numerous divinities all vying for attention would create division, envy, and jealousy. This, in his words, "would mar the harmonious concord of the whole, as many disposed in different ways of the shares allotted to each, and took no thought to maintain the whole world in the same state and according to the same principles." Such a state of affairs would lead to the "confusing of all things." And by "all" Constantine really means *all*. "The constellations would be in disarray, the seasons could not change in consistent patterns, the fruits of the earth could not grow, day and night would be confused." There has to be one ruler over all. The implication, should anyone miss it, is that there needs to be one emperor over all as well.

That does not mean that Constantine's speech is simply a power grab. It means that his religious commitment to worship the one God of heaven affected his sense that he himself was to be the one ruler on earth. As such he was completely committed to the Lord of all. His allegiance was completely Christian, as he himself declares in the oration: "My proper task is to hymn Christ through my way of life and the thanksgiving due to him from us in return for many great benefits" (*Oration*, 5).

Constantine was decidedly in favor of the "many great benefits" that were his through the worship of the Christian god. That may not sound like a disinterested view of theology or worship. But in an ancient context it is the least extraordinary thing about his deeply held commitment.

CONSTANTINE'S CONVERSION: IN SUM

Some historians have argued that if Constantine were really a Christian, he would have worked harder to convert his pagan subjects. That he clearly did not do. As Harold Drake has shown, however, this is no argument against his commitment to the Christian cause. It is evidence of the *kind* of Christian Constantine was and wanted to be. There were many, many Christians of his day—just as there have been many, many Christians in all the centuries that followed—who did not find it incumbent upon themselves to foist their Christian views on those who adhered to other religious traditions.[25] He had seen with perfect clarity the failure of forceful governmental intervention in religion, and he wanted no part of it. He was happy to support the Christians, to promote monotheistic piety of various kinds, and to allow people to worship God or the gods as they saw fit.

His conversion had serious repercussions. All the emperors of Rome from that time on—with one brief but notable exception—were Christian. Christianity was to take over the Roman world, becoming the official religion of the empire and eventually the dominant religion of the West.

Chapter 2

Back to the Beginning: The Conversion and Mission of Paul

Constantine's decision to worship only the god of the Christians may have been a major turning point in the history of the West, but it pales in comparison with a conversion that occurred nearly three centuries earlier. Had the apostle Paul not "seen the light" and become a worshiper of Jesus, the religion of Christianity, open to all people, both Jew and gentile, may never have developed into a worldwide phenomenon of any description whatsoever. It may well have instead remained a sect of Judaism fated to have the historical importance of, say, the Sadducees or the Essenes: highly significant for historians of Jewish antiquity but scarcely the stuff of world-shaping proportions.

It would be difficult indeed to identify two people more different than Constantine and Paul. Whereas Constantine was by far the most powerful, influential, and wealthy figure of the entire empire, Paul was an impoverished and embattled itinerant preacher unknown to most of the world at large. Constantine commanded the most powerful armies of his day and ran an enormous empire; Paul preached principally to lower-class day laborers in his workshop as a simple artisan. The magnificence and splendor of Constantine's life and surroundings beggar description; Paul's existence can be nicely summed up in his own words, where he compares himself with other supposed apostles:[1]

> Are they servants of Christ? I am a better one . . . with more numerous labors, more numerous imprisonments, with countless beatings, and often near death. Five times from the Jews I received the forty lashes minus one; three times I was beaten by rods, once I was stoned, three times I have been shipwrecked; a night and a day I have been adrift at sea; on frequent journeys, in danger from rivers, in danger from robbers, in danger from those of my own race, in danger from gentiles, in danger in the city, in danger in the wilderness, in danger at sea, in danger from the those falsely claiming to be brothers, in labor and toil, in many sleepless nights, in hunger and thirst, often without food, in the cold and naked. . . . (2 Corinthians 11:23–27).

We have, then, an exalted emperor and a beleaguered, impoverished craftsman. These are the two most significant converts of Christian history. Without the latter, this history would never have been written.

THE SOURCES FOR PAUL'S LIFE AND WORDS

Unlike for virtually anyone of equal insignificance at the time, for Paul we have rather good sources for his Christian life, including his conversion and his subsequent missionary efforts to convert others. These sources have come down to us in the New Testament. Later believers may have ascribed scriptural status to these books, but historians cannot discount them on these grounds. They are documents produced by people who, at the time, had no idea they were writing the Bible.

A number of these are writings in Paul's own name. Altogether we have thirteen letters, actual pieces of correspondence, allegedly written by Paul, along with several writings from outside the New Testament. Those that did not make it into the Christian canon are without question inauthentic, penned by later Christians claiming to be Paul in order to induce readers to heed their words. Modern readers would call such works forgeries; ancient readers called them equally denigrating things, if and when they realized they were being duped. Since the nineteenth century, scholars have recognized that even some of the letters in the New Testament fit this description. Six of the thirteen canonical Pauline epistles appear to be later productions by authors falsely taking Paul's name. Even so, that leaves us with seven letters almost certainly from Paul's own hand, invaluable sources for Paul's biography.[2]

One problem with these letters is that Paul is generally not interested in discussing what we ourselves might like to know. He did not write his correspondence principally to enlighten us about his conversion or his experiences in the mission field trying to convert others. As a rule, the letters are instead addressed to problems his converts were later having in their communal and personal lives, problems involving what to believe and how to behave. If a church of his—for example, the church in Thessalonica or in Corinth—was not experiencing a particular difficulty, Paul had no reason to address it. Moreover, in every case the original audience already enjoyed an intimate acquaintance with the story of how Paul—and how they themselves—had converted. For us to deduce that kind of information, we need to dig deeply into Paul's passing comments.

We are fortunate to have a second source of information as well, a narrative account of the spread of the Christian church over its first thirty years, starting from the days after Jesus's resurrection. This is the New Testament book known as the Acts of the Apostles, allegedly written by someone who had accompanied Paul on his missionary journeys. What better source could we hope for? This book actually describes Paul's conversion, on three occasions, and spends the bulk of its narrative describing his post-conversion missionary exploits.

The problem is that this historical narrative, in many, many instances, is not historical enough. Scholars have widely contended that the alleged author, an unnamed companion of Paul, could not have actually written it, in no small measure because both small details and larger narratives of the book are at odds with what Paul says about himself.[3] The dominant view of scholarship today is that the author produced his account at least twenty years after Paul had died—a growing number of scholars insists that it was written sixty years later—by an author without firsthand knowledge and a greater desire to tell a compelling narrative than an inclination, and an ability, to preserve solid, accurate, historical information.[4] As a result, anyone wanting to know what Paul really did, said, and experienced needs to use the book of Acts cautiously, grateful that it provides us any information at all but wary at every point. Scholars of Paul typically proceed, then, by focusing principally on the seven letters that indisputably came from his pen.

PAUL THE JEW

In order to understand Paul's conversion to faith in Jesus, we need a sense of what he converted from. Unlike Constantine, Paul was raised Jewish, not pagan. Twice in his undisputed letters Paul refers to his prior life. The first occurs in his letter to the churches in the region of Galatia, modern central Turkey. In order to establish his bona fides as an expert on the value and meaning of Jewish faith, Paul stresses that he himself started life as an avid Jew intent on pursuing the requirements of his religion with uncharacteristic zeal. It was this zeal that led him to persecute Jews who were declaring Jesus of Nazareth the messiah:

> For you have heard of my former conduct in Judaism, that I persecuted the church of God violently and was trying to destroy it. And I advanced in Judaism beyond many of my peers among my race, being especially zealous for the traditions of our ancestors. (Galatians 1:13–14)

In order to make a similar point in his letter to the Christians of the Macedonian church of Philippi, Paul gives a bit more detail:

[I was] circumcised on the eighth day, from the race of Israel, the tribe of Benjamin, a Hebrew born of Hebrews, according to the law a Pharisee, according to zeal, a persecutor of the church, according to the righteousness that comes in the law, blameless. (Philippians 3:5–6)

To make sense of Paul's Christian faith, we obviously need to know a bit about his Jewish origins. Jews made up something like 7 percent of the Roman Empire in Paul's day; everyone else, of course, was pagan. As is true today, Judaism was extremely diverse, with different Jewish groups both in Palestine and outside—in the so-called diaspora—evidencing a wide range of beliefs and practices.[5] Paul was definitely one of the outsiders: even though the book of Acts indicates that he was a highly educated rabbi trained in Jerusalem by the leading teacher of his day (Acts 22:3), Paul himself makes no reference to any pre-Christian Judean sojourn. Moreover, his native language is clearly Greek (the language of his letters), and at a relatively high level. We can assume then that Paul was born and raised outside Palestine, almost certainly in a large urban setting, where he could get an education. The book of Acts indicates that was the city of Tarsus in Cilicia (Acts 22:3), but Paul himself does not say.

Despite their wide diversity, Jews throughout the empire shared certain constants that made them recognizable and distinct from their pagan neighbors.[6] Most obviously, Jews were monotheistic, worshiping just their god, the god of Israel alone. This did not require Jews to deny that other gods existed: some thought they did exist but were not to be worshiped; others thought pagan gods were alive simply in the gentile imagination. In either case, they worshiped only their god.

In addition, Jews everywhere maintained that this one god, the creator of the universe, had chosen the Jews to be his people and given them a "covenant," a kind of contractual agreement or peace treaty. The covenant had first been extended to the Jewish patriarchs and then handed down to their descendants over the generations. In it God agreed to be distinctively the god of the Jews in exchange for their exclusive devotion, worship, and obedience. The covenant did not require or expect that Jews would go forth to convert others to their community. As we will see, Jews were by and large indifferent to what pagans chose to do with their devotional lives. But they saw themselves as the chosen people with a unique connection, secured by a kind of political or judicial agreement with the God who was over all.

This judicial agreement entailed specific legal requirements, found in the "law of Moses," located in the sacred Jewish Scriptures. These Scriptures, which later were to become the Christian Old Testament, contained books describing God's gifting of the law to the great prophet and deliverer Moses, back when God first saved Israel from enslavement and made them his people. The law included the Ten Commandments but many other requirements as well, both for how Jews were to live together and how they were to worship God. Among other things, Jews were commanded to circumcise their infant boys, observe the weekly Sabbath, and follow kosher food laws.

When Paul claims he was a Jew by birth, race, circumcision, and legal zeal, that is what he means. He rigorously followed the prescriptions of the law. He further declares he was a Pharisee. A scholar could write a long book on what that means exactly—many scholars, in fact, have done so[7]—but for our purposes it is this: Pharisees were particularly conscientious in following God's requirements. They devised oral interpretations of the law designed to enable the faithful to be certain to do all that God had demanded. Neither the written law nor these oral traditions were seen as a burden on the Jew. They were instead liberating: the Jew had learned from God how to live, and it was a pleasure to do so.

Like many other Jews of the time—including such figures as John the Baptist and Jesus of Nazareth—Pharisees held to a kind of apocalyptic worldview that had developed toward the very end of the biblical period and down into the first century. This view maintained that the world was not under direct divine control. For unknown reasons, God had ceded control to cosmic powers aligned against him who were responsible for all the pain, misery, and suffering experienced in the present. But God was soon to intervene to destroy these powers of evil and bring in a good kingdom in which his people would live a utopian existence. This kingdom of God would replace the wretched kingdoms of the current age. It would be a place of joy, peace, love, and prosperity, to be enjoyed by the faithful forever. In the meantime, the race of humans was stuck in this miserable cesspool of suffering and could only wait and hope for the day when God would bring a complete reversal of fortune for his chosen ones. The good news was that this day was not far off. It was coming very soon.

Jesus himself delivered some such message.[8] Paul, who never knew Jesus—who was, in fact, born and raised in a different country from Jesus, spoke a different language, and ascribed to a different, Pharisaic, form of Judaism—also held such views. These were two very different Jews. To be sure, they had significant points of contact: both were Jewish monotheists who belonged to the covenantal community obliged to obey God's law; and both were apocalypticists who understood that God was soon to bring about the cataclysmic end of this miserable world to establish his kingdom. But Paul did not hear about Jesus until sometime after his death. What he heard he did not like. Quite the opposite. What he heard stirred up his zeal. As he himself said, when he learned what the followers of Jesus were saying, he became a violent persecutor of the church and sought to destroy it.

On one level it may seem odd that Paul would be so opposed to one with whom, on the surface, he seemed so much to agree. On the other hand, our bitterest feuds are almost always with those closest to us. And religious violence, against those who are, broadly speaking, of the very same religion, is often the worst.

PAUL AS PERSECUTOR OF THE CHURCH

There is not a huge debate among scholars concerning the rough chronology of Paul's persecution of the church.[9] Jesus is almost always thought to have died around 30 CE; it may have been 29 CE or 33 CE, but it was sometime around then. Because of other pieces of relatively datable facts and a variety of specific chronological references in Paul's letters ("three years later" he did this, "fourteen years later" he did that—see Galatians 1:18; 2:1), it is almost always thought that Paul converted three or possibly four years after Jesus's death. So let's say 33 CE. That means Paul was persecuting the Christian church in its first three years of existence.

There is no way to know if his violent activities extended over just a few months or a couple of years. Moreover, we do not know where it was taking place. The book of Acts claims that it was in the region of Jesus's demise—especially in Jerusalem itself—and up north toward Damascus (Acts 8:1–3; 9:1–2), but there is good reason for doubting it. Paul himself claims that soon after his conversion he was "not known by sight to the churches of Christ in Judea" (Galatians 1:22). That makes it seem unlikely that he had been among them like a fox among the chickens. Moreover, he clearly indicates that he did not convert in Jerusalem but somewhere else, even though he does not say where (in Acts it was "on the road to Damascus"). As a result, we do not know how far the followers of Jesus had spread over the first couple of years or where Paul had heard of them.

It is not hard to guess *how* Paul had heard of them. The original followers of Jesus—the disciples who came to believe in the resurrection and those they soon convinced—were all Jews, through and through, in every way. They would have spread their religion by communicating with other Jews. That would have involved sharing their "good news" in Jewish contexts. Jews gathered every Sabbath in synagogues throughout the land of Israel, up in Syria and Cilicia, and in all nearby regions. In those settings, Jews who had come to believe in Jesus would be telling others he was the messiah who had died and been raised from the dead, just months or a year or two earlier.

It is important to reflect on why any such message might lead to violent persecutions not simply by Paul but, we must assume, by other Jews of his ilk. We are speaking of a strictly internecine religious persecution at this stage. The civil authorities were not yet concerned; there were no criminal activities involved. It was a persecution driven by religious animosity and almost certainly the animus derived from the nature of the message itself. Something about what the followers of Jesus—for simplicity, let's call them Christians, even at this early stage—were saying.[10]

The point of tension is not difficult to identify. It involved the Christians' central proclamation. The followers of Jesus were claiming he was the messiah. That was a problem for one rather glaring and obvious reason. The messiah could not possibly be a man who was crucified.

To make sense of early Jewish outrage over claims concerning the messiahship of Jesus, we need to cut through many centuries of Christian thinking, mountains of subsequent Christian theological speculation, and masses of Christian "common sense" about how Jesus came as the fulfillment of Scripture. Many Christians today have serious difficulty understanding how Jews in antiquity and throughout history, down till today, have rejected the claim that Jesus was the messiah. In this traditional Christian view it is very simple and clear-cut: the Jewish Scriptures themselves predicted the messiah would be born of a virgin in Bethlehem, that he would be a great healer and teacher, and that he would suffer an excruciating death for the sins of others and then be raised from the dead. All that is in the Jews' own Bible. Why can't they see that? Can't they *read*?

Not all Christians have thought this way, of course. Those who have done so have been trained to read the Old Testament in certain ways, to see references to a future messiah where Jews themselves have never detected any messianic prophecies.

Throughout history, when Christians have pointed to "predictions of Jesus" in the Old Testament, Jews have denied the passages involve messianic prophecies. Christians have long maintained, for example, that the ancient prophet Isaiah was looking ahead to Jesus when he declared, centuries before the crucifixion: "He was wounded for our transgressions, he was bruised for our iniquities, the chastisement for our peace was upon him, and by his wounds we were healed" (Isaiah 53:5–6). In response, Jewish readers have pointed out that Isaiah never indicates he is referring to a messiah figure. On the contrary he speaks of someone who has *already* suffered, and he does not call that one the messiah. More than that, earlier in his account he explicitly indicates who this "suffering servant of the Lord" is. It is the nation of Israel itself, which has suffered because of the sins of the people (see Isaiah 49:3).

In the days of Paul, among Jews who had expectations of what the messiah would be, there were never expectations that the messiah would suffer for the sins of others and then be raised from the dead. In fact, the expectations were quite the opposite.

We now know from the Dead Sea Scrolls a range of expectations of what the messiah would be like.[11] The term "messiah" itself literally means "anointed one" and originally referred to the king of Israel, who was anointed with oil during his coronation ceremony in order to show that God had chosen him to lead his people. In the first century, Jews did not have a king but were ruled by a foreign power, Rome. Many Jews considered this an awful and untenable situation and anticipated that God would soon install a Jewish king to overthrow the enemy and reestablish a sovereign state in Israel. This would be God's powerful and exalted anointed one, the messiah.

Other Jews maintained that the future savior of the Jews would be more cosmic in character, a kind of heavenly figure who would come on the clouds of heaven to judge the evil kingdoms of this earth and to establish, in their place, God's own kingdom instead. That kingdom would then be ruled by that cosmic judge or by someone he appointed as God's emissary.

Others thought the future ruler of the coming kingdom of God would be a mighty priest empowered by God to interpret the law correctly and forcefully as he guided the people of Israel in the ways of God apart from the oppressive policies of an alien force.

Despite their differences, all these expectations of the coming messiah had one thing in common: he was to be a figure of grandeur and power who would overthrow the enemies of Israel with a show of force and rule the people of God with a powerful presence as a sovereign state in the Promised Land.

And who was Jesus? He was a crucified criminal. He appeared in public as an insignificant and relatively unknown apocalyptic preacher from a rural part of the northern hinterlands. At the end of his life he made a pilgrimage to Jerusalem with a handful of followers. While there, he ended up on the wrong side of the law and was unceremoniously tried, convicted, and tortured to death on criminal charges. That was the messiah? That was just the opposite of the messiah.

There are good reasons for thinking that during his lifetime, some of Jesus's followers thought maybe he *would* be the messiah. Those hopes were forcefully and convincingly dashed by his execution, since the messiah was not to be executed. But some of these followers came to think that after his death a great miracle had occurred and God had brought Jesus back to life and exalted him up to heaven. This belief reconfirmed the earlier expectation: Jesus *was* the one favored of God. He was the anointed one. He was the messiah.[12]

This reconfirmation of a hope that had been previously dashed compelled these early followers of Jesus to make sense of it all through the ultimate source of religious truth, their sacred scriptural traditions. They found passages that spoke of someone—a righteous person or the nation of Israel as a whole—suffering who was then vindicated by God. These included passages such as Isaiah 53, quoted earlier. The followers of Jesus claimed such passages actually referred to the future messiah. They were predictions of Jesus.

This was for them "good news." Jesus was the messiah, but not one anybody had expected. By raising Jesus from the dead, God showed that his death had brought about a much greater salvation than anyone had anticipated. Jesus did not come to save God's people from their oppression by a foreign power; he came to save them for eternal life. This is what the earliest Christians proclaimed.

For the zealous Pharisee Paul, it was utter nonsense—even worse: it was a horrific and dangerous blasphemy against the Scriptures and God himself. This scandalous preaching had to be stopped.

We don't know exactly how Paul tried to stop it, since regrettably he never describes his persecuting activities. The book of Acts indicates he ravaged the gatherings of Christians and dragged people off to prison (8:3). That's inherently implausible: we don't know of anything like Jewish prisons and we can assume that Roman authorities were not inclined to provide cell space for Jewish sectarians who happened to be proclaiming a rather strange message.

Years later Paul does indicate, in the passage quoted at the beginning of this chapter, that on five occasions after his conversion he himself had received the "forty lashes minus one" (2 Corinthians 11:24). That is a reference to a punishment meted out in a synagogue when Jewish leaders found a congregant guilty of blasphemy and sentenced him to be flogged within an inch of his life: forty lashes were considered too severe, so the supreme penalty was thirty-nine. If Paul experienced this penalty—and we have no reason to doubt it—it would mean he was caught out in a Jewish context of worship. Possibly we can infer that he himself meted out this punishment on others before he had converted. If so, this would make sense of his claim that when he "persecuted the church," he did so "violently" (Galatians 1:13).

It is precisely Paul's original, vicious opposition to the Christian message that makes his conversion to the Christian faith so astounding and momentous. His was not a casual recognition that maybe he had been a bit too quick off the mark, or that perhaps he should have given it more thought. It was a life-transforming reversal, blinding in its intensity. The faith he had tried to destroy snared him and reversed everything he had ever thought—not about his Jewish faith and trust in the Jewish god, but about the person Christians were calling the messiah. Whatever caused this complete reversal, it was not simply life-transforming for Paul himself. It changed the course of human history.

PAUL'S CONVERSION

It is impossible to know exactly what led up to Paul's conversion or what happened at the time. We do have a narrative description in the book of Acts, and it is this description that provides the popular images of Paul being struck by a blinding light on the road to Damascus, falling to the ground, and hearing the voice of Jesus asking, "Saul, Saul, why do you persecute me" (Acts 9:1–19). The account of Acts 9 is retold by Paul himself on two occasions in the narrative

(22:3–16 and 26:9–18). The historical problems it presents have long intrigued and perplexed scholars. For one thing, the three accounts present numerous contradictory details. In one version Paul's companions do not hear the voice but they see the light; in another they hear the voice but do not see anyone. In one version they all fall to the ground from the epiphanic blast; in another they remain standing. In one version Paul is told to go on to Damascus, where a disciple of Jesus will provide him with his marching orders; in another he is not told to go but is given his instructions by Jesus. Clearly we are dealing with narratives molded for literary reasons, not with disinterested historical reports.

The other problem is that most of the details in Acts, contradictory or not, are absent from Paul's own terse description of the event: he makes no references to being on the road to Damascus, being blinded by the light, falling to the ground, or hearing Jesus's voice. I have already indicated the probable reason he provides no detail in his letters: his recipients had surely heard full descriptions of the moment from him earlier. As outsiders we have been largely left in the dark.

The closest thing to a description comes in the first chapter of Paul's letter to the Galatians. After he refers to his former zeal for the ways of Pharisaic Judaism and his consequent persecution of the Christian church, he says the following:

> But when God, who had set me apart from the womb of my mother and had called me through his grace, was pleased to reveal his son to me, so that I might preach him among the gentiles, I did not immediately consult with flesh and blood. Nor did I go up to Jerusalem to those who were apostles before me. But I went off to Arabia and again, then, returned to Damascus. (Galatians 1:15–17)

This description seems to suggest that the "revelation" Paul received occurred in Damascus itself and not on the road there. That's because he indicates that after his sojourn to Arabia—by which he does not mean the deserts of Saudi Arabia but the kingdom of the Nabataeans—he "returned" to Damascus. Despite its maddening brevity, the description does contradict at least one detail in the narrative of Acts 9: here Paul states that he did not consult with anyone about his experience right away. In Acts, that is the first thing he does, as he goes on Jesus's instruction to speak with a disciple named Ananias.

Then what exactly happened at this moment of conversion? All Paul says is that God was "pleased to reveal his son to me."[13] But what does that mean? That Paul was given a sudden revelatory insight into the true meaning of Jesus? That he experienced an actual revelation—an appearance of Christ?

It probably means both. In other places, Paul is perfectly clear: he had a vision of Jesus after his resurrection. He says so explicitly in 1 Corinthians 15:8. Just as Peter, James, the twelve apostles, and others saw Jesus raised from the dead, so too did Paul. In 1 Corinthians 9:1, he suggests that this is why he was an apostle: he had seen the risen Lord. The significance of the event for Paul was not simply that he witnessed something amazing one day. The vision completely revolutionized his thinking and turned him from being a violent persecutor of the Christian faith to being its most forceful and successful advocate. That was because Paul—whether on the spot or after reflecting on it for days, weeks, or months—came to see what it must mean. It must mean that God's entire way of dealing with the human race had changed. And Paul needed to tell people.

We obviously don't know what Paul actually saw. How can we possibly know? What he fervently claimed was that he saw Jesus himself, alive again. Believers would say that was because Jesus actually appeared to him. Unbelievers would say he imagined it. Either way, it is crystal clear that he believed he did see Jesus and that this radically changed his thinking.

THE IMPLICATIONS OF PAUL'S VISION

It is easiest to understand Paul's subsequent missionary activities and evangelistic message by realizing how an appearance of the living

Jesus would force him from "fact" to "implications." For him the "fact" was that Jesus was alive again, as he knew from having seen him. From there Paul started reasoning backward. This backward reasoning must have proceeded through a number of steps ending in a remarkable place: Paul came to believe that he himself had been chosen and commissioned by God to fulfill the predictions of Jewish Scripture. Divinely inspired prophecies delivered centuries earlier were looking forward to his day, his labors, and him personally. Paul cannot be faulted for thinking small.

Here is how the thought process appears to have worked.[14] Paul started with the "fact" that Jesus was alive again. Since Paul also knew that Jesus had died by crucifixion, his reappearance meant that he had experienced a resurrection. God performed a miracle by raising Jesus from the dead. If God raised Jesus from the dead, that would mean that Jesus really was the one who stood under God's special favor, the one chosen by God. But if he was in God's special favor, why would God let him be executed? Would God *require* him to be tortured to death? Is this what God does to the one he favors? What does he do to his enemies?

The matter was even more complicated for Paul, because Jesus did not die just any death or even just any excruciating death. He was killed on a wooden cross. That was a particular problem, because Paul knew full well that Scripture itself pronounces God's curse on anyone who dies on a tree, as Paul himself indicates in Galatians 3:13; quoting Deuteronomy 21:23: "Cursed is anyone who hangs on a tree." If Jesus was the one blessed by God, how could he be the one cursed by God? Paul drew what for him was the natural conclusion: Jesus must not have died for anything he himself had done wrong, since God favored him. He was not being cursed for his own deeds. He must have been cursed for the deeds of others.

As a good citizen of the ancient world, and a good Jew in particular, Paul was perfectly familiar with the theology of sacrificial death. Living beings, including four-footed animals, are chosen to be sacrificed for a variety of reasons: to honor God, to appease God's anger, or to cover over the sins of others. They are not killed because they themselves have done anything to deserve death. Jesus, then, must have been a sacrifice, one who suffered not because of his own misdoings but because of the misdoings of other people. Why was that necessary? As Paul continued to think backward, he concluded Jesus's death must not have been an accident or a gross miscarriage of justice. His death must have appeased God's anger toward others or covered over their sins. If that was the case, then his death must have been part of God's own plan for dealing with the human race. People needed a sacrifice for their sins, and Jesus provided it. God then honored Jesus's act of sacrifice by raising him from the dead.

Then came a further and all-important thought. If the salvation of God came by the death and resurrection of Jesus, this must be how God had planned all along to save his chosen people. That must mean that salvation could not come in any other way—for example, by the zealous adherence to the prescriptions of the Jewish law. If salvation could come by belonging to the covenantal community of the chosen people, or by keeping the Law of Moses, there would be no reason for God's messiah to have suffered an excruciating death. Following the law thus must have no bearing on how a person stands in a right relationship with God.

That in turn had inordinately significant implications. If the law had no bearing on a person's standing before God, then being a Jew could not be required for those who wanted to belong to God's people and enjoy his gracious act of salvation. The only requirement was trusting in the sacrificial atonement provided by Christ. That in turn meant that the message of salvation was not for Jews alone—although it certainly was for them, since it was through the Jewish messiah sent to the Jewish people in fulfillment of the plans of the Jewish god as set forth, Paul came to realize, in the Jewish Scriptures. But the message was not only for Jews. It was for all people, Jew and gentile. And it came to gentiles apart from observing the Jewish law.

Thus, to be members of God's covenantal people, it was not necessary for gentiles to become Jews. They did not need to be circumcised, observe the Sabbath, keep kosher, or follow any of the other prescriptions of the law. They needed only to believe in the death and resurrection of the messiah Jesus. This was an earth-shattering realization for Paul. Prior to this, the followers of Jesus—the first Christians—were of course Jews who understood that he was the messiah who had died and been raised from the dead. But they knew this as the act of the Jewish god given to his people, the Jews. Certainly gentiles could find this salvation as well. But first they had to be Jewish. Not for Paul. Jew or gentile, it did not matter. What mattered was faith in Christ.

Once Paul came to realize this, he was blinded yet again by a further insight. Throughout the prophets of Scripture can be found predictions that at the end of time God would bring outsiders into the fold of the people of God as gentiles flock to the good news that comes forth from his chosen ones, the message delivered through his Jewish people. The prophet Isaiah had said:

> In days to come, the mountain of the LORD's house shall be established as the highest of the mountains, and shall be raised above the hills; all the nations shall stream to it. Many peoples shall come and say, "Come, let us go up to the mountain of the LORD, to the house of the God of Jacob, that he may teach us his ways, and that we may walk in his paths." For out of Zion shall go forth instruction, and the world of the LORD from Jerusalem. (Isaiah 2:2–3)

The prophecy of Isaiah was coming true in Paul's own day. Or consider the words of the prophet Zechariah:

> Many peoples and strong nations shall come to seek the LORD of hosts in Jerusalem. . . . In those days ten people from nations of every language shall take hold of a Jew, grasping his garment and saying, "Let us go with you, for we have heard that God is with you." (Zechariah 8:22–23)

God had predicted that gentiles would come to the salvation that transpired in Jerusalem. Where had Jesus been killed? Jerusalem. How was the message to go forth? It would be preached by Jews, or a Jew, to outsiders. Paul may well have thought specifically of famous words about God's special servant, spoken by the Lord himself, again in the book of Isaiah:

> I am the LORD, I have called you in righteousness. I have taken you by the hand and kept you; I have given you as a covenant to the people, a light to the nations, to open the eyes that are blind, to bring out the prisoners from the dungeon, from the prison those who sit in darkness. . . .

> I will give you as a light to the nations that my salvation may reach to the end of the earth. (Isaiah 42:6–7; 49:6)

Who is this one who was "called in righteousness" to preach God's salvation as a "light to the nations"? Remember how Paul describes his conversion experience in Galatians 1: God "called me through his grace" and "in order that I might preach him among the gentiles" (Galatians 1:15–16). Paul was the one God had called to take his message of salvation afield. Paul's calling to preach was anticipated in the Jewish Scriptures. Paul himself was the fulfillment of prophecy. He was the one God had chosen to bring salvation to the world, through his proclamation of Jesus's death and resurrection.

A number of scholars over the years have suggested that, rather than speaking of Paul's "conversion," we should instead speak of his "call." Part of the logic behind this suggestion is that it is misguided to think Paul left one religion, Judaism, in order to adopt another, Christianity. It is widely acknowledged among Pauline scholars today that this is absolutely right. As Paul's recent biographer, J. Albert Harrill, has expressed it, "Paul thus did not change from Judaism to 'Christianity' in the sense of a faith apart from the religion of Israel."[15] In other words, Paul did not see himself as switching religions. He came to realize that Christ was the fulfillment of Judaism, of everything that God had planned and revealed within the sacred Jewish Scriptures. God had not abandoned the Jews or vacated the Jewish religion; Christ himself had not opposed the Jewish faith or proposed to start something new. Christ stood in absolute continuity with all that went before. But, for Paul, without Christ the Jewish faith was incomplete and imperfect. Christ was the goal to which that faith had long striven, and now he had arrived. And Paul was his prophet.

Even while granting that Paul saw himself principally as one who was "called," we should not jettison too quickly the term "conversion" for what he experienced. True, in his own eyes he did not stop being a Jew or think he was preaching a message at odds with Judaism. But he did "turn around"—the literal meaning of "conversion"—making a radical change in his understanding of that religion and, even more obviously, in his understanding of Christ, rejecting his earlier view of Jesus as condemned by God and coming to see him as God's messiah. And so possibly it is best to consider his experience as both a call and a conversion.

Whatever terms we use, it was a cataclysmic change, astounding in its heightened self-understanding. God had commissioned Paul to take this gospel message to the gentiles. For Paul, this was not merely an interesting career choice. It was the completion of God's plan for the human race. Paul's mission had been predicted by the prophets of old, in anticipation of the coming kingdom of God. Paul was to bring the history of the world to its preordained climax.

PAUL'S MISSIONARY STRATEGY

The received wisdom that Paul engaged in "three missionary journeys" derives from the accounts in the book of Acts. The final two-thirds of the book (chapters 13 to 28) are principally devoted to these journeys and the arrest and trials of Paul that came in their wake. In his own writings, Paul never mentions a specific number of missionary endeavors, but at one point he does intimate a missionary strategy. In what was probably the last of his surviving letters—and the only one addressed to a church that by his own admission he did not found, the letter to the Romans—he looks back on the missionary work already done: "I have completed my preaching of the gospel of Christ from Jerusalem to Illyricum" (Romans 15:19).

Here Paul is sketching an arc of missionary proclamation from the capital of Judea to the northwestern Balkans. As it turns out, nowhere in his letters does Paul indicate that he spent time in Jerusalem trying to convert anyone; on the contrary, he makes it quite clear that he understood himself to be the missionary to the gentiles, leaving the Jewish mission to the disciple Peter and others (Galatians 2:7–9). We also have no record of him taking his mission to Illyricum. We do, however, have clear and certain evidence that he established churches in areas between these two points.[16]

It cannot be stressed enough that Paul's mission was entirely to cities, at least so far as we know.[17] That only makes sense: Paul clearly wanted to reach as many people as possible. Unlike Jesus, who preached in hamlets, villages, and remote areas of rural Galilee, Paul focused on urban centers, where populations were the most dense. His letters mention Christian communities in such places as Corinth, Philippi, Thessalonica, Colossae, Laodicea, Ephesus, and the region of Galatia.

Among other things, this means he was traveling a lot. One scholar has pointed out that, in the book of Acts alone, Paul's journeys cover some ten thousand miles.[18] That is not implausible. The Roman road system was extensive and well maintained and it was a time of virtual peace on the interior of the empire. Ancient ships could cover a hundred miles a day; ordinary travelers on foot probably fifteen or twenty. On the whole, international travel was more popular and feasible in the Roman Empire than at any time in previous history, and more than in all the centuries to follow until the Industrial Revolution.

It is difficult to discern a pattern in Paul's travels, but his general principle appears clear. Either alone or, more commonly, with Christian companions, he would come to a new city, make converts, start a worshiping community, and instruct the new members in the basics of the faith. When he judged the church could survive and thrive on its own, he would then move on to the next place. He thus established churches in major urban settings one after the other—principally provincial capitals and Roman colonies—by converting gentiles to believe in the god of the Jews and in Christ as his son who died for the sins of the world and was raised from the dead.

Clearly Paul seems to have understood himself to be "planting" churches, as he himself states in his letter to the Christians in Corinth (1 Corinthians 3:6). Once planted, the church would grow by accumulating new members. After Paul journeyed onward he continued to be invested in the communal lives of the churches he left behind. That is demonstrated by the letters themselves as he responds to problems that have arisen in one community or another over what to believe and how to behave. He was not one to stay too long in one location. He had a gospel to preach and he needed to take it where it had not yet been proclaimed. As he writes: "Everyone who calls on the name of the Lord will be saved. But how can they call upon one in whom they have not believed? And how can they believe if they have not heard? And how can they hear without one who preaches?" (Romans 10:13–15) He was the preacher, the one who brought the word of faith.

The ultimate goal of his mission was, in his words, that "the full number of gentiles" would come into the faith (Romans 11:25). Paul saw himself as the one responsible for making it happen. We do not know his master strategy, given his inability to be everywhere at once. Possibly he planned to preach in one region and then the next—not in every city and town in the region, but in major urban centers—anticipating that the churches he planted would not just grow but would also fertilize the areas around them, leading to new growths and more expansion. Were that to work, the entire region, and eventually every entire region, would be filled with believers in Jesus.

When Paul wrote his letter to the Romans from the Greek city of Corinth, he indicated that he no longer had "any room for work in these regions" (Romans 15:23). He evidently meant in the entire eastern Mediterranean, since he then mentioned his plan to use Rome as a stopping point before moving on to preach in Spain. It appears that Rome was to be a base of operations from which to evangelize the western empire. Spain was as far west as he could go. Some scholars have plausibly argued that this was his ultimate objective. Recall that Isaiah had predicted the good news of God's salvation would be taken to "the end of the earth" (Isaiah 49:6, quoted by Paul in Acts 13:47). Was Spain the end of the earth? Paul may have well thought so, believing that, once he established the church there, the last days would be near when "the full number of the gentiles" had come in and "all Israel" would "be saved" (Romans 11:25–26). If so, this is heady stuff. In the words of one Pauline scholar, Paul himself had become "the central figure in the story of salvation."[19]

PAUL'S MODUS OPERANDI

It is difficult to know for certain how Paul conducted his mission on the ground. He was moving to cities that, so far as we can tell, he had never visited before, and trying to convert strangers to the faith. He apparently succeeded a good deal. But how did he do it?

We should not think that Paul staged "tent revivals" like a traveling American evangelist in the nineteenth or twentieth century. There is no reference to any such undertaking in his letters or even in Acts. The public speeches in Acts are almost always occasioned by a random and fortuitous event, such as a public miracle. They are not organized in advance.

It is theoretically possible that Paul acted on a more ad hoc basis, entering a public space and preaching, as it were, from a soapbox. But that too seems unlikely, both because the success rate would surely be inordinately low and because neither Acts nor Paul himself says anything of the sort.

More plausibly, it has been suggested that Paul would attend the local synagogue during services on Sabbath and use the occasion as a visitor in town to proclaim his good news about Jesus the messiah. After making some converts, according to this scenario, Paul would then use the synagogue as a kind of base of operations to begin reaching pagans in the community.

A strategy like this makes a good deal of sense. For someone new in town, the obvious first place to go would be where one could make contacts with people from similar backgrounds. And for a Jew who had just arrived, no better place would exist than one of the local synagogues. Moreover, as we saw at the outset of this chapter, Paul had been punished in synagogues, evidently flogged within an inch of his life on five separate occasions. Paul was no stranger to hostile Jewish environments, presumably in cities he was attempting to evangelize.

On the other hand, it cannot be overemphasized that Paul sees himself as a missionary not to Jews but to gentiles. In addition, it would have been very difficult to use a synagogue as a base of operations if everyone there, including the leaders who wielded the power and the whip, hated you and wanted to beat some good sense into you. Also, contrary to what one might think, there is little indeed to suggest that the communities of believers that Paul addressed comprised both Jews and gentiles. When he refers to his converts' former religious lives, it is to their worship of pagan gods. As he reminds the Corinthians: "You know that when you were pagans you were led astray by idols that could not speak" (1 Corinthians 12:2). So too when he recalls to the Thessalonians that they used to worship "dead idols" (1 Thessalonians 1:9). The entire letter to the Galatians is predicated on the fact that the readers are gentile Christians being told by false teachers to begin practicing the ways of Judaism. These are all churches filled with pagan converts. So where did Paul meet them?

Modern scholarship has landed on a solution that is both sensible and supported by Paul's own words.[20] In his letter to the Thessalonians, Paul recalls preaching while engaged in manual labor: "For you remember, brothers and sisters our labor and toil; during night and day we labored so as not to burden you, preaching to you the gospel of God" (1 Thessalonians 2:9). When he refers to his toil here, it is not to his toil of preaching: it was toil that kept him from having to be supported financially by others. He was working both a day and a night job. So too in his letter to the Corinthians, Paul stresses that he and his missionary companions engaged in a life of "labor, working with our own hands" (1 Corinthians 4:12). Later he reminds them how he and his companion Barnabas had "to work for a living" (9:6).

And so the question is, how are we to imagine the relationship between Paul's daily work and his missionary activity? New Testament scholar Ronald Hock has argued the most persuasive case: Paul was preaching on the job.[21]

Support for this view comes from the book of Acts, which indicates that Paul was a professional "tentmaker" (Acts 18:3). Some scholars have thought this word can have broader applicability, referring to some kind of leather-goods work. (Tents were made from animal skins, but so obviously were lots of other things.) There is no certainty on the matter. But it does appear that Paul was a craftsman of some kind. If so, we can have a good idea of how he proceeded from one town to the next establishing churches. If he was a leather-worker Paul would have had a mobile profession. He would have taken his knives, awls, and other tools of the trade with him from one place to the next. When coming to a new town, he would meet up with others in his line of work. Commonly the professions were centered in one part of the city or another. He would choose an apt spot, rent out a space for his workshop, probably secure an apartment in a floor above for living quarters (this was common in city dwellings: a multilevel building of this sort was called an *insula*), and open up for business.

It is in some such context that he would have "preached night and day" to the Thessalonians. People would come into his shop for business and he would talk to them about religion. Businesses as a rule were far more casual in that way than today. People could spend a long time in conversation. Paul, by his own account, was at it at all hours. Obviously he would not be able to convert someone the first time they met, on the spot. He was urging pagan people to give up every religious tradition and cultic practice they had ever known. That took time. But he had time. He had to work—he was at it before dawn to after dusk—and while working with his hands he was preaching the gospel.

One can imagine that he was rarely successful. But it would not take a lot of success to make a big difference. For one thing, it was a common feature of ancient life for the head of a household—the senior adult male—to make the family's decisions when it came to religion. Convert the head of the household, and you converted the entire family. Modern Christians might say that the wife and children of a convert should not really be counted as converts because it was not their choice. Even so, new religious traditions and forms of worship would be introduced into the household and everyone in it would participate. In many or even most situations, over a period of months or years, other members of the family would surely come over mentally and emotionally as well. Thus one convert could translate into numerous others.

One other factor to consider is the high population density of ancient cities. The modern city of Antakya in southeastern Turkey has just over two hundred thousand inhabitants and by most modern standards is crowded. In Paul's day it was called Antioch and it had twice that population. But you could walk around its circumference in an afternoon. The average population density in Roman cities was about two hundred persons per acre, matched today in only the densest inner cities. There was little space and even less privacy. One result was that news could spread very quickly indeed. And rumor. And gossip.[22]

If someone adopted a completely new set of religious traditions—abandoning the traditions and worship that everyone else followed more or less without question—any such conversion would no doubt spark comment, curiosity, and interest. Maybe enough interest to see what it was all about. More people would start showing up in Paul's workshop. He would not convert the majority of them by any stretch of the imagination. But he would convert some. Heads of the household would then convert their families. The church would be planted and start to grow.

Soon Paul would be satisfied that the planting season was finished, and he would head off to the next city to start all over again. This would go on for years, possibly for three decades. We will never know how many churches Paul started, but he is explicitly associated with about a dozen in his writings. Possibly there were many more.

We are still left with the question of what Paul would say to potential converts that would prove at all convincing. As we will see more fully in the next chapter, these people were pagans who worshiped numerous divine beings by local customs that had been handed down over the centuries and that everyone simply took for granted. Temples to pagan gods would be found everywhere throughout a major city, and in the temple would be idols—statues of the gods—that represented a kind of physical representation of the divinity itself. Outside the temple would be an altar on which to perform occasional sacrifices to the god—or, rather, to watch someone else do so. People could frequent as many temples of as many gods as they wanted. They would also worship their own family gods. And participate in worship of the emperor and of any of the gods that the Roman state itself promoted. In any city at any time there was a rich, fertile, and extraordinarily textured set of cultic traditions. Paul's mission was to convert people from these pagan traditions to be believers in Jesus. What did he say and how did he convince anyone?

PAUL'S MESSAGE

In his surviving letters, Paul never explicates the message he had delivered to his potential converts. Obviously there was no reason for him to do so: he was writing about other matters precisely to the people he had converted, who knew full well what he had said at the time, presumably over and over again. But he does on occasion make an allusive reference back to his preaching, and as scant as these recollections are, they provide an intriguing insight into what Paul said and the rhetorical strategy he used. We find the first such reference in the earliest of Paul's surviving writings, the letter of I Thessalonians.

In fondly recalling the time he had spent with the Christians of Thessalonica (in northern Greece), Paul has occasion to remember how they, as former pagans, came to join with him in his Christian faith, how they "turned to God from idols, to serve the living and true God, and to await his son from heaven, whom he raised from the dead, Jesus, the one who saves us from the wrath that is coming" (1 Thessalonians 1:9–10). The comment is terse but illuminating.

To convert to the Christian faith through Paul's gospel was both more and less complicated than converting to Judaism. It was more complicated because it involved not simply coming to believe that the Jewish god was the only one who deserved to be worshiped, but also to believe that Jesus was his son, who had been raised from the dead for salvation. Even in its briefest form, this is a two-step conversion—faith in God and faith in Jesus—not one step. At the same time, these two steps were somewhat less complicated than converting to Judaism, since the convert was not then expected to join the Jewish people by adopting Jewish customs and following Jewish laws, including, most notably, circumcision, Sabbath observance, keeping Jewish festivals, and following kosher food laws.

The first, and undoubtedly most difficult, step in converting pagans to Christianity was to convince them to turn away from the gods they had worshiped from infancy—gods that not just their immediate families but also all their friends, neighbors, fellow citizens, and, in fact, with the exception of Jews, everyone in their entire world worshiped. This would obviously be an enormous step. One would have to give up all the daily and periodic festivals, processions, sacrifices, prayers, beliefs, and practices attendant to all the traditional religions they had ever known. How did Paul manage to convince anyone to do it?

He shows how he did it in this concise recollection of 1 Thessalonians. He convinced the pagans that their idols—the statues of their gods—were "dead" and that they should instead worship the "living" God. For Paul, there was only God who was alive and active in the world. The others were completely dead and useless, inert and able to do nothing. It appears that when Paul preached to these pagans he employed the standard kind of attack on pagan gods that had been used by Jews for centuries. One of our earliest examples of this kind of attack, which shows both its rhetorical strategy and force, is in the Hebrew Bible, in a passage that Paul, with his rigorous training in Judaism, must have known intimately. It is found in the book of Isaiah, where the prophet mocks the gods of the pagans. He points out that a person who makes a god-statue, an idol, fashions it out of wood or iron, not realizing that this is all it is: wood or iron. It is not a god. It has no power. It can do nothing. It is human designed and human made. In his mockery the prophet points out that after the woodworker cuts down a tree for the material he needs to fashion his god:

> Then [the wood] can be used as fuel. Part of it he takes and warms himself; he kindles a fire and bakes bread. Then he makes a god and worships it, makes a carved image and bows down before it. Half of it he burns in the fire; over this half he roasts meat, eats it and is satisfied. He also warms himself and says, "Ah, I am warm, I can feel the fire!" The rest of it he makes into a god, his idol, bows down to it and worships it; he prays to it and says "Save me, for you are my god." . . . A deluded mind has led him astray, and he cannot save himself or say, "Is not this thing in my right hand a fraud?" (Isaiah 44:15–17, 20)

This kind of polemic would have seemed common sense to most Jews. Many pagans, it has to be admitted, would have found it either ridiculous or irrelevant, for a very simple reason. Pagans—at least, the reflective ones among them—did not consider their cult statues to be gods. They considered them to be representations of gods—visual aids, as it were—to help one focus on the reality of the god. Or, in a somewhat more sophisticated vein, they thought the cult statue was a focal point of divine energy, the place through which the god could manifest its power. But the item itself was not a god. It was an image or a conduit for a god.

Many pagans, on the other hand, may not have thought at this level of abstraction and may simply have taken the intellectual short-cut assumed by Jewish polemicists, thinking that idols really were gods. People like that would certainly be susceptible to the kind of critique leveled by Isaiah, by Jewish polemicists after his day, and by people like Paul, who in a different moment wanted to convince them that their own gods were lifeless, powerless, ineffectual—in short, dead.

Paul almost certainly preached some version of this message. And he proclaimed, by contrast, the glories of the living God, the one who created the heavens and the earth, the one who saved his people Israel from their slavery in Egypt at the Exodus, the one who did miracles through his prophets and who continued to do miracles among the living in Paul's own day. But Paul also had to persuade his listeners to believe in Christ. His message was not simply about the living God but also about the living Jesus.

In fact, Paul's message about the living Jesus may have itself been the medium through which he preached about the living God. The notion that God is living presupposes that God is active, not just in heaven but also on earth. A living God is a God who is involved in this world. He is a God who acts in ways that appear miraculous to mere mortals. In fact, his actions are miracles. Paul preached God's miracles as demonstrations of power available to all who believed. And he focused on one miracle in particular, as he himself indicates in the recollection I have quoted of his preaching to the Thessalonians. He preached that God had raised Jesus from the dead.

Paul's message to these converts began with a historical fact: Jesus was a Jewish prophet who was crucified by the Romans. There would be nothing incredible about that. Romans were crucifying people all the time. What makes this one instance stand out is what happened afterward. God raised Jesus from the dead. This is the heart and soul of Paul's proclamation. It is one that he could speak with enormous conviction, the kind of conviction that could win converts. Paul knew that God raised Jesus from the dead because he himself had seen Jesus alive afterward.

Paul could swear to it. He did swear to it. Moreover, he was a reasonable, intelligent, clear-thinking human being. We can assume that he seemed completely honest and ingenuous. He would have been straightforward and emphatic. With his own eyes he had seen the crucified Jesus alive again. This must have been convincing to people—at least some people.

Paul's potential converts must have wondered why God would allow his son to die, especially a death by crucifixion, the most torturous, horrific, and feared form of execution in Roman antiquity. So Paul's next step was to explain what the death of Jesus meant. We know how Paul explained Jesus's death because of another recollection of his missionary preaching in a different letter, this one not to the Thessalonians but to the church of Corinth, farther south along the eastern coast of Greece. Paul's first letter to the Corinthians is much longer and involved than the one to the Thessalonians. In it he deals with a large number of problems that the Corinthian church was experiencing. Near the end Paul has occasion to recall what he had preached to them—they too had been pagans—when first he converted them, a message that Paul indicates he had "received":

> For I delivered over to you among the most important things what I also received, that Christ died for our sins in accordance with the Scriptures, and that he was buried; and that he was raised on the third day in accordance with the Scriptures, and that he appeared to Cephas, then to the twelve. . . . And last of all, as to one untimely born, he appeared also to me. (1 Corinthians 15:3–5, 8)

This was the core of Paul's missionary message, as he himself says. Christ's death was not a miscarriage of justice or a tragic accident of history: it was all part of God's plan of salvation that had earlier been set forth in the Jewish Scriptures. Jesus died "for our sins." In this message Paul stressed there could be no doubt about Jesus's death, because after he died he was buried. But Jesus did not stay dead. God raised him from the dead, again in fulfillment of the Scriptures. Once more there could be no doubt, because he then appeared on several occasions to his disciples. Last of all he appeared to Paul. Paul saw him. He really was raised. If he was raised, God must have raised him. If God raised him, his death must have been by divine design. It was a death God planned and willed, because it was a death for the sake of the sins of others. It is the death and resurrection of Jesus that put a person in a right standing before the one and only God, a living God, who has done miracles in this world that he created.

But Paul's message did not end there. Recall from the passage in 1 Thessalonians that Paul reminded the Thessalonian Christians not only about what happened in their past—how they turned from their dead idols to the living God—but also about what was about to happen in their future. They turned to God and they now "await his Son from heaven . . . Jesus, who delivers us from the wrath that is coming" (1 Thessalonians 1:10).

The second coming of Jesus was absolutely central to Paul's preaching. It was not simply an afterthought. It was in fact a natural corollary to the declaration that Jesus had been raised. If he had been raised, where was he? Why wasn't he anywhere to be seen? Paul maintained that Jesus was no longer present because he had been taken up to heaven and given a position of divine glory. But he would not reside there forever. God's act of salvation was much, much larger than simply saving a few souls here and there. God's plan was to redeem the entire world.

It is crucial to remember that even before his conversion Paul was a thoroughgoing apocalypticist. He did not abandon his apocalyptic thinking when he came to follow Jesus; his apocalypticism was instead brought into his new faith and formed his framework for understanding it. This world was controlled by evil forces. That was why there was so much pain and misery here. But God was ultimately sovereign and was about to reestablish his control over the world. He was soon to enter into judgment and overthrow the forces of evil—along with everyone who sided with them—in order to bring about his good kingdom here on earth. The utopia to come was to be preceded by a cataclysmic act of destruction. God's wrath was about to strike. God would send a cosmic judge of the earth to destroy his enemies and set up his kingdom. And, for Paul, that cosmic judge was Jesus. It was Jesus whom the Thessalonians were to "await from heaven," because he was the one who would "save us from the wrath that is coming."

Paul's message, in a nutshell, was a Jewish apocalyptic proclamation with a seriously Christian twist. God was saving this world. He had destroyed the power of sin by the death of Jesus; he had destroyed the power of death by the resurrection of Jesus; and he would destroy the power of evil by the return of Jesus. It was all going according to plan. Paul knew for a fact that it was because with his own eyes he had seen that Jesus had been raised from the dead. He also knew that Jesus was soon to return. This time he would not come meekly.

PAUL'S MODE OF PERSUASION

It is not hard to see how Paul might convert at least some pagans with this message, given his confidence and self-assurance as one who had personally seen the resurrected Jesus. But was there anything else that made his message particularly persuasive? Here we have to rely on scant but tantalizing allusions that no doubt resonated clearly with the audience of Paul's letters, who knew full well what he was talking about, but whose meaning can only be surmised by those of us living two millennia later. In a later chapter we will see that Christian sources of the first four centuries consistently report one and virtually only one thing that convinced people to convert to the faith. They saw, or more often heard about, miracles that authenticated the Christian message. Miracles led to faith.

Let me be clear that I am not saying that Christian missionaries were actually performing the miraculous works ascribed to them in our sources: healing the sick, speaking with demons and driving them out, raising the dead, leveling pagan places of worship with a word, giving dogs human voices, and bringing smoked tuna back to life. (We will see these miracles later.) I do not think there is any way, given the nature of the historical discipline and the tools in the historian's chest, for a historian ever to claim that any of these things "probably" happened. Believers may think they did; nonbelievers will think they did not; and historians cannot arbitrate in that dispute (although theologians may want to give it a go). What historians can say—clearly, emphatically, and with a clear conscience—is that throughout history people have *thought* miracles happened. Most often they have thought this not because they saw miracles but because they heard about them.

Paul's converts heard about miracles. In fact, he suggests they saw him personally do miracles—or thought they saw him do them, which for our purpose comes to the same thing. Again, the references are allusive at best. But they do seem to point in that direction. In Paul's letter to the Romans, where he indicates he had preached the gospel throughout the eastern Mediterranean from Jerusalem to Il-lyricum, he claims he converted people not only "by word" but also by "deed, by the power of signs and wonders, by the power of the Holy Spirit" (Romans 15:18–19). It is hard to imagine what "signs, wonders, and Spirit-power" would be if not miracles.

So too, in his first letter to the Corinthians, Paul admits his speaking abilities were rather feeble but his words were backed up by incredible acts: "I was with you in weakness and fear and great trembling, and my word and preaching was not in persuasive words of wisdom but also in a show of the Spirit and of power" (1 Corinthians 2:3–4). Again "Spirit" and "power" as a supplement to his preaching. Then, more emphatically, in his second letter to the Corinthians, while reminding his readers of his apostolic ministry among them, Paul states that "the signs of an apostles were performed among you in all patience: signs, and wonders, and miracles" (2 Corinthians 12:12). What was Paul actually doing in these peoples' presence? We have no reliable record and no real clue. Whatever it was, it must have been stupendous. And it proved convincing. He was, after all, converting people and establishing churches, in city after city.

PAUL: IN SUM

I am all too aware of the problem of hyperbole, but I nonetheless stick to my claim: Paul was not simply the most significant convert of the first few years of Christianity, or of the first century, or of the early church. He was the most significant Christian convert of all time. One can argue that, without Paul, Christian history as we know it would not have happened.

It is not that Paul himself started Christianity. Christians were already around before his time. Otherwise he would not have had anyone to persecute. Moreover, contrary to what people often say, it is not that Paul invented the idea that Jesus's death and resurrection brought salvation. That is what the earliest Christians were proclaiming before Paul had ever heard of them. Instead, Paul is so significant because he came to believe—whether in a flash, as claimed in the New Testament, or over a period of time, as calmer reflection might suggest—that the death and resurrection of Jesus brought a salvation that was not tied to explicit Jewish identity; that the salvation of Christ was efficacious for gentiles as well as Jews; that pagans who came to believe in Christ did not first have to convert to Judaism and begin to follow the prescriptions of Jewish law and custom. Salvation had indeed come to the Jews, but it had gone forth to the gentiles. God was in the process of saving the entire world. Gentiles could remain gentiles—and presumably Jews could remain Jews.

What is more, Paul believed God had called him, and him in particular, to make this gospel, this "good news," known to the world at large. The prophets of old had predicted someone would come to bring light to the gentiles, enlightenment to the pagans. Paul was that one. He had a message and a mission, and it was not a small-time affair merely involving a leatherworker talking to customers in his shop. It was that, but it was also massively bigger. It was a fulfillment of the promises God had made through his prophets centuries earlier. Paul's mission would bring God's entire plan of salvation to completion. Once Paul had reached "the ends of the earth," the gentiles would have heard the message and the climax of history could arrive. Jesus would come from heaven, the forces of evil would be destroyed, and God's utopian kingdom would arrive. Paul's mission was of cosmic proportions.

The end, of course, did not come. But the Christian message continued to thrive after Paul's day. It does not appear to have thrived in Jewish circles. Nearly all the early Christians we know about—including those addressed in our earliest writings, those of the New Testament—came from pagan stock.[23] For reasons I have set forth in this chapter, most Jews simply could not accept the claim that Jesus, a lower-class itinerant preacher who was crucified for crimes against the state, was in fact God's messiah. Pagans proved more receptive to the message—not just in Paul's day, but in the decades and centuries to come.

Later we will consider how the message was preached after Paul and why it succeeded. First we need to gain an even clearer idea of what it was pagan converts were converting from. That will require us to explore more fully the world of Roman paganism, the world from which most Christians came and that they then confronted.

Chapter 3

The Religious World of Conversion: Roman Paganism

The earliest Christians were Jews. According to the New Testament, the first to believe in Jesus's resurrection were his eleven disciples (Judas Iscariot no longer being on the scene) and a handful of women, including Mary Magdalene (see Matthew 28; Luke 21; John 21). They were all from rural Galilee, the northern part of the land of Israel. One of the Gospels, Matthew, indicates that the disciples came to this belief (although some "doubted") sometime after Jesus's execution, when they had returned to Galilee (Matthew 28:16–17). That seems reasonable: they had made a pilgrimage to Jerusalem with Jesus to celebrate a Passover festival; things had not gone well there; and Jesus had been arrested, tried, and crucified for crimes against the state. It seems unlikely the others would have stayed in the city to see if the authorities would come for them next. They went back home, possibly in some haste.

Once these followers came to believe, they presumably told others in Galilee that Jesus had been raised, and these people converted. Eventually, when the heat died down, some of the disciples, if not all, returned to Jerusalem. We are not sure why. Did they, already at this early date, expect Jesus to return there? Whatever their reasons, we find them in Jerusalem in the book of Acts (Acts 1), and that's where Paul locates them as well (Galatians 1). It appears the city became the base of the Christian operation, with Jesus's disciple Peter and then his brother James taking charge of the small but growing community. That community would have principally comprised locals in the capital—that is, all Jews. Paul indicates that the earliest believers had undertaken a mission to convert Jews to the faith, headed by Peter (Galatians 2:7–8). That too is completely plausible.

It is usually assumed, then, that the first Christian community was located in the principal city of Judea. We do not learn much about the group in later sources, apart from the names of their leaders and a scant few legends associated with them. The truth is that, for reasons we saw in the previous chapter, the Jewish mission was never a huge success. In sources over the next four centuries we occasionally learn of a Jewish group of Christians here or there in the empire—in the Transjordan, in Egypt—but they never played a huge role in the ongoing life of the church at large. They were almost always on the margins.

The Jewish Christians were probably heading to the margins by the second part of the first century. We have seen that Paul himself was intent on establishing communities of believers on pagan soil, and he is the only massively effective evangelist we hear of in our first-century sources.[1] His churches, which appear to have grown even after he relocated to evangelize elsewhere, comprised exclusively or almost exclusively pagan converts. And not just the churches he founded. The one surviving letter from his pen sent to a community he did not start is to the Christians in the city of Rome, a church he had yet to visit. He explicitly addresses the Christians there as "gentiles" (Romans 1:13; 11:13). Scholars frequently argue that it was a strongly "mixed" church of Jew and gentile. It may have been that, but the letter itself indicates that the vast majority of the congregation were converts from paganism. In the greetings in the final chapter Paul names twenty-six people, several of whom indeed may have been Jewish: we can't tell just from their names. But he identifies six of them specifically as "of my race"—that is, Jews (Romans 16:7, 11, 21). That this is an identity marker of just these six seems to suggest that they stood out, for reason of their heritage, from all the rest.[2] The other twenty were probably former pagans.

Much the same can be said about the churches addressed by most of our earliest Christian writings. The vast majority of the New Testament books—including that "most Jewish" of our Gospels, Matthew—appear to be directed largely if not exclusively to gentile audiences, and most may well have been written by gentile authors.[3] The church by the second half of the first century was probably made up of predominantly pagan stock.[4]

We have already seen some indications of who such people were and what they believed in connection with Constantine, the most famous and significant pagan convert in the history of Christendom. We can now explore the matter in greater depth, as a prelude to showing, in the chapters that follow, how Jesus's followers managed to convince so many of these pagans to abandon their ancestral religious traditions in order to worship the Christian god alone.

THE "ISM" IN "PAGANISM"

Paganism, scholars have long argued, was not a single thing. Or, to put the matter differently, there was no such thing as paganism. What we call paganism was numerous things.[5]

The word itself would have made no sense to ancient people, including the very ones we call pagans. No one called themselves or thought of themselves, religiously, as a pagan—not because it was a derogatory term, but because it was not a term with any religious meaning. The idea that all the hundreds or even thousands of ways of honoring the gods involved some kind of unified "system" was simply not part of the ancient intellectual landscape. The religious designation "pagan" came into existence only after customs for acknowledging and worshiping the gods had been in place for millennia. It was deployed by Christians in its religious sense as a way of referring to others who did not follow their own practices of religious observation. Christians had to call non-Christians *something*.

Worshipers of the god of Israel were no problem: they could be called Jews. But what of everyone else? What of the 93 percent of the rest of the human race?

There are different theories about why Christians settled on the term "pagan" to describe the non-Jewish other.[6] Most commonly it is thought that the word derives from the Latin term *paganus*, which refers to a person who resides in the countryside. The idea, in this case, is that as the empire became Christianized in the fourth century and later, the sophisticated city folk were more likely to see the clear superiority of the Christian faith. Only country bumpkins (the *pagani*) continued to observe the backward customs of their ignorant ancestors.

Other scholars have argued, instead, that the term "pagan" originally referred to "civilian," as opposed to "soldier." In that case it would stand in contrast to the few, the strong, the brave: the soldiers of Christ. Those who were not in Christ's army were weak and morally out of shape.

Whatever the origins of the term, "pagan" was not a self-identity marker: in the early Christian centuries, no one in the Roman world would say, "I am not a Jew, I am a pagan." Being not a Jew—or later not a Christian—simply meant being what everyone else was: a person who accepted the existence of gods and worshiped them by following customs that had been followed since time immemorial. There were innumerable such localized customs. Modern people might call each of them a "religion."

As we have seen, ancient people would not call them that, since there was also no word for "religion." And in fact what we typically think today about religion simply did not apply to ancient modes of worship. If we were to define a religion as a coherent system of thought, belief, and practice, with a clearly demarcated set of theological views about the divine being(s) and a prescribed set of rituals to be practiced in reference to them, then none of the so-called pagan religions would probably qualify.[7] Certainly the totality of all the customs followed over the expanse of the Roman Empire cannot be lumped together into a unified whole and considered a solitary religion.

In Roman paganism (I will keep using the word for the sake of convenience) there were no set gods. Because the standard Greek and Roman mythologies are generally known, people today often still imagine there was just one ancient pantheon: for example, with Jupiter, the head god; Juno, his wife; Mars, the god of war; Venus, the goddess of love; and so on. It is true these gods were widely worshiped in the empire. But there was no set pantheon. Instead, there were different gods and various ways to worship them, depending on whether a person lived in North Africa, Egypt, Syria, Asia Minor, Greece, Gaul, Spain, Britain, or anywhere else. As a result, there was no universal mythology. Moreover, there was no single way to talk about the gods. There was no sense of a community of worshipers throughout the empire to which one would "belong." There were no organizations with empire-wide oversight over religious practices— no religious authorities who transcended particular localities. Trying to wrap our minds around this totality is difficult.[8]

RELIGION AND MYTH

It is often thought by people casually acquainted with the ancient world that Roman religion (and Greek religion as well) was focused on the famous myths that we still read today—that books such as Homer's *Iliad* and *Odyssey* functioned as the pagan Bible. The logic behind this view is that these literary works, along with writings of Hesiod and Euripides on the Greek side, or Virgil and Ovid on the Roman, reveal what people believed about the gods. The pagan myths seem comparable to the stories found in the Christian Bible, whether in the Old Testament with God's interactions with Israel or in the New Testament with the stories of Jesus. Since religion involves principally how we think about God or the gods, in this view, the myths tell us what ancient religion was like.

That common sense would not have made sense to most ancient Romans. It is true that myths were very important for helping people think about the gods. But ancient religion was less about what one thought and more about what one did. Traditional myths played little part in most ancient religious customs. Stories about the gods in great works of literature were usually taken to be just that: great stories. The educated classes in particular insisted they were not to be taken literally. Myths were not so much accounts of what happened in the past as amusing and always entertaining tales, or possibly highly allegorical narratives. As such, the myths formed the basis for a good bit of ancient literature, theater, and art, but they were not the "theological basis" for ancient religion, the equivalent of the Jewish Scriptures or the New Testament writings.

Pagan religions were almost entirely about practice, about doing things, about giving the gods their due—not through mental affirmations of who they were or what they had done, but through ritual actions that showed reverence and devotion.

RELIGION THEN AND NOW

In trying to conceptualize Roman pagan religions, one of the most important points to stress is that they differed enormously from how we think of religion today, at least in the context of the great monotheistic traditions of the West: Judaism, Christianity, and Islam.

Many Gods Instead of One God

To begin with, Roman religions were all polytheistic, accepting the existence of many gods and promoting their worship. As just mentioned, there were Romans, certainly at least among the highly educated, who did come to believe that one ultimate divine being ruled over all. But these were the exception to the rule, and even they acknowledged the existence of numerous other divinities that varied in grandeur, power, and function. Many Romans did acknowledge a pantheon of the "great gods" known from the famous mythical tales: Jupiter, Juno, Mars, Venus, Minerva, Pluto, and the rest. But this was not the full extent of the divine realm.

On the contrary, there were gods for every municipality and every family; gods with all sorts of functions: gods connected with love, war, livestock, crops, health, childbirth, and weather; gods associated with specific locations: mountains, streams, meadows, homes, hearths; gods of various abstractions, such as fortune, mercy, and hope; gods connected with elements of nature, like the moon, the sun, the sky, and the sea. Less grand and powerful divinities existed as well, including those known collectively (in Greek speaking areas) as *daimones*. These were not "demons" in the later Christian sense of fallen angels that inhabit human bodies and force them to do unpleasant things. They were low-level divine beings who were more active in humans' daily lives than the greater gods and who could be either nefarious or beneficent, depending on circumstances and their character or mood.

How many gods were there? They could not be counted. There were many divine beings in many places. And the same god could be in many different places. A god such as the Greek Zeus was worshiped in cities hundreds of miles apart, in different ways, and with different appellatives (Zeus Kasios, Zeus Ammon, Zeus Bennios). In any city there would be temples to a wide array of gods. The Roman architect Vitruvius recommended that a Roman city have temples to the gods of the Roman Capitol—Jupiter, Juno, and Minerva—as well as to Mercury, Isis and Serapis, Apollo, Liber Pater, Hercules, Mars, Venus, Vulcan, and Ceres. That was just to start. As one modern scholar has pointed out, we have coins from the city of Nicomedia (northeast Turkey) that advertise the worship of forty deities there. Those are just the ones mentioned on the city's surviving coins.[9]

Polytheism in Roman antiquity was normally an open and welcoming affair. New gods could be added and worshiped at will. It was simply accepted that people would worship the gods they chose: gods supporting the state, gods of the municipality, gods of various functions, gods of various locations, gods of the family. The gods themselves were at peace, which is one way in which Roman religion was at odds with Roman mythology, where the gods were constantly at one another's throats. Moreover, the god worshiped in one locality was often identified with a different god called by a different name worshiped in another locality.

Romans would frequently assimilate the gods of the people they conquered. This shows the remarkable openness of religious perspectives, and it made it possible for conquered people to continue living their lives with less cultural disruption. It also had the effect of submerging the identities of the other gods into the Roman system, just as the conquered people were also brought into a new form of governance and control.

Because of the open nature of polytheism, there was virtually no such thing as "conversion." Anyone who chose to begin worshiping a new god was welcome to do so and was not required or expected to leave behind any previous practices of worship or make an exclusive commitment to this one deity. Outside the world of Judaism, exclusivity—the insistence that only one god be worshiped—was practically unknown.

Many people today wonder what might have happened if Christianity had not eventually taken over the empire. Could another religion have done so? Some have argued that the mystery religion called Mithraism (discussed more later in the chapter) was Christianity's "competition"—that if the world had not become Christian, it might have become Mithraist. That is an intriguing idea, but on closer reflection it simply cannot be right. No one who started worshiping the god Mithras was required to stop worshiping Jupiter, Minerva, or Apollo. Mithraism may have spread, but it could not have destroyed anything to become the one and only option.

At the same time, as we have seen, there were increasing numbers of pagan henotheists in the Roman world who maintained that situated above this mass of divine beings and the cults that honored them was one ultimate divinity. We observed an example already in chapter 1 with Constantine, who, prior to his Christian conversion, committed to the worship of Sol Invictus, the Unconquered Sun. Such a move would not have seemed a complete oddity in his world. Those who did acknowledge one ultimate divinity and chose to focus worship on that one alone, however, were not expected to deny either that other divine beings existed or that people were justified in worshiping them.[10]

Pagans who tended toward henotheism did so for a variety of reasons. Sometimes, out of awe and wonder, a pagan worshiper would lavish such abundant praise on a particular god for being so incredibly powerful, wise, caring, merciful, just, and so on that there would be nothing left to attribute to any other god. So why not simply worship this one? Sometimes these various attributes would be converted into names or epithets for the divinity—he is the Greatest, Most Magnificent, Healer of All—to the same effect: there was no need then to name any other god. Possibly more frequently the hierarchy of power thought to exist among the various gods was taken to its logical extreme. The gods worshiped in large city festivals were greater than the *daimones* a farmer had to appease for the well-being of the crops; so too the great gods of the Roman pantheon residing on Mount Olympus were greater than the gods distinctive to individual cities. This pyramid of power could be imagined as going all the way to the top, above the great gods of state, to one who was the most glorious and powerful.

There cannot, of course, be two or more gods who are "most" glorious and powerful. And so sometimes this greatest god was worshiped as the One. In fact, he sometimes went under the name Theos Hypsistos (Greek for "the Greatest God"). We have abundant evidence that this god, sometimes alternatively called Zeus Hypsistos, was worshiped in parts of the empire by devotees who still recognized that it was perfectly legitimate to worship other, lesser gods should anyone choose to do so. For all pagans there were lots of gods, and all deserved adoration for their greatness, whether absolute or relative.

Cultic Acts Instead of Doctrine and Ethics

In the modern West, and most especially in some forms of Christianity, religion is all about what people believe and how they behave. Someone is in a right standing with God by acknowledging the validity of certain conceptual truths and by living as God wants. It is all about doctrine and ethics.

Traditional Roman religions were not like that. Pagan religions were about cultic acts. The word "cult" comes from the Latin phrase *cultus deorum*, which literally means "the care of the gods." A cultic act is any ritualized practice that is done out of reverence to or worship of the gods. Such activities lay at the heart of pagan religions. Doctrines and ethics did not.

That does not mean that pagans did not believe anything. Pagans had all sorts of views of the gods—different pagans with different views, often very different views. But these views were never collected into a set of propositional statements to be affirmed by the worshiping community or even by individuals in it, as eventually happened in Christianity ("There is only one God, the creator of all things"; "Christ is both fully human and fully divine"; "The death of Christ alone brings salvation from sins"; and so on). As Christianity came to develop, it was largely about the "faith"—that is, about affirming these statements. Pagans never had to affirm anything. As odd as this seems, pagans were not required to believe truths about the gods. Paganism was instead about performing the proper, traditional cultic acts.

Roughly speaking, there were three kinds of activities in pagan religions: sacrificial offerings, prayer, and divination.[11] Sacrifices involved offering an animal (which was then butchered), a less expensive food stuff (such as grain or wine), or some other gift (such as flowers or incense). Prayer involved invoking a god—for example, to give thanks or to make a request. And divination involved ascertaining the will of the gods through natural phenomena, such as the ritually observed flight of birds or, particularly alien to modern ways of thinking, the ritual examination of the entrails of sacrificed animals (for example, to see if the sacrifice had been accepted by the god).

Participating in pagan religions meant engaging in these activities, or—especially with animal sacrifice and divination—observing someone else do so. These various cultic acts did, of course, involve some basic ideas and beliefs about gods: the gods did appreciate offerings, for example, and could be influenced by them; they did answer prayers; and they did communicate their will through birds in the air or the entrails in bulls. Still, no one cared whether a participant actually believed these things were true. There were no propositional statements about a god that a participant in a cultic act had to affirm. There really were no doctrines. As a result, there was no such thing as "orthodoxy" (right beliefs) or "heresy" (false beliefs). There was instead an enormously varied set of ritual practices, each one formed by many years of custom and tradition.

Moreover—and this seems even more strange to many moderns—there was a scant role for ethics in the pagan cults. It is not that ancient people were less ethical than people today; it is that ethics had little to do with religion. If it had a "location" in ancient life, it was in philosophy. Philosophers talked a lot about how people should act toward one another, as members of a family, in relationships with friends and neighbors, as citizens of a city. Good behavior was part of being a worthwhile human being and a responsible citizen.

But it generally was not a part of religious activities. It is true that the gods would not accept some rather extreme forms of criminal activity: they condemned parricide, for example, and sometimes profligate licentiousness. And in a vague way the gods were thought to approve proper behavior and to disapprove bad. But most ethical activity had no relationship to cultic practices. Someone could mistreat their siblings, ruin their business associates, or carry on extramarital affairs, and it would have little real bearing on their religious life. The gods were principally concerned with prayers and sacrifices, and would reveal their will through natural phenomena.

This Life Instead of the Afterlife

Another key difference between traditional Roman paganism and some modern faiths is that, for most ancient religions, the afterlife was not a concern.

Ancient textual sources attest to a wide range of views about the afterlife. The classical writings of Homer describe a shadowy and vague type of existence for departed souls. Virgil speaks of the utopian existence coming to those who made it to the Elysian Fields.

Philosophers differed widely among themselves concerning what would happen to a person after death. Those who followed Pythagoras held to the transmigration of the soul. Adherents of Plato talked about rewards for the good and punishments for the wicked. The Epicureans were infamous for taking a hard line: there would be no life after death at all; instead, the body would dissolve into its original state as a mass of atoms and whatever there was of the soul would dissipate.

It is very hard indeed—impossible, actually—to know what most people thought. The vast majority of the population could neither read nor, more important, write, so we have no written record of their fears of death or anticipations of what, if anything, lay beyond. But we do have some material remains that are suggestive. Archaeologists have found numerous pagan tombs with "feeding tubes" through which nourishment could be occasionally funneled. This suggests the idea that some kind of divine spark continued its existence in the grave.

Ancient tombstone inscriptions are particularly fascinating. Many of them suggest that people expected death to be the end of the story, with no existence in any kind of great beyond. Today we are familiar with the funereal abbreviation "RIP" ("Rest in Peace"). Ancient Romans had something comparable, a seven-letter abbreviation that spoke volumes: "n.f. f. n.s. n.c." When spelled out, it stands for *non fui; fui; non sum; non curo*, which means "I was not; I was; I am not; I care not." The meaning is clear. There was no existence before birth. A person existed only after being born. After death there once more was no existence. And so the person could not be upset. The payoff: you have nothing to fear. You did not find it distressing before you were born, and you will not find it distressing after you die.

If that was the case—if there were no rewards or punishments—then gods were not worshiped to secure blessings in the afterlife. Worship was about the present life.

This life, for most ancients, was lived very near the edge. Simply surviving, let alone thriving, was an enormous struggle. This was a world that provided no protection from the ravages of weather: if it did not rain one year, the village would die of starvation the next. This was a world filled with disease and no way to handle it: a tooth abscess was often a death sentence. This was a world in which life itself was a life-threatening proposition: many children died in infancy; many women died in childbirth. Every childbearing woman in the Roman world had to bear an average of six children in order to keep the population constant.

There were numerous aspects of life that mere mortals simply could not control because of the forces of nature or of communal life: climate, the growth of crops, the fertility of livestock, health, personal safety in the home or while traveling abroad, acts of war. But the gods could control these things. That is largely why gods were worshiped: the gods had significant power and could provide what people could not provide for themselves. Gods worshiped properly would give the community and the individual what was needed to survive and thrive.

Some scholars have argued that ancient religion was principally concerned with averting the gods' anger.[12] But this divine anger was aroused almost always because of neglect. The gods—or at least one of them—had not been respected and worshiped properly or sufficiently. That was the main logic behind Roman persecution of the Christians. Because this group of miscreants refused to worship the gods, there was hell to pay. And so we have the revealing and oft-cited words of the Christian defender of the faith Tertullian:

> They think the Christians the cause of every public disaster, of every affliction with which the people are visited. If the Tiber rises as high as the city walls, if the Nile does not send its waters up over the fields, if the heavens give no rain, if there is an earthquake, if there is famine or pestilence, straightway the cry is, "Away with the Christians to the lion!" (*Apology* 40)[13]

To think that pagans worshiped the gods *only* to abate their anger, however, ignores far too much that we know about traditional religions. These were practiced not only as a kind of preventive medicine but also for positive outcomes, the many beneficences that gods could supply to those who could not provide for themselves. Consider the advice of one of the most famous elite agriculturalists, Cato, for addressing a god after an appropriate sacrifice had been offered on a field:

> That you may prevent, ward off and avert diseases, visible and invisible, death and destruction, ruin and storm, and that you permit the crops, corn, vineyards and plantations to grow and flourish, and that you keep safe the shepherds and their sheep, and grant good health and strength to me, my house, and our household.[14]

Chief among the beneficences sought, judging from surviving inscriptions and other material remains, was bodily health—so much so that one prominent scholar of antiquity has claimed that "the chief business of religion, it might then be said, was to make the sick well."[15] Virtually every god of the Roman pantheon, whatever else his or her primary function, occupation, or interest, could be and was invoked for healing. Even today people feel nearly helpless against the ravages of one epidemic, disease, or illness or another; prior to the invention of modern medicine, everyone felt that way, against each and every one of them. The gods had the power to help, though. As they could help in all other matters, personal, familial, civic, and imperial, if honored and worshiped appropriately.

Local Instead of Global

We today are accustomed to global religions. That does not mean that religion is practiced, or understood, the same way everywhere. Christianity in the hills of Croatia will differ significantly from Christianity in the hills of Kentucky. Even so, major forms of Christianity are widely considered transnational, with Greek Orthodox, Roman Catholic, Anglican, Lutheran, and other communities sharing practices, beliefs, and even leaders worldwide. So too, mutatis mutandis, with forms of Judaism and Islam. But it was almost never like that in the Roman world. Religious cults varied from one place to another. The few exceptions were notable principally because they were in fact so rare.

There was no "religion of Zeus" that could be found throughout the Greek-speaking eastern part of the empire. No head priest of Zeus or governing council had any say or any concern over how the practices were carried on in various localities. No international religious organizations of any kind existed.

Even those cults practiced in similar ways throughout the empire were the same more by the accident of propagation than by intention and design. The worship of Mithras mentioned earlier, for example, appears to have comprised a number of consistent elements whether practiced in Rome, Gaul, or Syria. But that was because of how it was spread: principally through the Roman army, as soldiers who adhered to the religion were reassigned to a different part of the empire. Moreover, Mithraism was a relative newcomer on the religious scene, not an ancestral tradition that had been in place for centuries. Most cults were age-old practices that had grown up locally. As international travel became more popular, there might be some influence of one regional cult over another—for example, in the taking over of the name of a god or the practice of a cult that worshiped him. But it did not happen consistently or regularly. Traditional religions were local affairs.

Customs Instead of Books

Modern Western monotheisms are all religions of the book: the Torah, the New Testament, the Qur'an. There was nothing like them in the Roman world.

There were, of course, books. I have already mentioned influential works of literature that helped provide ancient Romans with their various mythologies. There were even, in a few religions, sacred books. The famous Sibylline Books, for example, allegedly recorded prophecies of an ancient prophetess, a sibyl, and were consulted by especially appointed and trained priestly experts to determine the proper course of action for the leaders of the city of Rome in times of crisis. But there really was nothing like a Bible, a book that would give instructions about what to believe and how to act in one's daily life.

Instead, the many and various local religions practiced rituals that had been handed down for years or centuries. Customary observance was canonized in the sense that it came to form a body of tradition, but it was most often cited to justify or condemn specific religious practices. In particular, in Roman circles, specific appeal was made to the *mos maiorum*, the "custom of the ancients"—the established custom that determined proper behavior and practice. It was such oral tradition, rather than written texts, that normally provided guidance and precedent.

The Limits of Tolerance

Because most cults were viewed as proper and acceptable, few efforts were ever made by state authorities to restrict them. It did happen on rare occasion: merely a handful of known instances over centuries in which thousands of cults were in constant practice. This handful of exceptions is worth noting, however, especially given the fate of Christianity at the hands of Roman authorities in the years before Constantine. These exceptions show that the Roman state was massively tolerant, but not infinitely so. If religious practices were deemed socially dangerous—either causing physical harm or creating infectious social problems—the authorities might act.

The most famous instance occurred in Rome in 186 BCE, when the senate intervened to quash the cult celebrating Bacchus, the Roman god of wine and religious ecstasy. The suppression of the Bacchanalia is recounted two centuries later in the history of Rome produced by Livy (59 BCE–17 CE), in a passage some scholars have argued exaggerates the profligate activities of the group.[16]

Livy indicates that the Bacchic cult had come to Rome from Etruria and then spread "like an epidemic." It was, he claims, a wild and licentious affair that involved nocturnal sex rituals and ceremonial murder. Livy states that Bacchic meetings occurred at night under the cloak of darkness. They began with gluttonous banquets where the wine—Bacchus's drink—flowed freely and the sexes mingled promiscuously so that "all sorts of corruption began to be practiced, since each person had ready to hand the chance of gratifying the particular desire to which he was naturally inclined."

But it was not all fun and games. The evening events, Livy claims, would lead to "wholesale murders" that were concealed from public knowledge by the loud revelries: "No cries for help could be heard against the shriekings, the banging of drums, and the clashing of cymbals in the scene of debauchery and bloodshed."

It was through the testimony of an eyewitness that the Roman senate came to be alerted to these dangerous rites. Under threat of punishment the witness revealed that new inductees in the cult were always under the age of twenty. One of them would be introduced to the cult priests as "a kind of sacrificial victim." This hapless youth would then be taken into the midst of the frenzied Bacchics, who were shouting, singing, clashing cymbals, and beating drums to cover over the ultimate cultic act: ceremonial rape. Moreover, "anyone refusing to submit to outrage or reluctant to commit crimes was slaughtered as a sacrificial victim."

The senate was especially shocked to hear these practices were not a small-time affair but a massive movement involving not only the lower classes but also "men and women of rank." Moreover, they came to think it was growing at an alarming rate.[17] The senate stepped in and issued an edict to bring the festivities to a halt, rounding up those who had actively participated in the Bacchic rites—there were said to be seven thousand of them—and those who had "polluted themselves by debauchery or murder . . . were condemned to death." The senate then ordered the destruction of all the shrines dedicated to the worship of Bacchus, not only in Rome itself but throughout Italy, except, Livy indicates, those that had an altar or statue that "had been consecrated." This surely must mean that some sanctioned Bacchic cults were accepted as innocuous and thus allowed to continue. In fact, Livy goes on to say that anyone who considered Bacchic ceremonies "hallowed by tradition" and essential could submit an official request to be allowed to follow them. But "there was to be no common fund of money, no president of the ceremonies, and no priest." That is, there could not be a Bacchic organization, funding, or leadership. This edict, in effect, killed the cult, at least as insofar as it entailed drunken festivities involving rape and murder.

In sum, even though by modern standards Roman religion was incredibly diverse and tolerant, it was not endlessly so. There were limits. The limits were set by acceptable social norms. Degeneracy and criminal activities were not allowed and could be punished to the extreme.

Magic, Atheism, and Superstition

Roman officials were generally, or at least publicly, opposed not only to morally degenerate and socially dangerous cults but also to what they saw as a kind of pseudo-religion, the false manipulation of divine forces for selfish and often antisocial ends that went under the name "magic." Magic in antiquity was not a matter of tricks performed by a master of sleight-of-hand and deception. Magic was understood to be very real. It was thought to involve illicit and unsanctioned interactions with *daimonic* powers who could be swayed to accomplish miraculous results that might harm others or induce them to behave contrary to their own wishes.[18] These interactions might involve spells and invocations of dark forces in order to curse and even kill an enemy, to provide personal supernatural powers, or to make the village beauty fall helplessly in love at one's feet.

Scholars have long wrestled with how to define magic, especially in relationship to sanctioned "religion." The older view was that magic compelled divine powers to act but religion humbly petitioned them; that magic manipulated the powers of darkness but religion submitted to the powers of light.[19] In the second half of the twentieth century, however, scholars came to realize that it was difficult indeed to draw a clear and definitive line between practices one might call magical and others that might be called religious. Magic involves many of the same techniques and strives to attain many of the same ends as religion.

And so scholars had to reimagine ancient magic and began to think of it as the dark side of religion. Magic, in this understanding, would involve religious practices that were considered by mainstream opinion to stand on the margins, unauthorized, esoteric, secretive, nefarious, and dangerous, as opposed to cultic practices that, even if they look very much the same, were socially approved, public, open to scrutiny, licit, and, for the most part, wholesome.

However magic is defined, it clearly was known to exist in antiquity, as there is considerable evidence for it in both literary sources and archaeological finds, such as lead "curse tablets" in which a person invokes a divine attack on an enemy and papyrus texts that prescribe rituals and prayers that could have great magical effect.

In addition to forms of cultic practice perceived as socially dangerous, two religious extremes were widely disapproved of on both the state and popular levels: atheism and superstition. In a sense these phenomena were on opposite ends of the spectrum.

If we use the term in the modern sense, atheism was an exceedingly rare phenomenon in antiquity: very few people believed there were literally no gods. The word "atheism" itself, however, simply means "without the gods," and one could be "without" them while still acknowledging they existed. As Roman religion specialist James Rives has pointed out, atheism applied more normally to "anyone who rejected or neglected the traditional modes of honoring [the gods]."[20] That is to say, anyone who abjectly refused to participate in the worship of divine beings could be labeled an atheist. Such a person could expect a good deal of opprobrium and sometimes civil action. The Christians were often accused of being atheists. Obviously that was not because they denied the divine realm but because they refused to acknowledge (and act as if) it was inhabited by more than the one being they worshiped and refused to interact with it in traditional ways.

Christians also came to be accused of superstition, which for most Roman ancients was on the other end of the spectrum from atheism.[21] Superstition involved excessive fear of the gods and what they might do, leading to extreme and immoderate attempts to avert their anger.[22] In a scathing attack on superstition, Plutarch labels it as "a fear which utterly humbles and crushes a person, for he thinks that there are gods, but that they are the cause of pain and injury." He notes that fear of the gods gives a person no escape: it invades even sleep and death itself. Death in some ways is that which is feared the most, because of what might come afterward: "Rivers of fire . . . specters of many fantastic shapes . . . judges and torturers and yawning gulfs and deep recesses teeming with unnumbered woes."[23]

Unfortunately, the superstitious person thinks all this misfortune is deserved because "he is hateful to the gods, that he is being punished by the gods, and that the penalty he pays and all that he is undergoing are deserved because of his conduct." Such a one "assumes that the gods are rash, faithless, fickle, vengeful, cruel, and easily offended; and, as a result, the superstitious person is bound to hate and fear the gods . . . As he hates and fears the gods, he is an enemy to them. And yet, though he dreads them, he worships them and sacrifices to them, and besieges their shrines."[24]

For Plutarch, this is far worse than atheism, and much more despised by the gods themselves. As he puts it in a clever and convincing comparison:

Why for my part, I should prefer that people should say about me that I have never been born at all, and there is no Plutarch, rather than that they should say "Plutarch is an inconstant fickle person, quick-tempered, vindictive over little accidents, pained at trifles. If you invite others to dinner and leave him out, or if you haven't the time and don't go to call on him, or fail to speak to him when you see him, he will set his teeth into your body and bite it through, or he will get hold of your little child and beat him to death, or he will turn the beast he owns into your crops and spoil your harvest."[25]

Religion Past and Present: In Sum

Of all the features of Roman religion I have delineated here, those most analogous to modern experience are atheism and superstition. There are today, of course, many atheists who do not believe in any divine being at all and many other people who live their lives without giving any particular thought or attention to the divine. There are also plenty of monotheists who are highly superstitious in Plutarch's sense, stricken by dumb fear of what the divine ruler of the world will do to them either in this life or the world to come. At these points we are on familiar turf.

But Roman religions are highly unfamiliar in so many other ways. They involved many gods; they were all about practice, not about belief; they had no orthodoxy or heresy, no doctrines, almost no ethical requirements (with a few exceptions, such as a proscription of parricide), and no sacred "Word of God" giving instructions about theology or daily ethical practices. There were no trans-regional religious organizations or leaders. The religions on the whole were massively inclusive and highly tolerant. They principally entailed cultic activities of prayer, sacrifice, and divination. These are religions that would be scarcely recognizable in the modern Reform synagogue, the neighborhood mosque, or the Baptist church on the corner. Yet they were the dominant form of religiosity throughout all of Roman antiquity.

Their dominance was not restricted to some realm that we can wall off and call "the religious sphere." It is always to be remembered that throughout all of antiquity—in fact, until the eighteenth-century Enlightenment, and still in most parts of our world today—the religious and sociopolitical realms were not kept distinct. The state not only promoted and encouraged religious cults, it staffed them. In Rome itself, the priests of the major state priesthoods were political appointments held by professionals trained in affairs of the state. The emperor himself was the *pontifex maximus*, the "chief priest" over the state cults. As we will see in a moment, his predecessors were revered as gods. Religion infused the state; it infused life; it was virtually omnipresent.

THE OMNIPRESENCE OF RELIGION

Religion could be seen everywhere, in the temples and cult statues that dominated the landscape, both in the cities and in the country-side. We have a list of buildings in a papyrus document from ancient Alexandria. It enumerates 845 taverns, 1,561 baths, 24,396 houses, and 2,478 temples.[26] That would be nearly one temple for every ten houses. If that were true in my neighborhood, there would be five temples—or, in my Christian environment, churches—just on my relatively short street.

Numerous other holy places could be seen, apart from permanent temple buildings in the cities. Shrines could be located almost anywhere and could be small and roughly constructed—for example, at a crossroad or in the middle of virtually nowhere in the countryside. A typical home would have a small shrine to the Penates and Lares, who were gods of the family. (The Penates, for example, watched over the larder.)

The self-contained temples in the Roman world functioned differently from church, synagogue, or mosque buildings today. They were not places where the congregation would come together for worship. They were houses of the gods. The cult statue, representing the god, would be kept there, in a specially appointed room that normally was closed off and not accessible to the public. Sacrifices would take place not in this room, in the presence of the statue, but outside the temple, in front, on the altar. That is where people would gather together for the ceremony to hear prayers and music and to observe the slaughter.

These were normally festive occasions. Most people could not afford to eat meat on a regular basis, and a public sacrifice provided a rare and welcome exception. The priests who performed the ritual sacrifice would then butcher the animal in the temple precincts, after an expert examined the entrails to be sure the offering had been accepted by the god. Most temples had dining rooms, and if it was a large public ceremony with a number of sacrificial animals, as opposed to a small private occasion, there might be a distribution of the meat. On the inside, those celebrating were often joined for the meal by the god, in the person of the cult statue.

A temple to one divinity could house numerous cult statues of other deities as well. Statues could also be found in numerous other places. The surroundings of a middle-size temple, such as the Tychaean in Alexandria, Egypt, might be taken as typical. Not only did it have numerous gods within its walls; it was located near a bathhouse that held gods, and buildings nearby with niches in the walls for places for statues, "probably upward of a hundred different images of gods in and around this one intersection." Larger temples obviously would be associated with many more. The Acropolis in Athens was "absolutely packed with nearly one thousand years of dedicatory statues honoring both men and gods."[27]

As already intimated, cult statues were not actually worshiped. They were a kind of physical representation of the god to help focus the attention, or even a site through which the god could make himself present. As a rule, divine images had little to do with the sacrificial activities that played a central role in most cults. But they were often treated as holy objects: washed, dressed, and cared for; paraded through town with music and dancers; brought out to the god's worshipers on special occasions—special objects of reverence.

TWO SPECIAL KINDS OF CULTS IN THE EMPIRE

Among all the kinds of religious cults in the empire, two have struck specialists interested in the spread of Christianity as particularly significant and interesting: the various "mystery religions" and the imperial cult—the worship of the emperor.

Mystery Religions

The term "mystery religion" or "mystery cult" is normally applied to a range of cults that came from various eastern climes and that sponsored the worship of a foreign god or goddess, such as Demeter (in Greece), Isis (from Egypt), or Mithras (from Persia). To participate in the full range of religious activities in one of these cults (in addition to their public processions and sacrifices) a person was required to undergo a sacred initiation ceremony.[28]

Despite what one sometimes reads, we actually do not know a good deal about how these cults were organized, what specific cultic practices they entailed, how people were initiated into them, what these people were taught to understand about the deity at the center of the cult's worship, and what kind of myths were told about that deity. There is good reason for considering them "mysteries": only initiates could participate in the secret rituals of these cults, and initiates were sworn to silence, evidently with threats of serious divine reprisals and punishments for breaking their vow.[29] As a result, hardly anyone did.

For that reason, scholars deeply interested in these cults have had to base their views—and sometimes the highly detailed descriptions they spin out, often from whole cloth—on very slight evidence, including highly allusive references made in passing in ancient texts and the material remains that have been uncovered through archaeological discovery. In some instances, such as the worship of Mithras, archaeological finds are by far our most extensive and telling (though often ambiguous) evidence.

These cults naturally differed from one another in numerous ways, both in how they were practiced and to whom they were open. The mysteries of Mithras, for example, were restricted to men. No women were allowed. That, naturally enough, limited its appeal: it is hard to imagine Mithraism "taking over the world" if half the human race could not participate. Consistently among these cults, however, it is clear that an initiate in one could participate in others as well. None of them was "exclusive" in the way that Christianity was. Anyone who worshiped Mithras in an underground cave, where the god's sacred sites were always located, could also worship in a temple of Isis. Initiates participated widely in all kinds of other cults as well: civic cults, imperial cults, family cults, and so on.[30]

Even though initiation appears to have been a constant feature of mystery cults, the procedures would have differed significantly from one cult to the other. Becoming an initiate was thought to place a person in an unusually close and intimate relationship with the god or goddess at the center of the cult. A kind of personal relationship with a divine being was not something promoted or fostered in public cults. This may well have been the major attraction of the mysteries. This relationship was supposed to improve one's life in the present, and in some instances the relationship was understood to continue into the afterlife. It is not necessarily the case that the mysteries promised an afterlife to those who otherwise would simply not have one. Instead, for those who believed that life existed beyond the grave, a mystery cult maintained that the intimacy obtained with the deity in the present would continue after death, making the afterlife a far more enjoyable and pleasant experience.

Some of the mysteries—for example, Mithraism and the Isis cult—had communal leaders and a kind of "graded" membership by which initiates could "rise up" through the ranks, both to have greater authority in the community and to attain a yet closer relationship with the divinity. It appears as well that part of the periodic celebrations of these cults involved sacred meals that were shared together.

From all these features, as vague and underdetermined as they are, it should seem obvious why mystery cults have sparked the interest of scholars of early Christianity. Christianity too involved an initiation rite (baptism) that brought particular intimacy with the deity (Christ and God himself) and a hope of a greater afterlife; the Christian church had clear grades of authority, and one of its major rituals involved a weekly shared meal (which became the Eucharist).

As a result, scholars have often wondered whether we should consider Christianity another mystery cult—this one from another eastern region, Israel—and whether some of the other mysteries played any role in the development of Christianity.[31]

Those who have rejected such a suggestion have pointed out that Christianity is stunningly different in many ways from each of the mystery religions. Unlike Mithraism, for example, it was open to all people of both genders, not just to men, and in fact women played significant leading roles in the early years of the church. Unlike the others, it was exclusive and did not allow participation in other mysteries. Moreover, unlike them all, it also emphasized the importance of doctrine and ethics.

These are all strong points, but it is worth noting that any one of the mysteries could be selected—say, the cult of Cybele that is associated with Anatolia (modern Turkey)—and shown to be different in numerous ways from all the others. Each had its own distinctive features, sometimes extremely distinctive ones, such as only men being allowed to worship in underground caves. The fact that Christianity differed from other mysteries does not alter the fact that it also shared numerous features, probably more than it shared with other cults scattered throughout the empire.

The Imperial Cult

For many modern persons, the form of ancient cult that seems most alien involved the worship of political leaders. Such worship could take a variety of forms, but the one best known is the imperial cult: the worship of the emperor.

In trying to make sense of the worship of mere mortals, it is important to remember that ancient people had a sense of the divine that was different from what we have today. For the monotheistic traditions of the modern West, an enormous and unbridgeable chasm exists between the divine and the human. God is the Almighty and Eternal Creator of All "up there"; humans are peons fated for a brief and painful mortal existence down here. Ancient people, on the other hand, understood both the divine and the human realms to involve gradations of grandeur and power, and sometimes the two realms overlapped. There may have been the one ultimate all-powerful divine being over all, but below that one were the great gods and goddesses of ancient mythology and worship; below them were local divinities who were more closely connected with daily life; below them were family gods; below them were *daimones*; and so on. The divine realm was a continuum.

So too was the human. Some people are fantastically, even pre-ternaturally brilliant, beautiful, or powerful. They are not like the rest of us mere mortals. In that light, who could be more powerful than the Roman emperor? He was able to accomplish feats the rest of us could barely even imagine. The emperor was not Jupiter or one of the great gods. He was the emperor. But he, like other amazingly elevated human beings, could have a touch of the divine.

The worship of the emperor was precipitated by Julius Caesar, who advertised his family line as physically descended from the goddess Venus. After Caesar was assassinated in 44 BCE, his adopted son, Octavian, helped promote the claim that he had ascended to live now with the gods in the heavenly realm as a divine being. Caesar had been made a god. Octavian's declaration was not personally or politically disinterested. If his own father was a god, what did that make him?

Some fifteen years later, Octavian was to become the first of the Roman emperors, renamed Caesar Augustus. When he died, after a reign of just over four decades, he too was declared by the Roman senate to have become a divine being, and he was worshiped as such. The imperial cult that developed worshiped deceased emperors who had been declared deified by the senate. The senate did not actually make anyone a god but rather officially recognized that a deification had occurred. Deification came, of course, only to "good" emperors. The hopelessly inept or morally degenerate ones—think Nero or Caligula—did not receive the honor. Ironically some of the "bad" ones, including Caligula, were deemed awful precisely because of their megalomaniacal insistence that they were gods while still living.

It is often argued that the imperial cults offered prayers and sacrifices only to the deified, deceased emperors, not to the living. For the living emperor, offerings were made to his genius. The term "genius" is a little hard to define, but it means something like "guardian spirit," which, in the case of the emperor, inspired him and directed the course of his life. Thus, for example, we have a calendar of festivals observed by the Roman army from the third century CE that indicates that anniversaries of deified emperors were to be observed through sacrifices, whereas anniversaries of the current emperor were marked either by offerings to his genius or offerings to other divinities connected with his rule, such as the trio of divinities associated with the Capitoline Hill in Rome: Jupiter, Juno, and Minerva. Two centuries earlier, from 15 CE, we have an inscription found in a town near Sparta, Greece, that speaks of a festival on one day "for the God Caesar Augustus, son of the god, our Savior and Deliverer" and on the next day "for the emperor Tiberius Caesar Augustus, father of the fatherland." The wording is very important. Caesar Augustus, who had died the previous year, was God and son of God, the Savior and Deliverer. The current emperor, Tiberius, was "father of the fatherland." It was a big difference.[32]

There are other instances, however, especially in provinces in the East, where the living emperor was indeed worshiped as already divine. Scholars have long tried to make sense out of this discrepancy. Possibly the most persuasive view takes into account the fact that most people living in the empire, until the time of the emperor Caracalla (ruled 198–217 CE), were not actually citizens of Rome. Being a citizen was an enormous privilege and honor. In the provinces the honor was almost always granted only to highly placed and wealthy members of the local aristocracy. As a result, the majority of people living in the provinces were not citizens of Rome but still subject to Roman rule. One way to explain the discrepancy in the way the cult to the living emperor was practiced is to say that Roman citizens were

not expected to worship the living emperor but Roman subjects—
like most people in the eastern provinces—were. Most provinces in
the West, on the other hand, followed the lead of the city of Rome
itself by offering cult just to the emperor's genius.[33]

A previous generation of scholarship took a rather cynical view of
the imperial cult and maintained it was a ruse foisted on non-citizens
in the empire as a way of bringing them under control. There was
a clear logic to this idea. If people throughout the empire were required to participate in the worship of the ultimate ruler as a divine
being, were they likely to rebel? They may have wanted to resist the
authority of a mere mortal, but who would want to cross swords with
a *god*?

Despite the attractions of this view, it has waned over time as
scholars have realized from abundant evidence that most cults to
the emperor were not imposed on distant populations by the central
authorities in Rome but derived from local initiatives. It was a mark
of distinction to be allowed to build a temple in honor of the Roman
emperors. Cities competed for the honor. Local aristocrats who sponsored the movements and paid for the temples experienced exalted
personal status, as they were seen to be uniquely connected with the
mighty emperor himself. For local regional aristocrats who valued
status and prestige above all things, few honors could be considered
comparable.

The imperial cults, therefore, were localized affairs, and participation was voluntary. Apart from the fact that a city or region needed
official approval to start a cult, there was no centralized control, no
detailed set of rules they had to follow or leaders who oversaw the
entire operation empire-wide. In this, imperial cults resembled all
other cults of Rome. Roman religion did not involve interregional
organization, leadership, and governance. It was always carried out
on the local level.

At the same time, there was a general sense, promoted by authorities both in Rome and throughout the provinces, that faithful
adherence to the worship of the gods was vital to the healthy working
of the empire. People were expected to participate, even if this meant

simply showing up on an occasional feast day to watch a sacrifice and enjoying a meal of good meat and plenty of wine afterward. The worship of the gods was not intellectually, emotionally, or theologically separate from the sociopolitical realities of daily existence. Religion was part of life, fully integrated and interwoven with governance, social order, and daily experience.

ROMAN RELIGION: IN SUM

In many respects, the enormously wide-ranging cults of the Roman world represented different ways for different people in different parts of the empire to worship the gods. At the same time, there are a few features these cults do seem to share. They all subscribed to the existence of many gods and all were based on cultic acts of worship, such as sacrifice, prayer, and divination. As such, they were by and large inclusive. None of them insisted their god was the only divine being, or that this god was to be worshiped in only one particular way everywhere. As a corollary, these religions were highly tolerant of differences. So too was the Roman government, both centrally in Rome and throughout the provinces. There were exceptions, but only when a cult was judged to be morally degenerate or socially dangerous.

These exceptions help to prove a very important rule. Throughout the empire it was understood that the worship of the gods, in ways handed down through ancestral tradition, was important both for the proper working of the state and for the success and prosperity of the people who lived in it. The gods supported the empire, the city, the family, and the individual. The gods provided help for people who could not help themselves. They averted disaster. They showered beneficences among those who revered them and worshiped them properly.

It was in that context that Christianity arose. One of the leading questions historians of early Christianity have always tried to answer is how such a different understanding of religion could sprout, grow, and thrive in such an environment. Christians opposed the gods of the state, city, and family. They did not believe there were many gods but only one. They rejected the claims that emperors were divine. They did not accept the validity of other forms of worship. They did not think the traditional gods provided any benefits. They thought the gods were demons who had deceived virtually everyone in the known world.

The Christians themselves were widely considered strange. They were also known to revere, as the savior of the world, a lowly day laborer who had been crucified for crimes against the state. For a pagan in the early empire, it would have been virtually impossible to imagine that these Christians would eventually destroy the other religions of Rome. How they did so will occupy us in the chapters to follow.

Chapter 4

Reasons for the Christian Success

For over a century, since the pioneering work of the German historian Adolf von Harnack, scholars have widely believed that by the beginning of the fourth century Christianity probably made up 7 to 10 percent of the population of the Roman Empire.[1] Then Constantine converted and the numbers exploded. By the end of the fourth century, it is typically maintained, something like half of the empire's sixty million inhabitants claimed allegiance to the Christian tradition.[2]

If these ballpark figures are correct, then by 300 CE there would have been four to six million Christians in the world. Even though just a fraction of the empire, that is a lot. Suppose, for reasons I will adduce later, it is too many. Cut the numbers in half, so that, on hypothesis, there were two or three million in the empire. It is still a lot. And it raises the most obvious of questions. As we saw in chapter 2, Christianity started as a group of Jesus's male disciples and a handful of women—say, twenty people in the year 30 CE. How do we get from twenty to two or three million in under three centuries? And to go from there to thirty million in less than a hundred years, as most experts agree happened? That is absolutely extraordinary. How is it possible?

EXPLANATIONS FOR THE CHRISTIAN SUCCESS

Older scholarship was virtually unified on the question of why Christianity succeeded. It filled the spiritual vacuum created by the collapse of paganism, which fell under its own weight. At this point in antiquity, the view held, no one could any longer believe the ridiculous myths of the pagans or accept the bizarre cultic practices established by age-old tradition. The door was wide-open for the superior Christian faith to enter in and take over.

Thus, for example, in a multivolume discussion, *A History of the Expansion of Christianity* (1937–1945), Kenneth Scott Latourette spoke of "the decay of the older faiths." Christianity was lucky enough to emerge on the scene when "the traditional state and family cults of Greece and Rome had been losing their hold. Increasingly they were unable to satisfy some of the needs . . . of the population looking to religion."[3] So too, two decades later, a classic study of E. R. Dodds, *Pagan and Christian in an Age of Anxiety*, proclaimed: "One reason for the success of Christianity was simply the weakness and weariness of the opposition."[4]

Underlying these assessments of paganism is a moral judgment that most scholars of Europe and the United States would have found completely non-problematic: Christianity, with its rigorous monotheism and high ethical demands, was simply superior to anything on offer among the polytheistic cults of the Roman world. This is not just a commonplace of twentieth-century scholarship, however. It appears in the first critical examination of the rise of Christianity from relatively modern times, the massive and influential eighteenth-century work of Edward Gibbon, *The History of the Decline and Fall of the Roman Empire*.[5]

Gibbon insisted that paganism had grown weak and bankrupt. In his inimitable terms:

> An object much less deserving [than Christianity] would have been sufficient to fill the vacant place in their hearts, and to gratify the uncertain eagerness of their passions. Those who

are inclined to pursue this reflection, instead of viewing with astonishment the rapid progress of Christianity, will perhaps be surprised that its success was not still more rapid and still more universal.[6]

To be sure, as an eighteenth-century British scholar firmly ensconced in the ideological world of his day, Gibbon could not assign the enormous success of early Christianity to purely historical explanations. No, Gibbon conceded that ultimate success derived from its spiritual superiority and God's personal oversight: "Our curiosity is naturally prompted to inquire by what means the Christian faith obtained so remarkable a victory over the established religions of the earth. To this inquiry, an obvious but satisfactory answer may be returned; that it was owing to the convincing evidence of the doctrine itself, and to the ruling providence of its great Author."[7]

Even so, Gibbon devoted the bulk of his analysis to the "secondary causes of the rapid growth of the Christian church." No one can doubt that, in his own mind, these were what really did the trick. There were five of them:

- "The inflexible, and . . . intolerant zeal of the Christians." For Gibbon, such religious zeal for the implacable rightness of one's cause was otherwise unheard of in pagan antiquity.
- The doctrine of immortality. Pagans were desperate, Gibbon maintained, to learn that it was possible to enjoy a blessed ongoing existence after death.
- The miracles worked by the early Christians. These, he argued, convinced pagans that God really was on the side of the Christians.
- Strict Christian morality. In a religious world of lax morals, the Christians showed a superior way.
- Strong ecclesiastical organization. Unlike the pagan religions, Gibbon stressed, Christianity established an efficient

hierarchy of authority that advanced its cause. Christianity out-organized its competition.[8]

Many scholars since Gibbon's time have reiterated and affirmed his insights. But scholarship has advanced and we see things far more clearly today, even while acknowledging that subsequent research was built on the foundation he laid.

One issue scholars have wrestled with more vigorously since then is the fundamental question I raised in chapter 1: What does it mean to "convert"? Or, to ask it differently: What does one have to believe or do in order to be counted as a Christian? What if numbers of self-proclaimed Christians at the beginning of the fourth century continued to worship Roman gods, civic gods, or family gods, along with the Christian god? Should we call them Christian? What if members of a family were forced to adopt Christian ways because the head of the household, the paterfamilias, had converted, even though in their own minds and hearts they were still committed to the worship of Jupiter, Juno, Apollo, or others? Do they count as Christian? What if people who claimed to be Christian were not baptized, did not go to church, and basically did nothing at all to show that faith had any bearing on their lives? Were they Christian or not?

Much of the twentieth century saw scholars answering no in all such cases. As far back as the influential work of William James, *The Varieties of Religious Experience* (1902), experts argued that only a person who experienced a blinding-light experience that led to a radical change and a complete reversion of character and an unassailable commitment could be said to have had undergone genuine conversion.[9] One problem with this perspective is that it counts Christians based on psychological experiences and inner spiritual states that are inaccessible to historical knowledge. The historian's question is, how do we count? How do we know how many Christians there were, as opposed, say, to Jews, Mithraists, or worshipers of Zeus or Apollo? Historians are neither priests nor psychologists. They lack the capacity or resources to explore what a person really and genuinely believed, only to what they say about themselves and what they do in their lives. And, of course, for over 99.99 percent of the people who lived in antiquity, we have no access even to that.

For such reasons, many historians have moved to a broader definition of conversion and a more general sense of what it means to count someone as a Christian. As a rule, they do not include only those who were "blinded by the light" and then, on the spot, turned their lives around. Instead, they follow the very basic and more sensible path I set forth earlier: conversion can simply be considered an exchange of one set of religious beliefs and practices for another. Some people—possibly very large numbers of people—will not make the change instantaneously, completely, or with full commitment. But for our purposes, when it comes to Christian conversion, this kind of change *will* mean deciding to worship the Christian god, with the concomitant idea that Christ is somehow the Son of God and the savior.

For most of those who came to this belief, it meant abandoning the worship of the other gods. As we have begun to see, this made converting to the Christian faith different from anything else in the pagan world. Unlike devotees of traditional religions, Christians were expected to abstain from other cultic practices. Whether they always did so or not is another question, and one that is normally impossible to answer. But in the version of Christianity that was more or less authorized from its early centuries, conversion was not "both/and" but "either/or." Christians—at least the ones we are best informed about—understood their religion to be restrictive, not additive; exclusive, not inclusive.[10] It is this difference, I will be arguing, that ultimately mattered for the Christian mission. Enough people bought into this idea that it became one of the main reasons Christianity took over the empire.

ISSUES OF STRATEGY

How, then, did Christians go about convincing pagans? It is important to begin with a point too frequently overlooked. Potential converts to a new set of religious beliefs and practices will already have assumptions about the divine realm and how to interact with it, and a new religion cannot possibly expect to convert anyone without adhering in some degree to those assumptions. If Christianity were completely strange, no one would have had a way of conceptualizing it. It would have been not merely unattractive but unrecognizable. In order to convert pagans, Christians had to establish common ground with them. Moreover, they had to show the *superiority* of the Christian faith precisely at points of significant contact.

It is important, therefore, to consider not only how Christianity differed from other religions on offer but also what it had in common. The great historian of early Christian conversion Arthur Darby Nock once noted that "the originality of a prophet lies commonly in his ability to fuse into a white heat combustible material which is there."[11] We need to consider the combustible material that was available for Christians to stoke into a fire.

To start, we might reflect further on why pagans followed their religious customs in the first place. On one level, of course, most pagans practiced religion simply because that was what everyone had always done and what they themselves had been instructed to do since early childhood. Think about it in terms of a modern analogy. Why does everyone stand for the national anthem at a ball game? A lot of people, of course, think deeply about the moment with a sense of reverence. They reflect on the wars the country has fought, its struggles for freedom, and possibly their own involvement in those conflicts or the price paid by some of their relatives. But a lot of other people stand just because that's what everyone around them is doing and it is what they have always done. They may be thinking mainly about the game ahead or the hot dog they want to buy.

No doubt numerous pagans simply did what they had always done without giving it a great deal of thought. Others would have had clear and compelling reasons for doing what they did: the gods deserved to be acknowledged, worshiped, and thanked for all the many good things they had provided. Even more, the gods needed to be honored so that they would provide more good things, more benefits—even specific benefits, such as rain for the crops, safety for the home, and health for the family. Worshipers especially appealed to the gods for what they could not provide for themselves. In no small measure, worship was about acquiring access to this divine power.

Is there one divine being who has more of this power than the others? One who was above them all? Jews obviously worshiped one god, the god of Israel. What is not as widely known is the point I raised already in chapter 1: that some pagan polytheists also believed in one ultimate divine being.

THE WORSHIP OF ONE GOD

There should be some term that would differentiate between the be-lief in only one true god—the strict definition of monotheism—and the worship of one god to the exclusion of all others, who are seen, nonetheless, to be gods. That is the term I have already used and will continue to use, "henotheism."[12] I will contend that the growing pop-ularity of henotheism in the empire paved the way for the Christian declaration that there is in fact only one god and he alone should be worshiped.

Traditional Jews had long insisted on worshiping only their own ancestral god. As far as many were concerned, the pagan gods were not gods at all. Scholars have often maintained that the popularity of Judaism in the empire made the Christian mission possible: that pagans were widely attracted to the Jewish notion of one god; to the stress in Judaism on weekly fellowship, community, and sense of be-longing as part of the worship; and to the strict code of ethics in the Jewish tradition.

There may indeed be an element of truth in this claim, but a major caveat is necessary. The idea that Judaism was widely seen as "attractive" may be overly romantic. It is true that Jews did at-tract some outsiders into their ranks. That was the case with most cults, however, including the sundry mystery religions. On the whole, though, unlike most of the mystery religions, Judaism was looked upon with real suspicion in the empire. Jews were often thought of as superstitious and very strange indeed, even repugnant. They practiced circumcision ("You do *what* to your baby boys?"); they refrained from perfectly good foods; they refused to put in a full week of work; and they kept to themselves and did not interact with the greater society—for example, at civic festivals.

But it may be that precisely these perceived oddities were what made Christianity more acceptable than Judaism to the wider populace. Most Christians from gentile stock did not practice circumcision, keep kosher, or observe the Sabbath. They did, however, stress the worship of one god, high ethical standards, and community. Wasn't this the best of Judaism without its peculiarities?

In answering that question, we need to make a special effort not to think that somehow monotheistic faiths are inherently "superior" and that the movement away from paganism is somehow "progress." It is not progress. It is not regress either. I am not making any evaluative judgment or asking whether one religious system is better than another and closer to some kind of ultimate truth. I am simply asking if a new religion may have proved attractive to those who followed the traditional ways.

Scholars have long known of henotheistic tendencies among some ancient philosophers who had come to think that behind all the diversity of the world, above all the manifestations of what we know and experience, there must be one ultimate reality that makes sense of it all. This principle of unity could be understood to be the ultimate divinity, and so those philosophers stressed the "oneness" at the heart, or at the beginning, of all things.

The sense of one ultimate divinity could also be found outside the ranks of the professional philosophers, among the non-philosophical, highly religious as well. In an inscription found in the city of Oenoanda in southwest Asia Minor (modern Turkey) appears the self-declaration of a god who terms himself a mere angel in comparison with the one ultimate divine being. In response to the question of who or what is God, here is how he describes that One:

Born of itself, untaught, without a mother, unshakeable, not contained in a name, known by many names, dwelling in fire, this is God. We, his angels, are a small part of God. To you who ask this question about God, what his essential nature is, he has pronounced that Aether is God who sees all, on whom you should gaze and pray at dawn, looking to the sunrise.[13]

The "aether" (ether) that surrounds us all is God, but this god is not simply a material substance: God sees all and deserves universal worship. The other gods are his messengers, the "angels," who form part of that greater divinity. This is not a Jewish or Christian text. It is from a pagan.

We have seen that pagans might take several paths to arrive at such a concept of divinity. One is hinted at in the inscription, as God is said to be the one of "many names." Thus it was sometimes thought that all the names of divine beings were simply alternative designations of the ultimate divine being, who encompassed all the activities of all the gods and the names associated with them. Other pagans would cite all the great attributes of their favored god: he is the mighty one, the all-knowing one, the great healer, and so on. So much would be attributed to this one that there would be nothing left for anyone else, making that one, in effect, the greatest god there was.

Other pagans simply thought there had to be one god who was greatest. By the time of Christianity other cults proclaimed adherence to "the greatest" god, whether Sol Invictus revered by the emperor Aurelian, then Constantius, and finally Constantine, or instead the god explicitly called Theos Hypsistos ("the Greatest God"). One scholar has proposed an interesting hypothesis concerning the origins of the cult to this latter god by noting that Roman culture and religion were inherently competitive. Members of the aristocracy competed regularly, daily, for higher status, striving for greater position and rank. Cities competed with one another for prominence in their regions. Among other things, cities worked to stage the most lavish and interesting religious festivals to attract crowds from other places: the larger the crowd and the more glowing the accolades, the greater the sense of civic pride. Cult centers—such as oracles, where people could come to ask questions of a divinity and answers would be provided by specially appointed priests or priestesses, often in poetic verse—competed with one another for empire-wide attention and recognition. This was a culture, and these were religions, that were all about status, recognition, and prominence.

So too with the gods of a city. The city of Ephesus claimed it was the center for the worship of Artemis. The goddess was worshiped there better than anywhere else. She, for them, was the great goddess, greater than all other divinities.

The cult of Theos Hypsistos may well have emerged from some such context of competition.[14] This god needed no other name. He was literally "the Greatest God." He deserved more worship than any other. He is sometimes referred to in inscriptions as the "one" god.

Contrary to what you might think, the declaration that he is "one" does not mean this god's devotees believed he was the *only* god. We know this because of the way the term "one" is used in comparable ancient contexts. For example, if a benefactor to a community was especially generous, giving far more than anyone else had ever given the city, he could be referred to as "the one patriot and benefactor." That would not mean that no one else had ever given the city anything. It meant he was uniquely beneficial. Calling any divinity "the one god" functions the same way. In the words of one scholar, "it underlines the uniqueness of one particular God."[15] In no pagan context do we find the claim that there is only one god, to the exclusion of all others. But we do find claims that ultimately there is one god over all.

This is clear not only from ancient inscriptions—hundreds to Theos Hypsistos have been identified and studied—but also from the writings of ancient pagans.[16] Consider a statement made by a devout pagan, Maximus of Madaura, written in a letter to the church theologian Augustine near the end of the fourth century:

That the forum of our city is occupied by a gathering of savior gods, we see and assert. Who is so insane, so deluded, as to deny the utter certainty that there is one highest God, without beginning, without offspring in nature, like a great and glorious father? We invoke under many names his powers that are diffused through the created world, because, obviously, none of us knows his name: God is the name common to all religions. So it is that while we honor his parts (so to speak) separately, with various supplications we are clearly worshipping him in his entirety.[17]

Christians realized that many pagans were drawn to the idea of one ultimate divinity. Some two centuries earlier we have the words of the Christian defender of the faith Athenagoras of Athens: "We [i.e., Christians] are not the only ones who limit God to a single being [since] almost all those who have reason to speak about the principles of the world are unanimous, even if unwillingly so, that the divine is singular."[18] Soon thereafter we have the rhetorical question of the Christian apologist Tertullian: "Is it not generally held that there is one higher and more potent, as it were the world's chief ruler, endowed with absolute power and majesty?" (*Apology* 24).

In short, the Christian declaration that there was only one ultimate divinity would not have seemed completely extraordinary among pagans. Most pagans no doubt knew about the Jews in their midst: Jews appear to have numbered in the millions and were widely known and discussed. But even more, the notion of one god over all would have been broadly familiar from both philosophical and religious traditions attested with growing frequency in the empire.

When Christians spoke of this ultimate god, on the other hand, they insisted on two supremely important provisos. Unlike pagan henotheists, they maintained that this god was none other than the god of the Christians. And they insisted that anyone who chose to worship him was to do so to the complete exclusion of all other gods. One might think this exclusionary insistence would be off-putting and offensive in a world filled with gods, dooming the Christian mission to failure. On the contrary, it had just the opposite effect. It was this claim that led to the triumph of Christianity.[19]

CHRISTIANITY AS A MISSIONARY RELIGION

Even if pagans who adhered to one cult or another liked others to join them in their rituals of worship and welcomed them when they chose to do so, we have no evidence of organized efforts to make it happen. As a prominent historian of Roman religion, Ramsay Mac-Mullen, states: "Of any organized or conscious evangelizing in paganism there are very few signs indeed."[20] In fact, we don't know of any missionary religions in the pagan world.

Not even the mystery religions appear to have employed organized efforts to bring in devotees. It is sometimes said that the expansion of Mithraism presupposes some kind of mission, but that turns out not to be true. The religion spread essentially by word of mouth from friend to friend, family member to family member—at least among adult males.[21]

None of that is particularly surprising. What may be far less expected is that ancient Judaism also lacked any genuine missionary impulse. This claim cuts against what scholars had long argued: that the Christian concept of an evangelistic religion had been inherited from the Jews. But more recent scholarship has persuasively shown that this was not the case at all. Of course Jews typically did welcome anyone who seriously wanted to consider adopting their worship and ways. We do have records of pagans converting to become Jews. Among other things, this meant that converts, if men, were circumcised and, both men and women, went through the process of being admitted into the Jewish fold and agreeing to observe established practices of worship and custom.

There were other pagans who might be thought of as "Jewish sympathizers." These would be gentiles who chose, for rather obvious reasons, not to be circumcised and possibly not to follow the entire set of prescriptions in Jewish law. But they would have worshiped the god of the Jews and possibly him only, in synagogues with Jews, and participated in Jewish life as members of the community with a kind of secondary status. Sometimes these people are called "God-fearers" because they revered the one God even if they chose not to adopt certain Jewish identity markers.

Nonetheless, there is very little evidence to suggest that Jews actively *sought* converts or partial converts. Outsiders may have been attracted to aspects of Jewish worship and life, but most Jews were content to observe their traditional customs and forms of worship themselves and to let pagans do whatever pagans chose to do. This view has been argued convincingly by a number of recent scholars, including ancient historian Martin Goodman, who on the basis of a thorough examination of every significant piece of ancient pagan and Jewish evidence has concluded that the evangelizing mission of the Christian church was unparalleled and unprecedented: "Such a proselytizing mission was a shocking novelty in the ancient world."[22]

This mission of evangelism, as we will see, became a standard feature of the Christian movement and eventually, for many Christians, a contest for converts. But significantly, as Goodman explains, "For most of the period before Constantine's conversion, such Christians will have been running in a race of whose existence most of the other competitors were unaware."[23]

If the concerted attempt to win converts was not a standard feature of ancient religion, even Judaism, why did Christianity become missionary? Even though our ancient sources provide us with no firm answer, some informed intuition would suggest that surely it had to do with the nature of the Christian message. Christians as early as Paul—the first to undertake a worldwide mission—maintained that Christ died because it was God's plan to bring salvation to the world. Those who did not experience this salvation were lost, doomed to punishment. As an apocalyptic Jew, Paul, and then his converts, insisted God was soon to enter into judgment with this world. A cataclysmic act of destruction was to occur. Those who were in Christ would be spared the onslaught and be brought into God's eternal kingdom. Those who were not would be destroyed. Some Christians insisted the coming cataclysm was not simply an annihilation in which a person would cease to exist. It was to entail ongoing punishment, eternal torment.

At the same time, Christianity prided itself as a religion of love. Jesus was remembered as one who taught his followers to love God above all things, but also, next, to love their neighbors as themselves. By "neighbor" he did not simply mean the person next door. Everyone is a neighbor. Even an enemy is a neighbor. Christians were to love everyone in the world, even those who detested, opposed, and persecuted them.

If God commands his people to love others and, consequently, to act in ways that will benefit them, and if others are destined to the coming divine judgment unless they turn to God in repentance and begin to worship him alone, there is only one clear conclusion: Christians need to urge others to adopt their religion. It is the only way these others will be saved, the only way they can escape eternal punishment. It is therefore the only way a Christian can really show love for the other.

Christians then, starting at least with Paul, came to be missionary, convinced they had to convert the world. Goodman maintains it was Paul himself who came up with the idea. He was the innovator, "the single apostle who invented the whole idea of a systematic conversion of the world, area by geographical area."[24] At the same time, this is what makes it so striking and unexpected that, outside of Paul's work itself, we do not know of any organized Christian missionary work—not just for the first century, but for any century prior to the conversion of most of the empire. As MacMullen has succinctly put it: "After Saint Paul, the Church had no mission."[25]

That may be hard to believe, but in fact, if you were to count every Christian missionary about whom even a single story is told, from the period after the New Testament up through the first four centuries, you would not need all the digits on one hand: there is Gregory the "Wonderworker," who worked not worldwide but in a small area of third-century Pontus, a province in what is now northern Turkey; Martin of Tours, a fourth-century bishop who converted pagans in his own city of Tours in France; and Porphyry, a late-fourth-century bishop who closed pagan temples in Gaza and converted their devotees. We are not talking about armies of volunteers knocking on doors. We know of three, all in a different isolated region.[26] And, as we will see, even the stories told of them are highly legendary.

If Christians did not convert others through organized missionary efforts, how did they do it? The answer is simple: it was not by public preaching or door-to-door canvassing of strangers. They used their everyday social networks and converted people simply by word of mouth.[27]

Social networks are all the human connections we have by virtue of the fact that each of us is a living, breathing human being who has a life. We have family. We have friends. We have neighbors. We know people at work. We see acquaintances on the street, at the store, and at sporting events. We belong to clubs and organizations. We participate in the life of our communities. In short, we have numerous connections in numerous ways with numerous people.

The people you know from different points of contact often know many other people you also know. And they know people you do not know. Those people you do not know may know some people you know and certainly others you do not. Social networks all overlap but they are never the same from one person to the next. The community comprises everyone networked into it in a wide range of ways.

That was true in the ancient world as well. Christians did not associate only with Christians. In the early centuries, most of the people Christians would have known would have been non-Christians. The way Christianity spread was principally through these networks.

A Christian woman talks about her newfound faith to a close friend. She tells the stories she has heard, stories about Jesus and about his followers. She also tells stories about her own life, how she has been helped after prayer to the Christian god. After a while, this other person expresses genuine interest. Over time she considers joining the church herself. When she does so, that opens up more possibilities of sharing the "good news," because she too has friends. And family, neighbors, and people she sees in all sorts of contexts.

The woman converts. Over time she converts her husband. He insists the entire family—children, servants, slaves—follow the Christian religion. Three years later he ends up converting a business associate. That one requires his family as well to adopt the Christian faith. One of his teenage daughters eventually not only goes through the religious motions that her father requires (for example, saying prayers and going to the weekly church meeting) but becomes deeply committed. She converts her best friend. Who converts her mother. Who converts her husband. And then the next-door neighbor.

And so it goes. Year after year after year. One reason Christianity grows is that it is the only religion like this: the others are not missionary and they are not exclusive.[28] These two features make Christianity unlike anything else on offer. The people who become Christian are turning their backs on their pagan pasts, their pagan customs, and their pagan gods. That means that virtually every new Christian is also an ex-pagan. Every new addition to the church means one less adherent to the old, traditional religions. As Christianity grows, it is destroying paganism in its wake.[29]

CHRISTIAN EXCLUSIVISM

One way to understand Christian exclusivity is to think about the Christians' unusual approach to "choice." Of course everyone in the ancient world had to choose how to live, what to think, how to behave, and how to worship. In fact, pagan religions in recent scholarship have been portrayed as a kind of "marketplace," where "shoppers" would choose among competing options.[30] Just as you might choose to buy a fish, so you could choose a cult to follow. And at the market you might buy not only a fish but also some fruit, some grains, and some vegetables. At every point you make a choice. So too with religion: you can choose which cults to belong to and how often or rigorously to observe them.

For pagan religions, the cults you followed normally would not have provided a distinctive identity marker. If someone asked you how you identified yourself, you would not have said, "I'm a worshiper of

Apollo" any more than you would have said, "I'm a consumer of sea bass."[31] You might indeed have worshiped Apollo on occasion just as you might have sometimes eaten sea bass, but that was not how you identified yourself. In no small measure that was because your decision for Apollo and sea bass was just one of the many decisions you made all the time with respect to cult and cuisine.[32]

Christianity was different. The Christian god was not normally chosen as one of the gods to be worshiped. The choice in this case was exclusive. The choice specifically for one thing was the choice *against* everything else. It was eating sea bass and nothing but sea bass. And to most pagan minds, it probably seemed just as odd.

Scholars have long noted this distinctive feature of Christianity, especially since the days of Arthur Darby Nock, whose book *Conversion* is one of the true classics in the field.[33] Nock argued that the principal difference between pagan religions and Christianity was the difference between "adhesion" and "conversion." Within paganism one always had the possibility of adopting a new set of religious practices, but that simply meant "adhering" to it. There was no sense that a person who turned to a new cult had to turn away from another. That sense of completely turning to a new thing, and in so doing leaving behind the old, is what Nock meant by "conversion."

Nock was operating with an older sense of what conversion entailed: as the complete, heartfelt, emotional commitment to the new thing—the view I critiqued earlier in the chapter. All the same, Nock deeply understood that what traditional Christianity expected of a new follower had no precise parallel in paganism. He did acknowledge that something comparable to the concept of conversion could be found in the philosophical traditions of antiquity. At least some of the philosophical traditions were seen to be mutually exclusive: an Epicurean philosopher was not also a Stoic; a Cynic was not a Peripatetic. These were not airtight categories and there certainly were philosophically oriented people who borrowed from one school of thought or another. But, strictly speaking, a real disciple of Aristotle was not a follower of Epicurus. So Christianity was a bit like that.

One difference is that philosophical schools were not religious cults, even if they did discuss the divine and humans' relationship with it. There were also, however, rare instances in which followers of one divine being or another expressed deep and *virtually* exclusive devotion. No example is better known, or more fully exploited by Nock, than the devotion to the goddess Isis found in a popular work of Roman fiction, *The Golden Ass*, written by Apuleius, a North African author of the second century CE. Exploring this account can indeed help us understand the contrasts between pagan adherence and Christian conversion.

A PAGAN PARALLEL TO CHRISTIAN EXCLUSIVITY: *THE GOLDEN ASS*

The Golden Ass is a hilarious tale filled with joyous and rather raucous sex, nocturnal magical rites, murderous plots, wild escapades, narrow escapes, and, as it turns out, deeply felt religious experiences. As the title indicates, it is about an ass—or, rather, about a man who becomes an ass. The main character is named Lucius. On a journey to a new city, Lucius is hosted by a man whose wife is a witch, and Lucius is fascinated. After seducing the housemaid, Fotis, Lucius convinces her to allow him to watch her mistress practice her magical craft. Looking through a chink in the door, he sees the woman anoint herself with a magical portion to be transformed into an owl before flying off into the night.

Desperate to obtain such power, Lucius urges Fotis to retrieve the ointment for him. She enters her mistress's chamber and snatches the jar, but, rather unfortunately for Lucius (but luckily for the plot), she grabs the wrong one. When Lucius applies the ointment, he turns not into a noble owl but into a ridiculous ass, with his human mind intact but no human physical abilities. He can do nothing but bemoan his fate by braying loudly. Fotis, trained in the ways of her mistress, knows what Lucius the ass must do to be restored to his human self. He needs simply to eat some roses.

Before any can be found, in the dead of night, robbers break into the house, despoil its contents, steal the ass Lucius, load him with plunder, and drive him off to their stronghold. The rest of the long tale narrates Lucius's misadventures as a man trapped in a beast's body being handed over from one set of owners to another, over-worked, beaten, manhandled, and generally abused, though occasionally treated well. As part of the narrative, he is often privy to intriguing stories told by owners within hearing distance, all while desperately trying to locate a bunch of roses to consume, always to no avail.

The ribald and rowdy story takes an unexpected turn at the end. Lucius the ass has a deep religious experience that changes not only his outer life—literally, as he becomes a man once more—but even more his inner person. He becomes a devotee of the Egyptian goddess Isis.

By book eleven Lucius is more than fed up with his asinine existence. He escapes his latest masters, manages to find a quiet place on the seashore, and falls asleep, only to awaken to see the moon rise over the ocean. He knows that the moon was "the primal Goddess of supreme sway," so he immerses his head seven times in the water as a ritual act and invokes her, acknowledging that she might be any one of a number of divine beings: the goddess Ceres, Venus, Diana, or Proserpina. He ends his catalog of petitionary options by covering every possibility: "Or by whatever name and by whatever rites, and in whatever form, it is permitted to invoke you."[34]

Then he has an epiphany. The goddess appears to him. She informs him that she is the ultimate divine being: "I, the natural mother of all life, the mistress of the elements, the first child of time, the supreme divinity, the queen of those in hell, the first among those in heaven, the uniform manifestation of all the gods and goddesses—I, who govern by my nod the crests of light in the sky, the purifying wafts of the ocean, and the lamentable silences of hell." She goes on to indicate that various peoples have called her various things, but that her "true name" is "Queen Isis."

Isis promises to bring Lucius salvation—that is, to deliver him from his lowly beastly existence. Furthermore, she will enable him to worship her even after his mortal death. But there is a condition.

When she bestows her blessings upon him, he must be utterly devoted to her: "All the remaining days of your life must be dedicated to me, and . . . nothing can release you from this service but death. . . . [Y]ou should devote your life to her who redeems you back into humanity."

Isis is true to her word. She instructs Lucius that the next day, at a festival in her honor, he will find a priest bearing a bouquet of roses, which he will be able to consume to return to his human shape. He does so, and it happens. The rest of the book narrates how Lucius then devotes himself to the worship of the goddess. He goes through a prolonged and rather difficult period of preparation and then is initiated into her mysteries. The author cannot tell us exactly what is said during the ceremony, or exactly what happens—he is, after all, describing a "mystery" and he is not about to explain what actually happened in any detail. And so his account is both rapturous and frustratingly elusive. What is clear is that Lucius experiences the most glorious moment of his mortal existence, a kind of new birth, and he dedicates his life to serving Isis.

He later learns, however, that he has not reached the pinnacle of devotion. There is a higher level, a ceremonial induction into the mysteries of the divine husband of Isis, the "Father of the Gods, un-conquerable Osiris." Lucius is surprised: "For I had thought myself fully initiated already." But no, Osiris is the greater god and a new initiation is necessary. In part Lucius is dismayed, because partici-pating in these initiations is expensive. But he goes through with it.

Sometime later he learns that a third initiation is necessary. He starts wondering if this is a scam, but he decides to calm his suspi-cions. Afterward he realizes that in fact all is well: "At length, after the lapse of a few days, the Lord Osiris, the most powerful of the great gods, the highest of the greater, the greatest of the highest, and ruler of the greatest, appeared to me in the night, now no longer disguised by deigning to speak to me in his own person and with his own divine voice." And soon the book ends.

As Nock recognized, there are indeed numerous parallels be-tween what happened to the fictional character Lucius in his devo-tion to Isis in *The Golden Ass* and what happened to actual pagans who became Christian. Lucius recognizes Isis as the greatest of divine beings, one who is worshiped in heaven, on earth, and under the earth. In exchange for his devotion, she transforms his life. He is born again. In a sense, he becomes fully human—literally. Moreover, he is promised a life after death. In exchange, she demands a complete commitment. He is initiated into her cult, and he lives his life in adoration of her.

That does indeed sound very much like what happened to converts who joined the Christian community, recognizing the god of the Christians as the one ruler over all who was more powerful than all beings in heaven and earth, who could bring new life to one who was born again—not to mention life after death—in exchange for absolute devotion. But there is a very real and tangible difference. Lucius never had to think or act as if Isis were in fact the only divine being. On the contrary, she was *superior* to all others. As it turned out, not even that was right. There was one greater: Osiris. Were there yet others even greater? The author never says. When Lucius turned to Isis, he did not stop being a pagan who recognized the divinity of other divine beings. Nor did he make any commitment to worship her alone. His was not an exclusive devotion. It was simply a particularly intense devotion.

THE ADVANTAGES OF EXCLUSIVITY

And so Christianity was the only evangelistic religion that we know of in antiquity, and, along with Judaism, it was also the only one that was exclusive. That combination of evangelism and exclusion proved to be decisive for the triumph of Christianity. If it had been evangelistic but not exclusive, it may well have gained adherents, but paganism would have remained unaffected. Pagans would simply have begun to worship Christ along with whatever other gods they chose: Jupiter, Apollo, Diana, Mithras, Isis . . . take your pick. If, on the other hand, it had been exclusive but not evangelistic, Christianity, like Judaism, would have simply been an isolated and marginal religion without masses of adherents.

But it gained a massive following. Not at first, but over time, progressively adding to its ranks year after year, decade after decade. As it grew, paganism necessarily shrank. Unlike any religion known to the human race at the time, Christianity thrived by killing off its opposition.

No one has seen that better or argued it more convincingly than Roman social historian Ramsay MacMullen.[35] MacMullen explains with a hypothetical example that I will modify slightly. Suppose two persons were each promoting a new cult, one the worship of Asclepius and the other the worship of Jesus. A crowd of a hundred pagan polytheists gathers to hear each devotee extol the glories of his god. In the end, the two prove to be equally successful: fifty of the crowd decide now to worship Asclepius and fifty others decide to worship the Christian god. What happens to the overall relationship of (inclusive) paganism and (exclusive) Christianity? If our two hypothetical speakers are equally persuasive, paganism has lost fifty worshipers and gained no one, whereas Christianity has gained fifty worshipers and lost no one. Christianity is destroying the pagan religions in its wake.

This example, of course, is completely hypothetical and unlikely for all sorts of reasons. We do not know of pagan evangelists working a crowd. And even though Christianity was evangelistic, we don't know of public speeches aimed at conversion outside of the book of Acts in the New Testament and later comparably legendary accounts. Moreover, it does not appear that there ever were massive on-the-spot conversions to Christianity (a point on which I strongly disagree with Professor MacMullen). Christianity grew by one-on-one discourse as a person would convince a family member, friend, or acquaintance, who would convince another, who would convince another. How these people proved convincing will be the subject of the next chapter. For now, the point is that it is highly unlikely that anyone convinced fifty people at one time, let alone on the spot on the basis of a single public talk.

But the point still holds. Christianity necessarily destroyed the other religions as it grew, and it was the only religion in the empire doing so. As the church grew, the pagan world shrank until—after a couple of centuries—pagans realized they had a problem on their hands.

CHRISTIANITY AS AN "ALL-ENCOMPASSING RELIGION"

One other feature of Christianity that made it different from all the pagan religions throughout the empire is that it encompassed numerous aspects of life that had always been kept distinct.[36] Adopting the Christian religion did not mean simply participating in cultic activities, as was the case for other religions, whether imperial cults, civic cults, or family cults. For these pagan religions, the cultic acts *were* the religion. Cultic acts for Christianity, however, such as baptism, communion meals, prayers, hymns, and so on, were certainly important aspects of the religion, but they were only some of the aspects. Christianity also entailed an ethical code, a way of thinking about the divine, and a set of stories about divine intervention in the past. In the words of a scholar of ancient Rome, James Rives, Christianity was a "totalizing discourse."[37] That is, it involved a totality of a person's life. It was all-encompassing.

As a corollary, since Christians conceptualized their religion as a coherent system, they began thinking that everything outside their religion was a *competing* coherent system. Thus, relatively early in their history, Christians declared there were three kinds of persons: Christian, Jewish, and pagan. Being a pagan meant being some "thing." Paganism became an entity, granted its own "ism."[38] Everything not Jewish or Christian cohered together—even if there were hundreds, even thousands, of manifestations of this one thing, with enormous differences among them. That coherent whole was the rest of the world.

Because paganism was now seen as a recognizable "thing" standing as a competing force against Christianity (even though, for most of the first three hundred years, no one on the other side realized they were in a competition), it could be appraised, evaluated, and condemned. It could be contrasted with Christianity and judged to be deficient in everything that it practiced, believed, and taught. Pagans could be portrayed as unethical. As believing foolish things. As engaging in meaningless—or, worse, demonic—acts of worship. Comprising such features, paganism could be attacked. And over time it was attacked successfully.

REASONS FOR THE CHRISTIAN SUCCESS: IN SUM

A number of readers will have realized that I have been speaking in broadly general, even generalizing terms about Christians and Christianity, as if the early Christian movement were one thing, not lots of different things. The reality, as we know so well, is that Christianity was an amazingly diverse phenomenon throughout the first four Christian centuries, with different Christians advocating an enormous range of beliefs and engaging in strikingly different practices. This has been the subject of a large number of books in modern times, especially over the past forty years.[39]

If so, how can we make such broad generalizations as "Christianity was exclusive" or "Christianity was evangelistic"? I have made these statements fully knowing that Christianity encompassed a terrifically divergent set of beliefs and practices. There certainly were Christians, arguably the majority of them, who were not interested in evangelizing their next-door neighbors. And there were almost certainly large numbers of Christians who refused, either in their minds and hearts or in their daily lives, to be committed fully and exclusively to the Christian god alone.

In my view, all of that goes without saying. But I need to say it anyway, in part because in the long run I do not think that it matters for the case I am trying to make. For the argument I have been advancing, it is not important whether Christianity is reduced to some kind of essential entity that is necessarily evangelistic and exclusive. What matters is that broad swaths of it demonstrably were. That is the kind of Christianity that in the end became dominant in the empire.

I would like to make two concluding points about this eventually dominant form of Christianity. The first is that we know about it from the majority of written sources that have come down to us and these documents represent idealizations of later Christian leaders. This is the way the elite, highly educated Christian writers of the early centuries who produced our texts wanted to portray Christianity and possibly how they fervently wanted Christianity to be. This means these views represent the perspectives of the cultured leaders of the church.

But it also means they were the views of those who were in power. That is a point to consider deeply. In my judgment it would make no sense to think that the "official" line taken by leaders of the church was completely unrelated to the views held by numbers of average church people who possibly didn't think much about such things on their own. These are the views they were taught by those in power, and even if they are idealizations, they would represent idealizations held by other Christians as well, not simply by the elite authors whose works have come down to us. Again, for my purposes, it would not matter if everyone held these views as long as some did. And probably a significant number of Christians did.

My second point is that the distinctive features of this idealized Christianity that I have been presenting—that it was evangelistic, exclusive, and totalizing—can almost certainly be attributed to a number of the Christian groups of the first four centuries, not simply the one that became dominant. It is true that most of our surviving writings come down to us from sources that scholars call orthodox and proto-orthodox. The term "orthodox" refers to the form of Christian belief and practice that came to be dominant in the fourth century after Christianity began to expand and grow significantly. "Proto-orthodox" refers to the similar form of Christianity that was held by forerunners of the orthodox party in the years before its views came to dominate. In those years of pre-dominance there were varieties of Christian belief. But even some of these non-orthodox groups—call them heresies—were evangelistic and invested in converting Jews and pagans into their fold.[40]

Most of the converts into the proto-orthodox tradition—as well as most of the heretical traditions—came not from Jewish communities but from the ranks of the pagans. With such potential converts, Christians of different sorts made some common cause. They agreed with a growing number of pagans that ultimately there is one divine being above and beyond all others. For these Christians, this was not an unknown god, or one of the Roman pantheon, or simply "the Greatest God," Theos Hypsistos. It was the god of Israel, who had become the god of the Christians. These Christians also agreed with pagans that one of the chief reasons to revere this god was that he could provide numerous benefits to those who acknowledged his divinity and properly worshiped him. Divine benefactions had always been at the core of pagan religious devotion as they were at the core of Christianity.

What made these Christians different from those who adhered to traditional pagan religions was their concern and, for at least some of them, their passion to convert others to the worship of their god, their insistence that anyone who did so needed to turn away from the gods they had always worshiped, and their view that true devotion to God involved not just ritual acts but also ethical behavior and proper doctrinal understanding of who this god was. This was the form of Christianity proclaimed by the first known missionary to the pagans, the apostle Paul. It was the message proclaimed by our literate, elite, cultured Christian writers from the proto-orthodox tradition. It was the message that later orthodox writers of the fourth century insisted upon with unusual vehemence. And it is the message that eventually overtook the religious world of Roman antiquity.

One dominant question, though, is why anyone found the message convincing. Why were pagans persuaded to give up everything they had ever thought, change everything they had ever practiced, abandon all the gods they had ever worshiped, in order to join the Christian community and worship only the god of the Christians?

Chapter 5

Miraculous Incentives for Conversion

We have already seen that the church did not spread through a well-thought-out and highly organized missionary endeavor, a first-century parallel to British and American missions to deepest, darkest Africa and other "heathen" places in the nineteenth century. It spread by word of mouth, from one person to another, all deeply connected in their daily lives to social networks through which news could circulate and views could air. One place to start in considering the persuasiveness of the Christians is with the audience they were addressing: the pagan reservoir from which they were drawing most of their converts.

We wish we knew who these people were. It would especially help if we had some disinterested sources of information. But we do not. For the first 150 years of the church, virtually all our evidence comes from Christian accounts, which are obviously slanted in a particular direction and often make unverifiable claims about the masses adopting this new faith.[1] The first extensive discussion of the Christian movement from a non-Christian source—also not disinterested, of course—comes from the end of the 170s.[2] We do not have this source as a stand-alone document. It is a book quoted, instead, by a Christian author, the great theologian Origen of Alexandria, who cited it precisely in order to refute it. The book had been written by an otherwise unknown pagan intellectual named Celsus.[3]

Celsus's work was called *The True Word*. In it he assails Christianity as a foolish and dangerous religion that lacks all academic credentials and poses ominous problems, particularly because it leads people astray from traditional religions. Celsus's attack was direct and incisive. He had read the Christian Gospels and with rapier-like wit and clearheaded analysis tried to tear them to shreds, along with the Jesus they worshiped. Origen had his hands full in writing a refutation some six decades later.

Much could be said about Celsus's critique of the Christian faith, but for our purposes here, one point he makes is particularly trenchant. He argues—with obvious exaggeration—that Christianity is a religion of ignoramuses who are too thick to recognize either religious truth or valid argument. Christian proponents work especially hard to convert the foolish and the gullible. Here is what Celsus says in a rather amusing but mocking tone, a statement worth quoting at length:

> Wherever one finds a crowd of adolescent boys, or a bunch of slaves, or a company of fools, there will the Christian teachers be also, showing off their fine new philosophy. In private houses one can see wool workers, cobblers, laundry workers, and the most illiterate country bumpkins, who would not venture to voice their opinions in front of their intellectual betters. But let them get hold of children in private houses—let them find some gullible wives—and you will hear some preposterous statements. You will hear them say, for instance, that they should not pay any attention to their fathers or teachers, but must obey them. They say that their elders and teachers are fools, and are in reality very bad men who like to voice their silly opinions. . . . Now if, as they are speaking thus to the children, they happen to see a schoolteacher coming along, some intelligent person, or even the father of one of the children, these Christians flee in all directions. . . . These

Christians also tell the children that they should leave their fathers and teachers and follow the women and the little chums to the wool dresser's shop, or the cobbler's or to the washerwoman's shop, so that they might learn how to be perfect. And by this logic they have persuaded many to join them.

There is obviously a lot of elitist snobbery going on here. But there may be some truth as well. We have very little evidence to suggest that serious intellectuals converted to the Christian faith between the time of Paul and the mid-second century. Most converts would have been lower-class and uneducated. This was certainly true in Paul's own day. In a letter to one of his largest congregations, he explicitly reminds the Corinthians about their own constituency: "Consider your calling, brothers and sisters: Not many of you were wise by human standards, not many of you were powerful, not many of you were born to nobility. But God chose the foolish in the world to put to shame the wise; God chose the weak in the world to put to shame the strong" (1 Corinthians 1:26–27).

Some scholars over the past thirty years have stressed that, since Paul indicates not *many* of the Corinthian Christians were wise, powerful, or of the nobility, surely *some* of them must have been.[4] That is probably true, but Paul's entire point is that the vast majority of his converts were uneducated, powerless, and lower-class. Nothing in our early Christian sources suggests things had changed much in the century between Paul and Celsus.

On the contrary, it is striking that when Celsus claims that the ignorant lower classes—either literally or figuratively "children"—were particularly attracted to Christianity, Origen does not defend the faith by disagreeing. In his view, the fact that Christianity could be so successful despite its lack of intellectual force and impact on the highly educated classes shows that God must be behind the movement: it is not gaining converts because of its obvious intellectual superiority. The early-fourth-century defender of the faith, Lactantius, also indicates that most Christians were uneducated and "foolish" (*Divine Institutes* 5.1–2).

Celsus also mocks Christianity for being a religion not just of "children" but also of "gullible women." He clearly means this as a slur. It may simply represent a standard misogynistic charge leveled against a despised social group, but there are other indications that for some time the Christian faith drew more women than men into the fold. One piece of hard evidence comes somewhat later. As we will see, in 303 CE the emperor Diocletian inaugurated an empire-wide persecution. We are fortunate to have a report of personal belongings confiscated at the time from a church in the town of Cirta, North Africa: sixteen men's tunics, but thirty-eight veils, eighty-two women's tunics, and forty-seven pairs of female slippers. This datum is slight, but it has led one historian, Robin Lane Fox, to claim, though probably on too thin a thread of evidence, that "it is highly likely that women were a clear majority in the churches of the third century."[5]

By the middle of the second century one does start seeing isolated intellectuals convert to the faith: Justin in Rome, Tertullian in North Africa, Origen himself in Alexandria. These are clear exceptions to the rule. At the same time, it cannot be emphasized enough that *most* people in the Roman world by far were lower-class and uneducated, so it cannot come as a surprise that most Christians were. Still, the church may have had more than its fair share. Among other things, this suggests that most converts were not drawn in by the writings of the Christian literary elite or through public debates with well-educated proponents of the faith. Sophisticated argument was almost certainly not the principle engine of conversion.

There have been numerous attempts over the years to determine exactly what, then, was driving the Christian success. I do not need to enumerate all the options. It may be useful, however, to begin by considering two of the more intriguing but ultimately implausible ones.

THE ATTRACTIONS OF THE CHRISTIAN COMMUNITY

It is often thought and widely claimed that one of the main reasons pagans converted to Christianity was because of the inherent attractiveness of the church community. Pagan civic cults did not involve much community. They did entail ceremonies performed in public in the presence of others, but there were no weekly community meetings, opportunities for fellowship, or planned times of discussion, reflection, and sharing of concerns.

That was different within Christianity. Much like the Jewish synagogues out of which they grew, Christian churches entailed regularly scheduled weekly meetings. Converting to Christianity was not an isolated individualistic affair, a matter of private spirituality. It meant joining the church. The church was not a place: there were no buildings for Christian gatherings until the middle of the third century, so far as we know. Prior to that, and probably for a good while afterward, most churches met in private homes and in outdoor areas such as cemeteries. Rather than being a place, the church was a community. A tightly knit community. A community as tightly knit as the nuclear family. In fact, Christians were often encouraged to replace their families with the members of their new community. The founder or leader of the church was a "father"; fellow believers were "brothers" and "sisters" in one big family. Moreover, these were self-consciously communities of mutual love and respect. They provided material support for their needy members. They provided moral support for everyone who came.

Such, at least, were the claims of Christians who wrote about the church. Whether all this was entirely true is another question. But numerous scholars have maintained that the obvious attractions of this kind of community would have drawn in outsiders eager to join for the enormous social benefits. Classical historian E. R. Dodds once claimed that the nature of the Christian community "was a major cause, perhaps the single cause, of the spread of Christianity."[6]

Support for this view might seem to come from a comment by the late-fourth-century emperor Julian, known to history as "Julian the Apostate," since he abandoned his Christian faith to adopt and promote traditional pagan religions. Julian was the only pagan emperor after Constantine; he ruled for nineteen months, from 361 to 363 CE. He was, in fact, Constantine's nephew and had been raised in the church. But he rebelled upon taking office and was intent to re-convert the empire to paganism, as we will see more fully in chapter 9.

In one of his letters Julian laments the success of the Christian church and attributes it to the benefactions that Christians bestowed on others, expressing his wish that pagan religions could follow the Christian example of community and communal giving. In this citation he refers to Christians both as "atheists"—since they do not revere the gods—and "Galileans":

> Why do we not observe that it is their benevolence to strangers, their care for the graves of the dead, and the pretended holiness of their lives that have done most to increase atheism? . . . It is disgraceful that, when no Jew ever has to beg, and the impious Galileans support not only their own poor but ours as well, everyone can see that our people lack aid from us. (*Julian*, Letter 22)

And so, it has been argued, Christian communal life ultimately attracted adherents. There are, however, difficulties with this view. For one thing, as a young man Julian himself had been actively involved in the church and so knew of its workings from the inside. His was not an outsider's report. He may well have believed that charity drew people in, but it is striking that the advantages of church membership are never mentioned as a reason for conversion by any Christian on record. As Adolf von Harnack concedes, based on an exhaustive evaluation of all our literary sources: "We know of no cases in which Christians desired to win, or actually did win, adherents by means of the charities which they dispensed."[7]

That is not to say that benefits did not accrue to those who came into the church. On the contrary, there is good reason to suspect that numerous people found the Christian church very gratifying indeed, in no small measure for the social, emotional, physical, and intellectual benefits it bestowed. But there is a difference between benefits that might entice people to join the community in the first place and benefits that might encourage them to remain once they are there. Bringing someone in is not the same as keeping them in.

The early Christian churches were closed communities. Outsiders were not allowed to join in worship services. They did not know the inner workings of the church or the full advantages of what it had to offer. Indeed, as we will see later, stories about what happened within Christian communities could be considerably repugnant rather than attractive. In short, we have little evidence to suggest that people widely, if at all, joined the church because of the communal benefits they would receive. Something else probably made the Christian religion attractive.

SUPERIOR HEALTH CARE

One benefit of joining the church, which has been recently touted as particularly important for Christian growth, was the availability of better health care. This was one of the many controversial proposals set forth by sociologist Rodney Stark in his popular discussion *The Rise of Christianity: A Sociologist Reconsiders History* and was the thesis behind a more extensive treatment by Hector Avalos, *Health Care and the Rise of Christianity*.[8]

Despite Avalos's in-depth discussion of how early Christians organized, managed, and implemented health care, he never mounts an argument to show how the Christian health care system attracted converts or led to church growth. Stark, on the other hand, applies his sociological training to the question and makes some intriguing suggestions. He points out that epidemics swept through the Roman world on more than one occasion during the period that Christianity was gaining members. The terrible plague that ravaged the empire during the reign of Marcus Aurelius killed, Stark avers, between a quarter and a third of the entire population of the empire. The emperor himself was one of the fatalities.

Stark notes that Christian sources celebrate the eagerness of Christians to minister to the sick in times of illness. Stark claims this was unlike the pagans, who, as a rule, simply let the sick fend for themselves. He goes on to point to studies that indicate that even without access to modern medicine, simple nursing—caring for someone who is ill—can have a drastic effect on survival rates. Stark concludes that Christians emerged from epidemics far more intact as a population group than pagans, so their relative numbers grew through nothing more than the decision to nurse the sick.

This is an intriguing perspective, but it has not proved widely persuasive, for several reasons. For one thing, Stark unrealistically and uncritically assumes that when Christian sources praise Christians and malign pagans for their health care practices, they are giving factual information. For him, a Christian author is simply stating historical reality when he praises fellow Christians for acts of love far superior to anything found elsewhere, and maligns outsiders for neglecting even their dying family members. Historians of early Christianity are never this sanguine when it comes to our sources. One always needs to consider their obvious biases.[9]

Beyond that, there is a fairly obvious reason for doubting that Christian nursing practices in times of epidemic led to growth in the church. If our sources are indeed to be trusted that Christians tended to the sick more often than pagans did, that would surely also mean that Christians were more often infected.

As it turns out, early Christian texts bemoan precisely this fact: Christians frequently died because they acquired the diseases they were trying to heal. This is a point that Stark, naturally enough, glosses over. But it is clearly stated in the eyewitness accounts, nowhere more grippingly than in a letter written by a mid-third-century bishop of Alexandria, Egypt, Dionysius, as quoted by the church historian Eusebius. In this letter Dionysius refers to an epidemic that "came out of the blue" and notes how the Christians dealt with it in their community:

> Heedless of the danger, they took charge of the sick, attending to their every need and ministering to them in Christ, and with them departed this life serenely happy; for they were infected by others with the disease, drawing in themselves the sickness of their neighbors and cheerfully accepting their pains. Many, in nursing and curing others, transferred their death to themselves

and died in their stead. . . . The best of our brothers lost their lives in this manner, a number of presbyters, deacons, and laymen.

Dionysius claims that the care of the sick continued postmortem, leading to yet more deaths within the community:

> With willing hands they raised the bodies of the saints to their bosoms; they closed their eyes and mouths, carried them on their shoulders, and laid them out; they clung to them, embraced them, washed them, and wrapped them in grave clothes. Very soon the same services were done for them, since those left behind were constantly following those gone before.[10]

We have no indication from outsiders that they were drawn to the church because of the improved possibilities of health care, and it seems unlikely that a Christian inclination to stay in intimate contact with the contaminated led to a growth in Christian numbers. We should therefore look elsewhere to discover what attracted converts to the church. The best place to begin is the actual accounts of conversions from the early church. These are relatively abundant and scattered throughout the decades and centuries with which we are concerned. Moreover, these narratives are unambiguous about what attracted outsiders to the faith. The Christians did amazing miracles.[11]

MIRACULOUS CONVERSIONS TO THE FAITH

As I pointed out earlier when discussing Paul, I am not saying that Christians really did miracles. A modern-day believer may think they did; a nonbeliever will think they did not. Either way, it is safe to say that Christians were *believed* to do miracles. It is consistently reported that this belief is what led outsiders to convert to the faith.

To understand how it worked, it is important to recall a key point at which ancient pagans and Christians agreed with respect to human interaction with the divine. Participating in worship was believed to have real benefits. Among pagans, gods were worshiped, on one hand, simply because they were great and deserved to be acknowledged and revered for who they were. At the same time we have constant testimony that failure to participate in worship could lead to dire consequences: the gods could and occasionally did make life very unpleasant for communities that failed to grant them their divine due. Even more than that, the gods were worshiped because of the great benefactions they could give: they controlled the weather, caused the crops to grow, made the livestock multiply, healed the sick, and protected travelers from harm. The gods could provide what humans needed but could not provide for themselves. The gods had superhuman powers, and, in no small measure, worship allowed people to access that power.

Why, then, would a pagan decide to worship a new or different god? Because of the beneficences that god could provide. Why worship the Christian god? For the same reason: he too could do miracles, and even better ones. But in this case there was a catch. Anyone who came to worship the Christian god was expected to forgo the worship of the other gods. That was the Christian message from the beginning, as we saw from the first surviving letter of our very first Christian author, Paul, who reminded the Thessalonians that they had turned from their "dead idols" (i.e., gods who were powerless) "to the living God" (1 Thessalonians 1:9). How could one tell this god was living? Because he was active in the world. He was doing things, through humans, that humans could not do on their own. He was performing miracles. And so, as we have seen, Paul spoke of the "signs and wonders" that he himself performed on the mission field (Romans 15:18–19); of the proofs of his message that came "in demonstration of the Spirit and of power" (1 Corinthians 2:4); "of the signs of a true apostles . . . performed among you with signs and wonders and miracles" (2 Corinthians 12:12). These words of Paul's are borne out time and again in our accounts of Christian conversion from the pages of the New Testament up through the fourth century. Christians do miracles; that convinces outsiders that God is on the Christians' side; as a result, the outsiders convert.

Take the very first account we have of the spread of early Christianity, the New Testament book of Acts. The conversions begin, naturally enough, with Jews, just weeks after Jesus's death. They happen because of miracles. The first episode occurs already in chapter 2, the famous account of the coming of the Holy Spirit on the Day of Pentecost. Pentecost was an annual Jewish festival that occurred fifty days after Passover. In this account, that would be just under two months after Jesus's death and resurrection. In the story there are by this time a 120 believers, all gathered together in Jerusalem, awaiting the Holy Spirit that the resurrected Jesus promised would come upon them. It does so in a show of power. The believers hear the noise of a loud rushing wind, tongues of flame appear above their heads, and they all begin to speak in foreign languages they do not know. An exceedingly curious crowd gathers: Jews from around the world who are at the festival. All of them hear the gospel of Christ proclaimed in their own tongue. It is a great miracle, and the crowd is "amazed and perplexed."

The miracle is followed by a sermon delivered by the head apostle, Peter, who explains that the onlookers have seen a fulfillment of the prophecies of Scripture. Jesus, who was killed "by lawless people" just weeks before, had been a great miracle worker. After his death an even greater miracle occurred: God raised him from the dead. The person that they, the Jews, had crucified has been made Lord of all. The Jewish crowds cry out, asking what they should do. Peter tells them all to repent and be baptized in the name of Jesus Christ. They do so: three thousand people convert on the spot (Acts 2:1–41).

From that point on we learn that "many wonders and signs were done through the apostles" (Acts 2:43). As a result, their numbers grew day after day.

The next main episode comes in the next chapter and involves another miracle. A man lame from birth is begging for alms at the Jerusalem temple. The apostles Peter and John pass by and, in response to the man's request for money, Peter tells him he has something even better to provide. He heals him on the spot. The crowds all marvel, inspiring Peter to launch into another speech about Jesus as a fulfillment of Scripture. At the end of it all, another five thousand convert (Acts 3:1–4:4). Needless to say, things are going extremely well for the Christian movement. Just two months in and they have won over eight thousand people. At this rate there won't be any non-Christians left in Jerusalem.

The narrative continues with more miracles and more conversions. Some of the miracles are truly astounding, not your garden-variety healings or exorcisms. Peter becomes so powerful that his shadow will cure anyone it falls upon; needless to say, the lame and crippled line the streets of Jerusalem for the opportunity (Acts 5:14–15). Later, Paul converts and he too becomes not just an evangelist but an effective miracle worker. Even his handkerchiefs and aprons have the power of healing, leading many to flock to the faith (Acts 19:11–20).

These accounts from the book of Acts set the stage for later narratives of the apostles and their successors outside the New Testament, in noncanonical and highly legendary reports. The basic story line of these evangelistic endeavors is the same: these Christian preachers of the gospel are empowered by the Christian god to do things that mere mortals can only dream of doing. These miraculous deeds convince outsiders that the Christian god is more powerful than any other. This leads them to convert, abandoning their older practices and joining the Christian ranks.

A PAUSE FOR MIRACULOUS REFLECTION

Before looking at these tales, we need to pause. How are we to credit the Christian stories of miraculous conversions? Anyone who wants to accept them at face value will say they happened. But what about everyone else? We are confronted with three inescapable facts, all of which need to be accounted for. First, it cannot be denied that people did convert to the Christian faith, eventually in massive numbers. Second, the early Christian accounts of conversion, starting with the New Testament, attribute conversions to the great miracles being performed. Third, many people today—almost all non-Christians but a lot of critical Christians as well—do not think these miracles really happened.

In explaining all three facts, one option is simply to claim that conversions happened (since they did indeed happen) for reasons other than what our sources say. A skeptic might attribute them instead to the attractions of community or to superior health care or the like. That is a common line to take. But we should not abandon our sources too quickly. As we will continue to see, they abundantly attest that the conversions took place precisely because of miracles.

And so an alternative might suggest itself. When people believe in miracles today, it is rarely because they have actually experienced one. Some people claim they have, but not most. In fact, most people who believe in miracles have not even observed one, let alone been the beneficiary of one. What all believers in miracles do have in common is that they have heard of miracles. Often they have heard of miracles from others who claimed the miracles happened to them. More often they have heard of miracles from others who claimed they personally observed them happen to someone else—or who claimed to know someone who knew someone else who knew someone else who observed them.

Most believers in miracles today have only heard about miracles. It is reasonable to assume that this is why most people in early Christianity believed in miracles. They heard stories such as those found in the book of Acts. These are literary narratives, not disinterested historical records. They are accounts that had been told by word of mouth before someone wrote them down. Many people today believe the Holy Spirit really did come upon the disciples on the day of Pentecost and made them speak in tongues—a great miracle. They believe it because they have read the story in Acts 2.

We might suppose this is how it worked in early Christianity. People heard the stories. Most people did not believe them. Some, after hearing enough stories repeated time after time, began to consider them possible. Eventually they came to believe them. They then converted. It is not necessarily because the apostles and their followers were really doing miracles. They may have been or they may not have been. But when told with enough conviction, the stories certainly proved convincing to others. And there is proof: people did convert, and the reason stated was almost always the same. The words of the Christians were backed up by stories of miracles.

APOCRYPHAL TALES OF CONVERSION

Once we move outside the New Testament, the tales of conversion-inducing miracles continue. Few are more intriguing than the conversion of the entire city of Edessa in Syria, allegedly because of miracles worked by Jesus's follower Thaddeus.

In no small part the tale intrigues because it starts with Jesus himself, before his death, and a personal letter he sent to the king of Edessa, Abgar, in response to the king's written request to be healed—the only piece of correspondence ever attributed to Jesus himself.[12] The two letters are cited by the fourth-century church father Eusebius, who claims to have found them in the archives of Edessa and to have translated them from their original Syriac into Greek. In his letter to Jesus, King Abgar indicates that he has heard of Jesus's miracles. He implores him to come to Edessa to heal him of his illness and, at the same time, to escape the animosity of the Jews in his homeland. In his reply, Jesus blesses Abgar for "believing without seeing" (an allusion to John 20:29), but informs the king that he cannot come because he needs to fulfill his mission (that is, by being crucified). After his ascension, however, he will send an apostle to heal the king.

Eusebius quotes both letters in full and then tells the tale that transpired later as he discovered it in the archives.[13] After Jesus's resurrection, his disciple Judas Thomas sent Thaddeus, one of the followers of Jesus during his public ministry, to heal Abgar. He does so but does not stop there. He "began in the power of God to cure every disease and weakness, to the astonishment of everyone." Indeed: "Many other fellow citizens . . . Thaddeus restored to health, performing many wonders and preaching the word of God." The crowds of Edessa were "amazed . . . by his wonderful miracles" and as a result "from that day to this the whole city of Edessa has been devoted to the name of Christ, providing most convincing proof of our Savior's goodness to them."[14]

Similar tales of the miracle-working powers of Jesus's followers are found in several books collectively known as the Apocryphal Acts of the Apostles. These are legendary narratives of the exploits of the apostles during their missionary endeavors in the years after the crucifixion. Any one of these accounts yields numerous instances of astounding and conversion-inducing miracles. Here I mention just a couple that are illustrative.[15]

The Acts of John narrates the miraculous ministry of John the son of Zebedee while spreading the word abroad. Some of the episodes serve no evangelistic purpose but have purely entertainment value in showing the remarkable abilities of this man of God. Of these, probably the best known is the incident of the bedbugs. We are told that after a long journey John and his companions come to a country inn for the night. Upon lying down, John discovers to his dismay that the bed is infested with bugs. Since he needs his rest, he orders the creatures to leave him in peace. His companions find this amusing, until the next morning when they get up to find a large throng of bedbugs awaiting John's command at the door. He wakes up and tells the bugs that they can now return to their home, and they obediently do so.[16]

Most of John's miracles are performed not for the benefit of a good night's sleep but in order to convert the masses. None is more impressive than his effortless destruction of the temple of the great goddess of the Ephesians, Artemis.

Artemis was the patron divinity of the city of Ephesus, on the west coast of what is now Turkey. The Ephesians' dedication to her is celebrated even in the New Testament, in a scene in which her devotees cause a riot in protest against the missionary work of the apostle Paul (Acts 19). In the Acts of John we have another apostolic encounter. This time the goddess—or at least her temple—does not escape unharmed.

John arrives at the magnificent temple of Artemis and there he confronts a large crowd of pagan worshipers celebrating the goddess's birthday. Ascending a platform, John challenges them to a kind of spiritual duel: they should pray for their goddess to strike him dead; if she proves unable to do so, he in turn will pray to God to kill them. Since everyone in the crowd knows that John is able to do great miracles—he has already publicly raised the dead—they cry out for him not to do it.

John urges them all to convert and then prays that the deity of the place yield up to God himself. Immediately the altar of Artemis splits apart, the sacrifices all fall to the ground, the "glory of the temple" (whatever that is) is broken, as are the seven idols in the shrine. Half the temple falls, the roof caves in, and the priest of Artemis is killed in the collapse. The god of the Christians obviously means business, and he is patently more powerful than the greatest divinity in town.

Immediately the pagan crowd delivers the expected response for such tales of Christ's mighty apostles: they all cry out, "There is only one God, that of John, only one God who has compassion for us; for you alone are God; now we have become converted, since we saw your miraculous deeds."[17] Readers might wonder how conversions can occur so suddenly, with almost no instruction about what the people are converting *to*. But there it is. John encourages the crowd, explaining that God is more powerful than Artemis, and his words now have an added effect: the people rush to destroy what is left of Artemis's temple, crying out, "We know that the God of John is the only one, and henceforth we worship him, since we have obtained mercy from him. . . . We have seen that our gods were erected in vain." To make the conversion story complete, the pagan priest who had been killed inside the falling temple is then raised from the dead by the power of God and becomes a believer in Jesus.[18]

In a different set of apocryphal Acts we find comparable powers attributed to the disciple Peter. One of Peter's famous animal tricks involves a talking dog. Peter comes to Rome to confront an enemy of the faith—not a pagan, in this instance, but an arch-heretic, Simon Magus, who is ruining the faith of Christian believers in the capital of the empire by convincing them through his own spectacular miracles that his false teachings are true. Miracles convert. Most of the Acts of Peter involves miracle contests between the true apostle of Christ and the wicked corrupter of the faith.

When Peter arrives in the city, he learns to his dismay that one of the great leaders of the faith, Marcellus, has brought the nefarious Simon under his roof. Peter is barred from entering—the heretic fears his power—but he is not to be deterred. He lets loose a large dog on a chain and endows it with a human voice. The dog enters the house to tell Simon Magus that Peter is waiting for him outside and is not in a conciliatory mood. Returning to Peter, the dog gives Simon's reply: This will be a showdown. The animal then breaths his last and dies. The result is a massive conversion: "When the multitude with great astonishment saw the talking dog, many fell down at the feet of Peter." Others, for whom one amazing feat is not enough, ask him for another miracle, and Peter responds by bringing a smoked tuna back from the dead, tossing it back into the water to swim. Once again "very many who had witnessed this followed Peter and believed in the Lord."[19]

In the miracle contests between Simon Magus and Peter that follow, one fantastic deed trumps another, until eventually everyone has taken a side, either with the heretic or the apostle. At one point Simon and Peter are brought together for an official contest in the arena before all the people of Rome, including senators and prefects of the city. To ensure a fair match, the chief prefect sets the rules of engagement by sending in a slave and giving the two competitors their instructions. Simon is to kill the slave (supernaturally) and Peter is to revive him.

Simon complies by speaking a word in the slave's ear, and he drops down dead. The prefect is more than a little disturbed, in no small measure because the slave is a favorite of the emperor's and now the prefect realizes that he is to blame for his death. He pleads with Peter to do something, and, naturally enough, Peter complies. Informing everyone present that God "is doing many signs and miracles through me to turn you from your sins," he takes the slave by the hand and raises him from the dead. Then comes the expected response: "When the multitude saw this they cried, 'There is only one God, the God of Peter!'"[20]

Such accounts can be found throughout the entire corpus of the Apocryphal Acts of the Apostles.[21] But not only there.

OSTENSIBLY HISTORICAL ACCOUNTS

In addition to such legendary tales of apostolic adventures, we have two narratives from the early Christian centuries that describe missionary activities of later evangelists, one active in the third century and one in the fourth. Even though these are presented as ostensibly historical accounts, they more easily align themselves with "tales of a holy person," that is, an idolizing biography known as "hagiography"—a highly pious and legendary kind of writing that celebrates the miraculous deeds of a Christian saint.

The Life of Gregory the Wonderworker

The third-century figure of Gregory "Thaumaturgus"—that is, the "Wonderworker"—is known to us from a biographical sketch produced over a century after his death by a namesake, Gregory of Nyssa (335–94 CE). Gregory of Nyssa was a major theologian in the Christian church, most famous for his contributions to the ongoing discussions centered on the doctrine of the Trinity. His narrative of the Wonderworker shows how, in the fourth-century imagination, the earlier conversion of the pagan masses came through clear and compelling demonstrations of divine power. The god of the Christians routed the gods of the pagans in a series of direct confrontations. The *Life of Gregory the Wonderworker* declares that whereas he could find only seventeen Christians when he arrived in New

Caesarea, a city in the region of Pontus (northern Turkey), when he completed his missionary campaigns, only seventeen pagans remained.

The account's first episode provides a foretaste of what is to come. The entire region is said to have been filled with pagan temples, altars, and idols. When Gregory arrives, a violent rainstorm forces him to enter a pagan temple. It is filled with the filthy stench of sacrifices, and he purifies it by making the sign of the cross and invoking the name of Christ, putting the terror of God into the resident demons—that is, the pagan gods. Gregory spends the night in the temple saying prayers and singing hymns. The next morning, when the custodian of the temple arrives, the demons appear to him and inform him that they are now barred from the temple. He is furious with Gregory, but the saint tells him that his god has the power to order the pagan demons at will.

The temple custodian asks for proof, so Gregory tears off a piece of paper and writes a command to the demons: "Gregory to Satan, Enter!"[22] The custodian places the message on the altar, and only then is he able to perform his customary sacrifices. "When these things happened he began to grasp the fact that Gregory possessed a divine power, by which he appeared to have overwhelming superiority over the demons." He asks for a further demonstration of divine power, and the saint is more than happy to comply. Outside the temple is a large boulder, far too heavy for a human to lift. Gregory orders it to move. It levitates on its own and glides through the air to settle in another place. "When this had happened, the man straightaway believed in the word, and left everything (including his family) to follow Gregory." The *Life* explicitly states that "he was converted to the true God," not "by some sound or word," but by the great miracle.

That was just the beginning. Soon "the inhabitants of the town poured out en masse as to some account of a new marvel, and all were eager to see who that Gregory is who, though a human being, has power like an emperor over those whom they deemed gods, apparently able to order the demons to and fro like slaves wherever he might will." By the end of Gregory's impressive displays of divine power, virtually the entire region converts.

The Life of Martin of Tours

Within about twenty years of Gregory of Nyssa's description of the remarkable missionary endeavors of the Wonderworker, the Christian writer Sulpicius Severus (c. 355–420 CE) produced an account of another missionary saint, Martin of Tours, in Gaul, modern France. In this case, however, the subject was a contemporary of the author. He was, in fact, the author's spiritual mentor. Sulpicius claims he based his narrative on personal interviews with the saint.

Here too we find numerous accounts of amazing deeds, as Martin is empowered by God to cast out demons and raise the dead. But it was the miracle of a falling pine tree that converted the masses.

Martin comes to a village with a pagan temple and begins to chop down a sacred tree because, he maintains, it is dedicated to the resident demon. A crowd of pagans gathers and objects to his proceeding—naturally enough, as it is a desecration of their sacred site. After an angry exchange, one of crowd offers to chop down the massive tree if Martin agrees to stand beneath it to see if he can avoid being crushed. Martin is not one to back down from a challenge. He stands beneath the tree, the pagans cut it down, and it begins to fall with a loud noise; but before it can land on the saint, he makes the sign of the cross and then "you would have thought it had been repelled by a kind of tornado. The tree fell in a different direction, so that it almost flattened the country men who had been standing all around the place." The miraculous aversion of disaster has its desired effect. "It was agreed that on that day, salvation had come to those regions. For there was almost no one from that immense multitude of pagans who did not believe in the Lord Jesus, and who did not renounce the impiety of their error."[23]

As Martin travels around from one village to another, destroying more pagan temples, the miracles continue to occur. In one site the villagers stand by helplessly as he tears their sacred place down to the foundation, smashes its altars, and reduces the idols "to dust." Once he is finished, the pagans realize they have been frozen in place and unable to move, transfixed by a divine power to prevent them from interfering with the man of God. As a result, "nearly all of them believed in the Lord Jesus, claiming openly and confidently that they should worship the God of Martin and forsake the idols that had been unable to assist either them or others."

The Miracles of Salvation

Some thirty years after the death of Martin of Tours, Augustine of Hippo, the greatest theologian of Christian antiquity, published his famous *City of God* in twenty-two books (416–22 CE). Augustine had a clear sense of why the great miracles of Scripture had been recounted: "The miracles were published that they might produce faith, and the faith which they produced brought them into greater prominence."[24] But some people—possibly a large number of people— wondered why such miracles no longer happened. Augustine had a witty response: "I might, indeed, reply that miracles were necessary before the world believed, in order that it might believe. And whoever now-a-days demands to see prodigies that he may believe, is himself a great prodigy, because he does not believe, though the whole world does."

Augustine is not content to leave it at that. He proceeds to recount miracle after miracle that occurred in his own day, some of them, he claims, in his very presence, seen with his own eyes: people cured of blindness, gout, paralysis, cancer, hernia, and "rectal fibula." These miracles may not be widely talked about, Augustine avers, or even known, but they continue to occur. They reveal the power of God, which continues to work in the present. Augustine's readers then can rest assured that God is still very much active in the world, and because of these manifestations of divine power, people can believe.

Augustine was writing very much at the end of the period I am covering in this book, and his stories provide a fitting conclusion to the period, begun with the letters of Paul and the book of Acts. Throughout those first four Christian centuries converts did not need to see divine displays of power with their own eyes. They needed simply to hear about them. And they certainly did hear about them, from the pages of Scripture, from apocryphal accounts of Jesus's apostles, from narratives of great evangelists such as Gregory and Martin, and, possibly most frequently, from stories orally circulated about this or that great thing that the god of the Christians had done for his people in response to their prayers.

But miracles come in different packages. There are two related phenomena that contributed to the spread of the Christian faith as well, if we can credit our ancient sources to any extent at all. Both also relied on manifestations of awesome power from the God over all. One of them relates to the specific message Christians delivered to the lost, the other to their own refusal to depart from that message, even in the face of torture and death.

THE TERRORS OF THE AFTERLIFE

One of the reasons stories of miracles proved so effective in making converts is that Christians combined them with the claim that God's manifestation of power in the present foreshadowed what he would do in the future. Life was filled with pain and suffering: people were starving; they were afflicted with blindness, loss of hearing, paralysis, the ravages of disease, or abject poverty; they were attacked by hordes of evil demons. Life could be—and for many it was—a wretched existence, a cesspool of misery. But God's miracle workers cured these ills. They could multiply the supplies of food, cure the body's deficiencies, heal any disease, and overpower the demons. Moreover, all that was merely a prelude to what was to come. After this life humans could enter into a world of sheer joy, free from the trials, tribulations, defects, plagues, and forces of evil of this world. There was a world to come, and those who sided with God would inherit it, to live a utopian existence for all eternity.

Alternatively, they could reject the power of God and be subject to the ravages of sheer evil, physical torments that made the miseries of the present pale by comparison. This horrific existence would not last a mere human life span of fifty or sixty years. No, the torments would never end. It would be everlasting hell.

And so people had to choose. God had shown what he could do. It was also quite clear what the forces of evil could do. Which would people prefer? Christian preachers were forthright and stark about the options. As the third-century church father Cyprian wrote to one of his correspondents, a man named Demetrius, "An ever-burning Gehenna will burn up the condemned, and a punishment devouring with living flames. . . . Souls with their bodies will be reserved in infinite tortures for suffering." There will not be "either respite or end to their torments. . . . Too late they will believe in eternal punishment who would not believe in eternal life."[25]

In the second century, accounts of the afterlife begin to appear in Christian texts, often presented as guided tours of the realms of the blessed and of the damned. In these a saint is shown the ecstasies of the saved and, especially, the torments of the lost, presented with barely concealed voyeuristic glee. Roman historian Ramsay Mac-Mullen has called these accounts "the only sadistic literature I am aware of in the ancient world."[26]

The earliest surviving example is called the *Apocalypse of Peter*. In it Jesus himself gives his disciple Peter a glimpse of what life will be like for those who refuse the path of righteousness, who are not baptized as believing Christians, who instead follow the ways of sin. In the realms of the damned Peter sees blasphemers hanged by their tongues over eternal flames. Men who committed adultery are similarly suspended, but by their genitals. Women who have performed abortions on themselves are sunk in excrement up to their necks forever. Those who slandered Christ and doubted his righteousness have their eyes perennially burned out with red-hot irons. Those who worshiped idols are chased by demons off high canyons, time and again. Slaves who disobeyed their masters are forced to gnaw their tongues incessantly while being burned by fire.

The alternative, Peter sees, is to enjoy the utopian life of heaven, surrounded by flowers and all good things for eternity, in the presence of the saints, who literally glow with happiness in the midst of fantastic gardens full of beautiful trees laden with gorgeous fruit that fills the air with their perfumed fragrances.

So: Which option will you choose?

There is a good deal of evidence to suggest that, far more than the glories of heaven, it was the tortures of hell that convinced potential converts. The hellish vision is certainly one that obsessed a number of Christian authors, some of whom delighted in thinking how their enemies among the pagans would roast forever. Consider the Schadenfreude expressed by the early-third-century apologist Tertullian:

> What sight shall wake my wonder, what my laughter, my joy and exultation? As I see all those kings, those great kings, welcomed (we are told) in heaven, along with Jove, along with those who told of their ascent, groaning in the depths of darkness. And the magistrates who persecuted the name of Jesus, liquefying in fiercer flames than they kindled in their rage against Christians. Those sages, too, the philosophers blushing before their disciples as they blaze together.[27]

This is not to mention the charioteers, the poets, and the actors who will prove to be "lither of limb by far in the fire."

Unrepentant pagans recognized the rhetorical force of these descriptions. Thus the second-century critic Celsus pointed out that Christians succeeded in their proselytizing because they "invent a number of terrifying incentives. Above all, they have concocted an absolutely offensive doctrine of everlasting punishments and rewards, exceeding anything the philosophers . . . could have imagined."[28] Christians too declared the effectiveness of divine terrors. As Augustine declared: "Very rarely, no never, does it happen that someone comes to us with the wish to become a Christian who has not been struck by some fear of God."[29]

In an earlier context I pointed out that most pagans appear not to have subscribed to the idea of any afterlife whatsoever. When Christians put forth their doctrines of heaven and hell, these may have come as news to many in their audience. But that is sometimes how effective propaganda works. It creates a new problem that it then resolves, eliciting a previously unknown need that it then satisfies. In his classic study of conversion, Arthur Darby Nock noted, "prophetic religion has to create in [people] deeper needs which it claims to fulfill."[30] Or, as Ramsay MacMullen has declared more recently: "What Christianity put forward was the fearful novelty of a God who would burn them alive in perpetuity for their very manner of life. . . . [T]he flames of hell illuminated the lessons of Christianity as much as the light of Grace." Indeed: "We see these horrors used as the chief, perhaps the only, argument for conversion."[31]

The horrors of hell may have been the argument, but it was the miracles that made the argument persuasive. God had shown, and continues to show, what he can do to counteract the ravages of pain, misery, and suffering. Anyone who refused to side with him now would pay a price later. Or as one group of Christian martyrs is said to have proclaimed to the pagan hordes who were enforcing horrible torments upon them in the public arena: "You condemn us, but God condemns you."[32] The tortures experienced by the martyrs lasted but minutes, or at most hours. The tortures experienced by their tormentors would last for all eternity.

The very point is made by one of our first recorded Christian martyrs, Polycarp, the second-century bishop of the city of Smyrna. When being threatened by torment and death, the faithful Christian declares that the punishment is mild in comparison with the alternative: "The proconsul said to him, 'If you despise the wild beasts, I will have you consumed by fire, if you do not repent.' Polycarp replied, 'You threaten with a fire that burns for an hour and after a short while is extinguished; for you do not know about the fire of the coming judgment and eternal torment, reserved for the ungodly.'"[33]

Is it possible that such willingness to experience intense pain in the form of martyrdom also contributed to the persuasiveness of the Christian message? That was certainly the claim of several early Christian writers.

THE MIRACLE OF MARTYRDOM

Justin Martyr earned his "last name" by being one of the earliest Christian intellectuals to suffer the ultimate penalty for his faith. At one point in his writings Justin alludes to his conversion, indicating that originally it was Christians' martyrdom that showed him they deserved to be believed.[34] They were willing to die for what they held dear. Of how many people can that be said? Or, to put it differently, how many martyrs for Zeus do we hear about?

As a Christian, Justin claimed that the church grew precisely because it was attacked by pagan officials: "The more we are persecuted, the more do others in ever-increasing numbers embrace the faith and become worshippers of God through the name of Jesus. Just as when one cuts off the fruit-bearing branches of the vine, it grows again and other blossoming and fruitful branches spring forth, so it is with us Christians."[35]

Some decades later, Tertullian gave a fuller explanation. Tertullian's fifty-chapter *Apology* (i.e., defense of the faith) is one of the clearest and most forceful intellectual justifications of the Christian faith to emerge from the early centuries. At the end of the book, Tertullian issues a challenge to rulers who persecute Christians, concluding with one of his most memorable and most frequently cited lines:

But go to it! my good magistrates; the populace will count you a deal better, if you sacrifice the Christians to them. Torture us, rack us, condemn us, crush us; your cruelty only proves our innocence. That is why God suffers us to suffer all this. . . . But nothing whatever is accomplished by your cruelties, each more exquisite than the last. It is the bait that wins people for our school. We multiply whenever we are mown down by you; the blood of Christians is seed.[36]

Tertullian goes on to explain why Christian blood bears fruit: the Christians' ability to endure such pains, their tough-minded obstinacy in the face of suffering, convinces others they stand for the truth: "For who that beholds it is not stirred to inquire, what lies indeed within it? Who, on inquiry, does not join us, and joining us, does not wish to suffer, that he may purchase for himself the whole grace of God, that he may win full pardon from God by paying his own blood for it? For all sins are forgiven to a deed like this."

On the heels of Tertullian's *Apology* came one from a Latin-speaking Christian named Minucius Felix, who stated the matter concisely. It was not possible for the martyrs of Christ to "endure torments without the aid of God."[37] In other words, Christian endurance was not only a marvel of human strength; it was a miracle.

In the overall scheme of things, Christian martyrdoms probably inspired only a few conversions. Surviving pagan authors who noted that Christians often resisted official pressure to recant typically considered this resistance not as miraculous endurance but as sheer stubbornness. That is the judgment, among others, of the emperor Marcus Aurelius, who could not understand such stupidity.[38] Even more significant, martyrdoms would rarely lead to conversions because they were themselves relatively rare. The vast majority of pagans—including the millions who eventually converted—never saw a martyrdom, as recent scholarship has shown.[39] As the most prolific and one of the best-traveled authors of the first three Christian centuries, Origen of Alexandria, stated in no uncertain terms: "Only a small number of people, easily counted, have died for the Christian religion."[40]

On the other hand, as was true of other miracles, divinely empowered endurance of pain would not have had to be observed in order to be known. When Christians told stories about martyrdom they particularly highlighted the miraculous abilities of the tormented faithful to withstand pain with a pleasant disposition. Miracles come in many guises and can easily be magnified in the telling. Martyr miracles may well have featured prominently in the tales of those who shared the glories of their faith with potential converts.

INCENTIVES FOR CONVERSION: IN SUM

Christians of the first four centuries did not stage massive evangelistic rallies involving altar calls with thousands of people coming forward to commit their lives to Christ. They spread their religion simply by word of mouth within their various networks of personal relationships, with converts telling their families, friends, neighbors, and other associates of the "good news" they had come to believe. What persuaded people were not so much the new doctrines that were being propounded or the reports of Christian ritual activities or even the many virtues of these communities of faith. What made the difference were the amazing stories that verified the Christian message. From the beginning, starting with the astounding life and ministry of Jesus himself and continuing through the work of his apostles and then their successors, the power of God had been manifest in real and tangible ways. God was at work, and his followers could prove it through the miraculous activities they engaged in.

Few people could claim to have observed any of these spectacular miracles of faith. But that was not necessary. All that was needed was belief that such things had in fact happened, and possibly that they continued to happen. This kind of belief could be won by Christian storytellers. These were not professional orators, just simple people telling what they themselves had heard and believed. The more the stories were told, and told with conviction, the more listeners were likely to think they might be true.

These stories were accompanied by the insistence that God's power manifest in the world now simply foreshadowed what was to take place in the hereafter. The people of God were about to enter an eternity of joy, peace, and glory. But those who refused to accept the message would pay an ultimate price. The sufferings of the present age were nothing in comparison with the torments that awaited those who rejected the truth and continued to worship the minions of evil. For all such people there was only the fearful prospect of everlasting agony.

We know this was a convincing message because it eventually took over the Roman Empire. Still, it did not do so overnight. And it did not do so through massive conversions of pagan crowds at any one time, despite the legendary accounts that have survived. Individual Christians would need only to convert a family member on occasion, or a friend or neighbor. Over time, that would add up, because whoever became a Christian was lost to paganism.

Chapter 6

The Growth of the Church

Nearly everyone agrees that approximately half the Roman Empire claimed allegiance to the Christian faith by about 400 CE. The empire as a whole is thought to have comprised some sixty million people at the time, making the numbers of Christians staggering. Even so, recent scholars have demonstrated that no massive conversions would have been needed for the church to attain such high numbers. All that was needed was a steady and plausible rate of Christian growth.

EXAGGERATIONS OF OUR SOURCES

In determining that rate, we are hampered by a number of factors, not the least of which are the exaggerations in our various literary sources, both pagan and Christian. Even today, with scientific methods of calculation, it is difficult to gauge the size of a crowd, and widely ranging estimates are often determined by an observer's enthusiasms ("We had thousands rallying to our cause") or fears ("Our opposition is mobilized and massive").

Without access to modern methods of determining demographics, ancient sources relied on generalized and often idealized superlatives. We have seen this already in Livy's account of the suppression of the Bacchic rites in Rome in 186 BCE, where it was reported to the senate that the profane practices of the cult had infected the masses of Rome like an epidemic. From these reports one might think the entire population was imperiled. Are we talking about a fifth of the populace? A fourth? No, when Livy actually gives the numbers of those involved, it adds up to seven-tenths of 1 percent of the population of the city. Not much of an epidemic.

Pagan sources mention Christians with striking infrequency in the second century, but when they do so, they suggest frightening numbers parallel to those of Livy's Bacchanalia. The early-second-century governor of the Roman province of Bithynia-Pontus (in modern Turkey), Pliny the Younger, is the first pagan author of any kind to refer to the existence of Christians. In a letter addressed to the Roman emperor Trajan written in 112 CE, Pliny discusses the threat posed by Christians to the traditional cults and indicates that he has, as a result, initiated an official proceeding against them. These Christians, he tells the emperor, are "many of all ages, every rank, and both sexes."[1] That certainly sounds serious, as, indeed, Pliny wanted it to sound. He needed the emperor to realize that the measures taken to stamp out the cult, including judicial executions, were altogether justified.

Just a few years later, the Roman historian Tacitus produced his famous *Annals* of Rome, an account of the empire from the reigns of Tiberius to Nero that was published around 120 CE. Tacitus mentions Christians in the context of the great fire of Rome under Nero in 64 CE. Nero's actions during and after the fire raised suspicions that he was responsible for it. Possibly he wanted parts of the city destroyed so he could implement some of his own architectural designs. Those burned out of house and home were not pleased. In order to shift the blame, Nero scapegoated the Christians, rounding them up as the culprits and executing them in rather grisly ways, as we will see in chapter 7. In his reference to the Christians charged with the crime, Tacitus indicates that it was "an immense multitude" (*Annals* 15).

Such comments are almost certainly exaggerations of scornful opponents. If Christianity were such a large threat at this stage of imperial history, we simply cannot explain why most Roman authors have little or, more frequently, absolutely nothing to say about them. Apart from a few other very brief references (in Suetonius, Lucian of Samosata, Galen), Christians simply do not appear, and certainly not as a sizable presence in the Roman world. On the contrary, in the rather full account of the empire from 180 to 238 CE written by the third-century Roman historian Herodian, in which he details the careers of the emperors and the threats they had to confront, Christianity is never mentioned at all. They were no threat.

If the very occasional references to Christians in the pagan sources of our period are exaggerated, the numerous references in texts written by Christians themselves are far more so. That is true from the very beginning, starting with our first account of the Christian movement, the New Testament book of Acts. Right after Jesus's resurrection, in Acts 1:14, we are told that the Christian cohort consisted of the eleven remaining disciples, several unnamed women, Jesus's mother, and his brothers. But then, in the very next verse, we learn that "in those days" there were 120 believers. How did a hundred people convert in the space of a verse?

The conversions continue apace soon after this. As we have seen, on the day of Pentecost, just fifty days after Jesus's crucifixion, Peter converted three thousand Jews (Acts 2:41); soon thereafter, he converted another five thousand (Acts 4:4). In the next chapter, multitudes more convert (Acts 5:14). At this rate the entire empire will be Christian by the year 50.

No Christian author is more profligate in his exaggerations than the apologist and theologian Tertullian, writing about a century after Acts at the end of the second and beginning of the third century. In his defense of the Christian faith, the *Apology*, Tertullian claims that pagans are aghast at the massive conversions to the faith: "The outcry is that the state is filled with Christians—that they are in the fields, in the citadels, in the islands" (*Apology* 1). In another work he indicates that "our numbers are so great—constituting all but the majority in every city" (*To Scapula* 2).[2] His most famous statement absolutely revels in the sheer dominance of the Christian religion:

> We are but of yesterday, and we have filled every place among you—cities, islands, fortresses, towns, market-places, the very camp, tribes, companies, palace, senate, forum,—we have left nothing to you but the temples of your gods. . . . For if such multitudes of men were to break away from you, and betake themselves to some remote corner of the world, why, the very loss of so many citizens, whatever sort they were, would cover the empire with shame. . . . Why, you would be horror-struck at the solitude in which you would find yourselves. . . . You would have to seek subjects to govern. You would have more enemies than citizens remaining. For now it is the immense number of Christians which makes your enemies so few,—almost all the inhabitants of your various cities being followers of Christ. (*Apology* 37)

One counterweight to these excessive claims appears in the more sober assessment of other Christian authors who, despite also having reasons to celebrate the turning of entire populations to the Christian faith, knew that, alas, it simply had not happened. This includes such writers as the Latin apologist Minucius Felix, some years after Tertullian, who indicates that Christians "are still few" (*Octavius* 23) and the widely traveled and highly informed Origen, from the first half of the third century, who acknowledges that many people in the empire, let alone barbarians outside of it, had never even heard of the Christian faith (*Commentary on Matthew* 24:9).

As a result, modern experts have not been swayed by the exuberant claims of authors such as Tertullian. Pagan religions of the first and second centuries were not being widely demolished by the unstoppable forces of the Christians. As British historian Robin Lane Fox has pointed out, "By c. 200, Christians still wrote polemically as if the gods had fallen silent, but they were ignoring the contrary facts at the sites to which they referred."[3] These contrary facts come by way of hard evidence—literally hard, in the presence of inscriptions chiseled in stone—that pagan religions were flourishing (indeed, resurging) in the second and third centuries CE.[4] Christianity was not taking the empire by storm at the time of the apostles or in the days of Tertullian. The Christians remained a tiny fraction of the population up into the third century.

THE NATURE OF OUR DATA

It is difficult to know exactly how quickly Christianity grew because we have very few hard data. But we have some. One particularly important statement appears to be a disinterested record of fact concerning the situation of the church in the city of Rome in the middle of the third century. The statement comes in a letter by the bishop of the church, Cornelius, in which he provides some much-welcome hard numbers: the church of Rome, he informs us, had at the time 46 presbyters, 7 deacons, 4 sub-deacons, 42 acolytes, 52 exorcists, readers, and doorkeepers, and 1,500 widows and other needy persons under church support (Eusebius, *Church History* 6.43).

This is a significant data point. The great historian of early Christianity Adolf von Harnack claims: "So far as regards statistics, this passage is the most important in our possession for the church history of the first three centuries."[5] In a city of around a million people, the church had 155 clergy (counting the bishop himself) and provided charitable support to 1,500 people. The 46 presbyters would each have had charge of a smaller community that met for worship, so that at the time there would have been that number of actual churches (gatherings, not necessarily buildings) in the city. On the basis of these data, Harnack surmises that the church in Rome totaled approximately 30,000 persons.

In a footnote, however, he acknowledges this figure might be too low. We know from the fourth-century bishop of Constantinople, John Chrysostom, that his own church of 100,000 provided material support to some 3,000 needy persons—that is, to about 3 percent of the total. If a comparable rate applied to the church of Rome some decades earlier, the church may have numbered something like 50,000. If that is a closer approximation, the church would have comprised about 5 percent of the population of the city.

In his exhaustive treatment, Harnack cites and analyzes every reference to Christianity and Christian churches in every surviving text of the first three centuries. As just one other example, he notes that in the same letter Cornelius mentions a regional synod of church officials attended by sixty bishops from Italy. From this reference Harnack surmises (on grounds he elucidates) that there were probably about a hundred bishops altogether in the region in the mid-third century—meaning about a hundred churches just in Italy.

On the basis of his survey, Harnack comes to some significant statistical conclusions, the most frequently cited of which is one with which we are by now familiar: by the beginning of the fourth century, probably 7 to 10 percent of the empire was Christian. As one contemporary expert, Harold Drake, indicates: "Almost everyone is willing to admit that this number feels about right."[6] If it is indeed right, and the population of the empire was approximately 60 million, then Christians would have numbered somewhere between 4 million and 6 million, most of them located in the eastern provinces.

There are some reasons for suspecting, however, that the number may be on the high side. One of the most startling and disturbing recent analyses has been provided by Yale historian Ramsay Mac-Mullen. The study is predicated on the fact that, after his conversion, Constantine sponsored the building of numerous churches both in Rome and throughout the empire. Moreover, as Christians came out of the woodwork and large numbers of wealthy people began to convert, numerous other churches were built. MacMullen's study tries to determine how many individuals these churches could accommodate during a weekly worship service, based on the actual size of the building and the space required for the human body. This is a novel approach to determining how many Christians there were, or at least how many Christians there were who would have been worshiping in the church structures at the time.[7]

The numbers are shocking. MacMullen shows that "out of some

255 churches in some 155 towns and cities, wherever the remains survive for the record, the expected attendance ranged between a mere 1 per cent and 8 per cent of the general population."[8] This is not in the second or third centuries, when Christianity was known to make up a small fragment of the overall population. It is the fourth century, when the church is widely thought to have been taking over the world. Why is there not more room for worship?

MacMullen points out that in a typical fourth-century city of 20,000 persons, there was, so far as we can tell, an average of only one church that could, with rare exception, accommodate only 350 to 400 people (2 percent or less of the population). Moreover, he stresses that the church sizes were not restricted by limited funds. On the contrary, funding was abundant. Churches were built to accommodate the numbers of worshipers who could be expected to attend.

These findings based on archaeology are hard to explain, even for MacMullen. Given what we know from our literary sources, they simply cannot mean that the church was not growing at all. It was demonstrably growing, and there are other explanations for the size of the actual church buildings. Possibly most Christians simply did not go to church every week. Or ever. Possibly they continued to meet more often in homes, attending the one church building in town on only rare occasions. Possibly Christians preferred to meet in outdoor spaces. We do know that Christians often gathered together in cemeteries. Were these their primary meeting places? Did most Christians not see a need to meet together much at all? The reality is that we simply cannot know.

But MacMullen's surprising findings may suggest that Harnack's conclusions, based on an analysis of strictly literary sources, may be a bit too sanguine. Possibly 7 to 10 percent of the empire by the year 300 is an overestimate.

Pointing in the same direction is the fact, too infrequently considered, that in its first three centuries Christianity succeeded principally in urban settings, but the bulk of the population was rural—by a typical calculation, probably 80 to 90 percent of the empire. These countryside masses were by and large not converted until the fourth century, and even then rather slowly. This makes it even more difficult to determine how much of the total population, urban and rural, was Christian by the year 300. It seems altogether unlikely, based on both the literary and material evidence, that it could be as high as the 10 to 20 percent range. If Harnack's numbers may overreach, possibly it is most reasonable simply to halve his figure and think generally of something like 2 to 3 million Christians in the year 300. Possibly it was slightly less. As we will see in a moment, given the rate of Christian growth, surprisingly enough, the exact number does not matter much.

THE DEMOGRAPHICS OF CONVERSION

First, it is important to consider several matters of demographics. The vast bulk of the ancient population comprised lower classes. The very upper crust of the aristocracy—the senators of Rome, the next level down known as the equestrians, and the local elite of cities throughout the empire called decurions—altogether made up just over 1 percent of the total population. With respect to the other 99 percent, there was not much of a middle class to speak of in Rome's noncapitalist, preindustrial society. There were, to be sure, large differences in wealth, even in a world where the great majority of people were living on the economic edge. But the majority of people did live on that edge, including most of the people coming into the Christian faith. Pagan intellectuals such as Celsus may have mocked Christians for being attractive principally to the poor and uneducated, but the reality is that this was most of the population.

For reasons I have already explained, it proved much easier to convert people in urban settings than in rural ones. The urban centers were packed with people. Rome itself had a population of nearly two hundred persons per acre, and the number on the ground was much higher than that, since about a quarter of the city was public space without housing. Such dense populations made human interchange much more frequent than in rural settings. As MacMullen points out, "the narrower one's house, the more time would naturally be spent among one's neighbors, the more intercourse and friendliness, the more gossip and exchange of news and sense of fraternity."[9] And, accordingly, the more opportunities for conversion, as information about this new cult could spread like wildfire, no less quickly than rumor and gossip.

It is clear that Christianity grew at different rates in different cities and regions. Both literary and archaeological sources confirm there were far more converts in the East than the West in the first three hundred years; it was not until the end of the second century that western provinces began to be seriously Christianized at all. Rome itself was an obvious exception. Moreover, some parts of the East— for example, Asia Minor—saw Christian growth much more quickly than others.

Egypt is a good example. One of the fascinating studies of the Christianization of Egypt was undertaken by a Roger Bagnall, at the time a professor of ancient history at Columbia.[10] Bagnall applied an interesting method for determining how quickly Egypt became Christianized. It had to do with a field called "onomastics," the study of personal names. As Christianity spread throughout the empire, Christians started giving their children Christian names. As an obvious example, Peter was not a name at all in antiquity before Christians arrived on the scene. The name Peter is based on a nickname given to one of Jesus's disciples, Simon son of Jonah (John 1:42). It is a word that means rock. We are not sure why Jesus wanted to call Simon "the Rock," but he did, and years afterward Christians would sometimes give their children the name of this famous disciple. Non-Christians had no inclination to do so.

Some names are thus definitely Christian, and if enough documents survive from any region—such as tax records, marriage certificates, and land deeds—it is possible to determine what people are named at different periods of time and on that basis to calculate how many of those people were Christian (based, at least, on the naming practices).

As it turns out, we see very few traces of Christianity in Egypt before the middle of the third century, unlike, say, the city of Rome, which had a large church already in Paul's day. For most of the time prior to the conversion of Constantine, Egypt was almost entirely pagan. It was not completely so, as we know of some Christians and Christian literary activity there, especially in Alexandria. But Christians were hugely outnumbered by pagans until the end of the third century.

Then there was a striking shift. On the basis of his initial analysis, Bagnall argued that Christians had become half of the population sometime between 318 and 330 CE; 75 percent of the population by the middle of the fourth century; and 90 percent by the end of the century. These results, he maintained, can be confirmed from other evidence: records in our surviving papyri, inscriptions, and literary sources such as the hagiographic tales of the Egyptian saints.[11]

Thus, the growth of Christianity in Egypt did not parallel the situation in Rome, or Antioch, or Jerusalem. Each place was different. This idea that Christianization was wildly uneven throughout the empire is not new or controversial. Already Harnack had differentiated rates of growth, as he identified some places where, by the year 312 CE, Christianity was nearly half the population (for example, Asia Minor, Armenia, Cyprus); where it was less than half but very strong (Antioch, parts of Egypt, parts of Italy, Spain); where it was very sparse (Palestine, Phoenicia, Arabia); and where it hardly existed at all (upper Italy, middle and upper Gaul, Germany).[12]

These basic findings have been confirmed by further analyses in recent times, as cited, for example, by Frank Trombley, a leading expert on the Christianization of the empire, who not only reconsidered all of the literary evidence adduced by Harnack but examined scattered inscriptions, remains of papyri, and archaeological findings. These kinds of evidence allow us to speak more authoritatively about the presence of Christianity in specific cities, towns, and rural areas. Trombley noted that the newer evidence tends to support the findings of Harnack but also provides some important nuance. Among other things it appears that major cities serving as capitals of provinces—places such as Rome, Antioch, and Thessalonica—did not become predominantly Christian until the middle of the fourth century; fairly large regional towns in the provinces at the time were often roughly balanced between pagans and Christians then. But many places, such as Athens, Delphi, and Gaza, remained predominantly pagan, even into the early fifth century.[13] The growth of Christianity, in short, was uneven. People converted in different numbers in different times and places.

THE RATE OF CHRISTIAN GROWTH

Still, it may be possible to calculate some very rough sense of the rate of Christian growth over the first few centuries. That will require a bit of number crunching, and there is no one better at crunching numbers than a sociologist. It was indeed a sociologist, Rodney Stark, a specialist in modern religious movements, who made the first serious attempt at establishing Christian growth rates in the first several centuries in his popular book *The Rise of Christianity*.[14]

Because the discussion of Stark's analysis requires statistical computations—not the most scintillating of reading—I have relegated it to the appendix, beginning on page 287. Suffice it to say here that Stark's numbers need to be nuanced for a variety of reasons, even if his overall thesis appears to be rock-solid: the triumph of Christianity over the pagan religions of Rome did not require a miracle from on high. It required a steady growth in the church, one convert after the other, year after year, for the first three centuries.

Once Stark's numbers are appropriately tweaked, it is clear that Christianity was growing only at a rate—very roughly—of 30 percent or so per decade for the majority of this period. In other words, if there are a hundred Christians this year, there need to be another thirty or so ten years from now. The results of the calculations explained in the appendix can be cited here. The following gives a rough estimate of the number of Christians at key moments of the movement, starting right at its beginning immediately after Jesus's death:

30 CE—20 Christians
60 CE—1,000–1,500 Christians
100 CE—7,000–10,000 Christians

150 CE—30,000–40,000 Christians

200 CE—140,000–170,000 Christians

250 CE—600,000–700,000 Christians

300 CE—2.5 million–3.5 million Christians

312 CE—3.5 million–4 million Christians

400 CE—25 million–35 million Christians

To non-statisticians, these raw numbers—especially toward the end of the chart—may look incredible. But in fact they are simply the result of an exponential curve. If 25,000 to 30,000 Christians were added in the half century between 100 and 150 CE, then at the very same rate of growth, during the half century between 250 and 300 CE, something like 2 million or 2.5 million Christians would be added.

The enormous numbers provided by a steady rate of growth can be seen especially at the end of the graph. If there were just 2.5 million to 3.5 million Christians in the year 300, the church would have to grow only at a rate of 26 percent to reach 30 million by the year 400.

The nature of this exponential curve can be seen in the following tables:

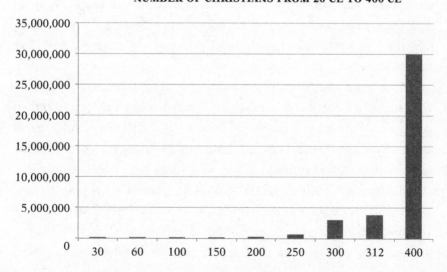

NUMBER OF CHRISTIANS FROM 20 CE TO 400 CE

NUMBER OF CHRISTIANS FROM 20 CE TO 400 CE

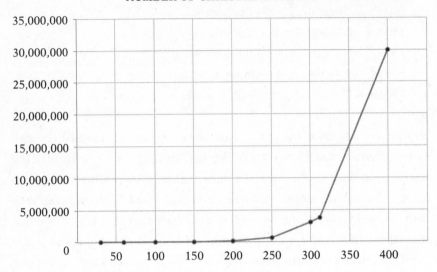

I need to stress that we are not talking about implausible rates of growth, even though the numbers at the end of the period are staggering. For the fourth century, if the rate really was around 25 percent per decade, that would only mean that every hundred Christians would need to convert just two or occasionally three people a year.

In that regard, it is important to remember that conversions include everyone who begins to adopt Christian practices. If the head of a household converts, and he brings his wife and three children into the fold so that they too adopt the new faith, then you have five new members.

We know these kinds of "family conversions" occurred from the very beginning of the Christian movement. They are recounted in the book of Acts as a matter of course as if there was nothing at all unusual about members of a household joining the paterfamilias (or even the materfamilias) in the faith. And so, when Paul and his companions are in Philippi, they convert a wealthy woman named Lydia, and immediately "she and her household were baptized" (Acts 16:14–15). Soon thereafter an unnamed jailer learns he must believe in Jesus to be saved, and "he and his entire family were baptized without delay" (Acts 16:33). I am not saying these accounts are necessarily historical. But the author of Acts saw nothing at all unusual in an entire family joining in the new faith of the head of the household.

It would thus be a relatively simple matter for the church to grow at a rate of 2.5 percent per year—the rough rate of growth we are hypothesizing for the fourth century. It would simply mean that every group of a hundred Christians would have to witness one male adult convert, along with his small family, every two years. That would make the church grow from 3 million to about 30 million in just the fourth century. The rate of growth does not have to be vastly different if at the beginning of the century there were only 2 million Christians (just under 3 percent a year).

SOME IMPLICATIONS

In a discussion of Christian growth in the first four centuries, Roman historian Keith Hopkins drew out some intriguing implications of the numbers of conversions that had been discussed by Stark. I have tried to provide some nuance for these numbers while allowing broader figures, but for the most part they are not radically different from Stark's, and many of the implications are very much the same.[15]

I have already discussed the exaggerated claims of various ancient sources. We can now consider these in light of more sensible estimates. Clearly the book of Acts cannot be right that within two months or so of Jesus's death there were some 10,000 Christians in Jerusalem; nor can Tertullian be right that around 200 CE the majority of people in the empire were Christian. Not even close.

Suppose our figures are roughly correct that in the year 100 there were possibly 7,000 to 10,000 Christians. How does that figure in the overall population of the empire? Were Christians likely to have been seen as a growing threat? Recall, the empire (by rough calculation) numbered something like 60 million. If there were 10,000 Christians, that would make the Christian portion of the population about 0.0167 percent—that is, $\frac{1}{60}$ of 1 percent. The vast majority of Romans had never heard of Christians. The idea that Christians were about to take over would have been laughable.

If by 200 CE Christians numbered in the vicinity of 160,000 people, that still would be just a tiny fragment of the population: 0.267 percent, or somewhat over ¼ of 1 percent. Even though the church was growing by relative leaps and bounds, it still would have been a completely unknown quantity to most Romans. It was only in the third century that the numbers began to grow significantly (think compound interest), and then to avalanche in the fourth.

In Hopkins's study he poses the interesting questions: How many actual Christian communities were there in the early decades, and how many writings did they generate? Both are very hard to answer. In his comprehensive survey of all of our surviving literary sources, Harnack was able to identify about 50 Christian communities by name by 100 CE. How many communities were not mentioned by our sources? I would assume most of them. So were there 150 communities in the empire by then? Or 300? We don't really know.

But suppose there were 50. Hopkins plays with the figures and comes up with some fascinating ideas. We know that early Christian communities were in contact with one another, often simply by writing a letter, one community leader to another (often in the name of the community itself). And so Paul wrote letters to his communities and we know that his communities wrote letters to him, as he himself indicates in 1 Corinthians 7:1.

Let's say that, between the years 50 and 150 CE, these 50 known communities each wrote just two letters a year. That's not much. I would think they wrote more. But Hopkins asks us to suppose they wrote on average only twice. That would mean that over that century there would have been 10,000 Christian letters sent back and forth. How many of these letters do we have today? About 50.

Hopkins's numbers seem to me—and probably to him—far too conservative. Suppose there were actually 200 communities in the year 100. That seems plausible: if there were just over 8,000 Christians, then that would mean each community would have, on average, about 40 members. It is hard to imagine a community being much larger than that, since Christians were still meeting in private homes, and few places could accommodate even three dozen persons. But suppose there were 200 communities, and suppose they each wrote a letter just once every three months, or four a year. That would mean that there would have been 80,000 Christian letters produced in the period, represented now in just the 50 that survive. The sheer number boggles the mind.

Hopkins is also interested in the question of how many people in these communities could actually read or write these letters. He points out that, as a rule of thumb, any ancient community would be made up of 30 percent adult males, 30 percent adult females, and 40 percent children. The people who could read would be found principally among the adult males. The best indications suggest that maybe 20 percent of the adult male population could read. If the numbers in the preceding paragraph are right—that an average community consisted of forty people—then twelve of those would be adult males. That would suggest that just two or three people in the community were literate.

Those would be the ones who did the writing. And the reading. Letters sent back and forth to the churches would not have been read *by* most Christians but *to* them by the literate two or three. One of those two or three would in almost every instance have been the "bishop" or leader of the church. He (always a male, so far as we know) would be a leader precisely because he had the skills needed to lead, and those skills would have involved some degree of education. Thus although Christianity was from the outset a religion that depended, to an unusual extent, on literature, most Christians were illiterate, as was most of the population of the empire. Those without an education were dependent on others for the reading—and interpretation—of the texts that were used in their communal worship.

THE GROWTH OF THE CHRISTIAN CHURCH: IN SUM

Even though the numbers of Christians and the rates of growth are, of necessity, rough estimates, they do appear to coincide with the surviving data, both the literary evidence evaluated at length by Harnack and others after him as well as the material remains from Christian antiquity: inscriptions on stone, writing on papyri, and an assortment of archaeological finds.[16] We may not be able to chart Christian growth with precision, but we can do so approximately, and even these imprecise finds are highly suggestive.

Several points bear repeating. It would not take a divine miracle for Christianity to win over the empire. Christians may well want to claim it was a miracle, that it was ultimately God's doing. The historian has no way of evaluating that claim. But the triumph of Christianity would not have required supernatural intervention. It would have required a steady rate of growth as people converted for reasons I laid out in the preceding chapters.

There was no need for massive conversions at large evangelistic rallies. We have almost no record of any full-time evangelists after the days of Paul, of missionaries or organized missions of any kind. People converted because they knew other people who were Christian—people connected to them in their daily lives, members of their families, friends, neighbors, coworkers. Many Christians were quite happy to talk about their new faith, about the great miracles that had been worked by and for those who believed, the divine power that was more readily available to those who worshiped the Christian god than to anyone who worshiped any other divine being. These Christians proved convincing. Not massively, just occasionally. That is all it took.

Perhaps most surprising is the fact that the ultimate triumph of Christianity did not require the conversion of the emperor Constantine. As I have been stressing throughout this book, that conversion was indeed important, one of the most breathtaking moments in Christian history. Christianity went from persecuted minority to favored religion, nearly in one fell swoop. Certainly this opened the floodgates in the sense that now the upper classes within the Roman administration—that rarefied 1 percent of the educated, cultured, and wealthy elite—could see their way to adopting the Christian faith. Christian buildings could now be constructed with no dread of reprisal. The masses could join the faith without fearing for their lives or property. And Christianity grew enormously—from, say, two and a half or three million at the beginning of the fourth century to thirty million at the end.

But it would be a mistake to think that it was Constantine's conversion alone that facilitated the Christianization of the empire. If Christianity had simply continued to grow at the rate it was growing at the of the emperor's conversion—or even less—it still would have eventually taken over.

It is impossible to say what would have happened if Constantine had not converted. One could argue that, had the Romans been even more determined to stamp out the faith, they could have done so. Or one could argue the opposite: that even more rigorous Roman opposition would have hardened the Christians' resolve and made them more fervent in the propagation of their religion, making true Tertullian's claim that the blood of martyrs was the seed of the church. We will never know what might have happened.

But we do know what did happen. Constantine converted at an opportune moment. Christianity was poised to grow exponentially even as its rate of growth slowed. The masses did begin to pour in. The emperor showered favors on a religion that excluded the possibility of all other worship. From that point on, looking at the matter in hindsight, the pagan cults of Rome were doomed. An exclusive commitment to the one God of the Christians destroyed the other religions in its wake. Within eighty years of Constantine's conversion, the transformation would be both massive and official. Rome would become predominantly and officially Christian.

Chapter 7

Christians Under Assault: Persecution, Martyrdom, and Self-Defense

E ven though the church experienced remarkable growth during its first three centuries, the empire's transition from paganism to Christianity was by no means smooth. The pagan world did not yield to this new faith quietly. From the very beginning, with the pre-Christian activities of Paul up until the conversion of Constantine, Christians encountered firm, sometimes even feverish opposition. Some of this opposition entailed nothing more than social shunning and verbal attack. But sometimes it involved actual physical assault, either by enraged mobs or by Roman officials intent on punishing those who claimed the name of Christ. Eventually the imperial authorities tried to stamp out the religion altogether. In this chapter we will examine these setbacks along the road to Christianity's triumph.

At the outset I need to stress that organized opposition to the Christians came, for the most part, in isolated incidents. The church did not experience perennial violent persecution. The idea that Christianity was an illegal religion under constant surveillance by a state apparatus that inflicted martyrdom on many thousands of believers, forcing the church underground into the Roman catacombs—all this is more the stuff of Hollywood than of history. Christianity was not declared illegal in the empire before the middle of the third century. There were no empire-wide laws or decrees issued by the central authorities in Rome that proscribed the faith. Christians did not, as a rule, go into hiding. For the most part they lived perfectly normal lives in the midst of other people who practiced a wide variety of other religions. The catacombs were not meeting places for Christians forced to congregate in clandestine cells for fear of violent persecution. Persecution itself was rare, and there were relatively few casualties.

But it did happen on occasion, and there were indeed some ghastly incidents involving trials, tortures, and horrific executions. One might wonder why they happened at all. There were thousands of other religions in the empire. No one was required to worship just one god or another. It was no crime to add a god to the hundreds already revered—not even the god of the Christians. Nor was it a crime to consider a human being, such as Jesus, a god. Many pagans did so with impunity. Given the wide variety of religious cults in the empire, and the abundant tolerance in open display every minute of every day, both among the general populace and by the ruling authorities, why would Christians occasionally find themselves—or, more commonly, hear of others—arrested, tried, and tortured? And why was the judicial goal not to get them to confess to a crime they had committed but to force them to stop committing it?

First, we should recall that even though Roman authorities were highly tolerant of religious differences, they were not infinitely so, as the Roman suppression of the Bacchic rites in Rome in 186 BCE demonstrates. Any religious cult perceived to be flagrantly immoral or dangerous to society was subject to official intervention. Its members could be tried and punished, and the cult itself could be locally proscribed. The Christians discovered this early in their history. On occasion throughout this period—most dramatically, as we will see, in 250, 257 to 258, and 303 to 313 CE—authorities intervened to disrupt the Christians' religious practices and force, or try to force, its adherents to abandon the faith. This was not because the Christian religion was illegal per se; it was because the Christians were perceived as dangerous, either to the social well-being of a local community or, eventually, to the ongoing health of the entire empire.

EARLY PERSECUTION OF THE CHRISTIANS

We have already discussed the persecution of Christians by the Jewish antagonist Paul, who experienced violent opposition himself after his conversion. That discussion will suffice for the question of how and why non-Christian Jews, in the early years of the church, opposed the movement. In this chapter we shift our focus to Roman persecution. As one might expect, the earliest references to such persecution come to us in the New Testament and are once more related to the missionary work of the apostle Paul.

Just as Paul tells his readers in Corinth that he had on five occasions "received at the hands of the Jews the forty lashes minus one," he says that on three other occasions he was "beaten with rods" (2 Corinthians 11:24–25). This was a form of Roman corporal punishment. Paul never explains the nature of the charges or of the judicial proceedings leading to these punishments. We do, however, find several episodes in the book of Acts that address the issue.

As we have seen, Acts is not a disinterested historical account of what happened in the early years of the Christian movement, even if it is often uncritically read in that way. The episodes it narrates may or may not have occurred. But for it to "work" as a piece of literature in its own first-century setting, Acts certainly had to be plausible to its readers. Even if its accounts of what happened in the lives of Paul and the others may not be accurate in their specifics, they do represent the sorts of things that could have been expected to happen. These would include Paul's experiences of Roman persecution.

One of the earliest episodes can illustrate the point. In Acts 16, on his second missionary journey, Paul and his companions are in the city of Philippi, where they encounter a young female slave who is possessed by a demon that allows her to predict the future. Her owners make a nice income from her peculiar abilities. But she hounds and publicly maligns Paul, who, after several irritating days, exorcises the demon (Acts 16:16–18). The slave's owners are incensed at having lost their business. Seizing Paul and one of his companions, they drag them before the local magistrates and charge: "These men are Jews and they are disturbing our city; they are proclaiming customs that we as Romans are not allowed to accept or practice" (Acts 16:20–21). The crowd joins in on the attacks, and the magistrates decide that punishment is in order. They sentence the apostles to be stripped naked, beaten with rods, and thrown in prison.

As one comes to expect in the book of Acts, later that night God intervenes on behalf of his chosen ones, causing an earthquake that shakes off their shackles and opens the doors of the prison, allowing them to walk out free.

The divine earthquake may not be creditable, but the general tenor of the persecution is. The views and activities of the Christians are seen as "un-Roman," harmful, and dangerous, leading local magistrates to take appropriate action. These actions are not based on laws that had been passed against the Christians. There were no such laws. Followers of Jesus were sometimes considered troublemakers and treated accordingly. Roman officials had the authority to deal with such issues on their own, with rather broad latitude. They could punish those causing problems—or even those thought likely to cause problems—without having to consult legal codes or precedent.

Other sources show that it was not long before simply being known as a Christian could lead to serious opposition. Within the New Testament we find the little book of 1 Peter, one of the real gems among the early Christian writings. Comprising a mere five chapters, this book places an unusually strong focus on the issue of anti-Christian opposition.[1] The word "suffer" occurs more in this book than in the entire twenty-eight-chapter book of Acts.

We learn here that some Christians are paying a price for their faith. We need to assume this means some kind of local opposition, as there is no indication whatsoever that the author has in mind an empire-wide persecution. But the suffering was real:

> Beloved, do not be surprised at the fiery trial that has come upon
> you as if it is something unexpected, but insofar as you share in
> the sufferings of Christ, rejoice, so that you may also rejoice and
> find joy when he is revealed in glory. You are blessed if you are
> reproached for the name of Christ. . . . None of you ought to suf-
> fer as a murderer, thief, evil-doer, or mischief-maker. But if you
> suffer as a Christian, do not be ashamed, but glorify God by this
> name. (1 Peter 4:12–14)

The author is vague concerning what this suffering entailed. It is
clear, in any event, that it was awful: he calls it a "fiery ordeal." And
it could come upon the community simply because it was Christian.
This kind of suffering was acceptable and pleasing to God, whereas
criminal and mischievous activity obviously was not.

Some light may be cast on this "ordeal" by an earlier comment in
which the author tells his readers they are no longer to live according
to "human passions but by the will of God." The Christians' friends
and neighbors do not appreciate this kind of new lifestyle. But the
author insists:

> The past time is sufficient for doing what the gentiles prefer,
> going about in licentiousness, desires, addiction to wine, rev-
> eling, carousing, and lawless idolatry. They are surprised when
> you no longer accompany them in wild profligacy and they ver-
> bally attack you. (1 Peter 4:3–4)

It may well be that in the early stages of the Christian movement, as
converts moved their allegiance from families, friends, and neighbors to their new Christian community, they upset and angered those
left behind, who then abused them for it. It is hard to know exactly
how this might have led to corporal punishment, but it may be that
the secretive meetings of Christians and their antisocial behavior
began not only to upset individual members of the wider community
but also drew the attention of local magistrates, who suspected nefarious activities.

Questions of legitimacy eventually concerned not only the ethical and social activities of the Christians but even more their religious cult itself, the worship of just one god and the refusal to participate in the religious life of the larger community. That this became the salient issue in pagan opposition to the Christian community becomes crystal clear from sources outside the New Testament.

THE PERSECUTION OF PLINY

The first detailed account of a Roman judicial proceeding against Christians foreshadows what was occasionally to happen in subsequent years. It comes to us in the early-second-century letters of Pliny the Younger, Roman governor of the province of Bithynia-Pontus in northwest Asia Minor.

This Pliny is called the Younger because he was adopted by an uncle, Pliny the Elder, an equally famous Roman official and author best known for his scientific writings on natural history and for dying during the most catastrophic natural disaster of his time. Following the eruption of Mount Vesuvius in 79 CE, Pliny the Elder attempted a sea rescue of some who were trapped and he died in the cataclysm. His nephew recorded his own observation of the volcano from afar, along with numerous other incidents in his life, in a large collection of his letters in ten books. They are among the most extensive, informative, and intriguing sets of correspondence to come down to us from the ancient world.

Book ten contains sixty-one letters Pliny exchanged with the emperor Trajan from 110 to 113 CE. Particularly important for our purposes are letters ninety-six and ninety-seven, the first containing Pliny's only references to Christians and his judicial proceeding against them, the second setting forth the emperor's very brief response.

Pliny wrote letter ninety-six because Christians had been brought to his attention, and he was not certain that his treatment of them followed acceptable protocols. There obviously was not a "law" against Christians or any official procedure for dealing with them, or Pliny would not have needed to inquire. He knew that something was to be done, but he was not sure what. As he says at the outset of the letter: "It is my regular custom, my lord, to refer to you all questions which cause me doubt, for who can better guide my hesitant steps or instruct my ignorance? I have never attended hearings concerning Christians, so I am unaware what is usually punished or investigated, and to what extent" (Pliny the Younger, *Letters*, 10.96).

Clearly there had been official proceedings against Christians before, but they must have been relatively few and far between. Pliny, a highly placed Roman official, had never attended one and did not know what they entailed. He asks the emperor whether the age of a Christian should be a matter of consideration, whether a Christian who has recanted the faith should still be held liable, and whether it is simply the name "Christian" that is actionable or if, instead, actual crimes attendant to the name are to be punished.

He goes on, then, to explain how, in the absence of any law or known precedent, he has proceeded. When a person was accused of being a Christian, Pliny would simply ask if the charge was true. If the person confessed, he then gave the person two chances to recant, under threat of execution. If the person persisted in remaining a Christian, Pliny ordered execution on the ground of obduracy in the face of imperial power, for refusing to obey the orders of a Roman official. Christians who could show they were Roman citizens, however, were sent to Rome for trial, one of the privileges of citizenship.

What the term "Christian" actually *meant*, and why it was a capital offense, becomes clear in Pliny's fuller explanation of his procedure. If a person claimed not to be a Christian, Pliny made them prove it. He brought cult statues of the gods and of the emperor into the courtroom and ordered the person to do obeisance, to offer up a sacrifice of wine and incense, and to curse the name of Christ. Anyone who refused was obviously a Christian and was taken off for execution. Those who complied were acquitted of all charges.

This was a clever test, and it showed why the term "Christian" itself was punishable. Those who genuinely claimed that name would refuse to worship the gods and the emperor himself. They did not follow cultic practices acceptable to Rome. That was both dangerous and actionable. Pliny therefore knew a simple way to see whether someone really was a Christian or not. Non-Christians would have no qualms about participating in a traditional cult; Christians who persisted in their views would rather die first.

Then there arose the question about what to do with Christians who chose not to persist in their views. What should happen to someone who admitted to being a Christian previously but who recanted? Pliny decided that such a person was not guilty of an offense and should be released unharmed. This is extraordinary. It means that Christianity was not a crime like any other crime. Anyone who commits murder cannot escape a judicial penalty by claiming that even though he had committed murder in the past, he was not murdering anyone in the present, and so he should not be punished. Murder, like all other crimes, is punishable for having been committed. Romans did not treat Christians that way. *Having been* a Christian was not a crime. *Being* a Christian was. Anyone who recanted and returned to traditional ways was acquitted.

Pliny's logic was followed by later Roman officials as well. It was the logic of religious observance. Refusing to worship the traditional gods was not simply a matter of personal preference. It was a social and political issue as well, in part because, when not revered, the gods could bring communal disaster. Obdurate members of nontraditional cults who refused to participate in the religious life of the community therefore constituted a threat. Those who recognized the error of their ways, however, no longer posed a threat, and so did not need to be coerced into obedience. The gods were happy, the officials were happy, and the community was happy. There was, then, no need for punishment.

In his letter Pliny goes on to indicate that his interrogations of Christians revealed important information about their cultic practices. His comments show not only what Christians were doing in their communal services but also, by inference, what they were wrongly suspected of doing. Pliny indicates that the Christians came together to worship at dawn and in their gatherings they sang antiphonal hymns to Christ as God. They also bound themselves by oaths to engage in highly ethical activities: they agreed to commit no crime, no theft, no adultery; they agreed never to break their word or to withhold money from someone who had deposited it with them. The Christians would then disband and gather again later to share a meal together, of food that Pliny indicates was "common and harmless."

These comments about Christian activities may seem rather straightforward and banal, yet they are anything but that. An understanding of Christian writings of the second century makes it quite easy to read between the lines to see what Pliny is actually saying. He is, in effect, indicating that the common rumors in circulation about Christian worship practices were unfounded. As we will see later in this chapter, Christians were accused of engaging in wild nocturnal rituals that involved profligate immorality, infanticide, and cannibalism. Pliny found nothing of the sort. The Christians were committed on oath to being unusually ethical and they ate regular food—not human babies—in their periodic celebrations.

Pliny appears not to have believed his own findings at first. He identified two slaves who served as "deaconesses" or "ministers" in the community and had them tortured to find the truth. In Roman antiquity it was believed—quite contrary to our own way of thinking—that only under extreme torture would a person necessarily speak truthfully. In judicial proceedings involving slaves, it was actually required that they be tortured. Pliny wanted the truth. But when tortured the slaves revealed nothing scandalous "other than a debased and boundless superstition."

Nonetheless, Pliny indicates the problems caused by this superstition were indeed significant. It had affected "many of all ages, every rank and both sexes" and was widespread: "The infection of the superstition has extended not merely through the cities, but also through the villages and country areas" (Pliny the Younger, *Letters*, 10.96). In fact, the local pagan temples had been virtually deserted and there was almost no demand for sacrificial meat. That had all been rectified, however, by his intervention. Now that he had acted, the temples were once more crowded and the meat markets were beginning to thrive.

Pliny clearly wanted the emperor's approbation for his way of proceeding, and he received it in a terse reply. Trajan does not invoke any imperial law that was to govern the case—the clearest indication of all that no such law existed, since, if it had, the emperor, of all people, would surely know. On the contrary, Trajan indicates that in dealing with Christians: "No general rule can be laid down which would establish a definite routine." Pliny's procedures were fine. In particular, anyone who denied being a Christian and proved it "by worshipping our gods," even if previously suspected of adhering to the aberrant faith, was to be acquitted.

Trajan does stress two provisos. Christians were not to be sought out. There was to be no witch hunt, no tracking down of criminals. Second, Trajan emphasizes, accusations could not be made anonymously. If someone had a charge to bring, they needed to bring it in person and stand by their claim: "Documents published anonymously must play no role in any accusation, for they give the worst example, and are foreign to our age." With that, Trajan's reply ends.

It should be clear that there were simply no established procedures for dealing with Christians in the early second century. Pliny's approach was clever and effective, but it was also ad hoc. He was not following precedent, because he did not know any precedents. Some scholars have argued, however, that his procedure itself became a kind of precedent. Later officials acted in similar ways. Christians were to be forced to recant their faith and worship the traditional gods. Anyone who refused was guilty of a crime—ironically, to our modern thinking, a crime without a law—and was to be punished accordingly, sometimes with torture and death. This did not happen frequently. But it did happen on occasion. It happened because people knew what being a Christian involved and, possibly even more, because they suspected what it involved.

That Pliny was not alone in his understanding of what being a Christian entailed is shown in writings of second- and third-century

Christian intellectuals, who occasionally discussed their treatment at the hands of Roman officials. Among other things, these discussions show that Christians were known to be atheists engaged in regular acts of grotesque immorality.

THE CHRISTIAN ATHEISTS

It may come as a shock to learn that Christians on trial in the Roman world were maligned and punished for being atheists. Christians? Atheists? Aren't Christians precisely the opposite of atheists?

They may be in modern times, when Christians believe in God and atheists believe there is no God. But the situation in antiquity was different. Virtually no one would ask a friend, "Do you believe in God?" In its barest form, the question presupposes a theology that almost no one held: namely, that there is, or may be, one divine being in the universe and that it is possible to accept his existence or not. In the ancient world, any such view would have been considered bizarre at best.

Nonetheless, the term "atheist" was used. Only rarely did it refer to someone who denied the existence of any divine being at all. Rather, it was used either to refer to those who thought the gods were radically disinterested and uninvolved with human affairs— that was the view of the Epicurean philosophers—or to those who did not ascribe any true divinity to the traditional gods. No one who participated in the regular religious life of the empire fit that category. The Jews were a partial exception, but even most Jews were completely open to gentiles worshiping their pagan gods in any way they chose. The charge of atheism principally came to be applied, after the Epicureans, to Christians. They insisted not only that theirs was the only god but also that a person needed to worship this god alone. None of the other gods was really a god. Worse still, Christians did not engage in widely recognized and accepted cultic acts, especially sacrifice. Because of their idiosyncratic views and practices, Christians were considered to be without the gods. They were the atheists.

That this was not just a slur but an actual judicial charge becomes clear from the writings of the "apologists," the intellectual defenders of the faith, including the witty but relatively obscure Athenagoras of Athens, who lists "atheism" as the first accusation typically leveled against the Christians (*Plea Concerning the Christians* 3). So too the second-century Justin—who was himself eventually to be martyred for his faith—clearly states: "This is the sole charge you lodge against us, that we do not worship the same gods as you do" (*1 Apology* 24). We have seen the reasons this would be a charge warranting punishment, not simply a religious concern. Religion was not stored in a separate compartment, apart from social and political life in antiquity. Not revering the city or state gods meant not being faithful to the city or state. On one level it was the ancient equivalent of refusing to say the Pledge of Allegiance. But it was far more dangerous. The gods could harm the communities that refused to give them their due. Recall the chilling words of Tertullian on why pagans feared and despised the Christians:

> They think the Christians the cause of every public disaster, of every affliction with which the people are visited. If the Tiber rises as high as the city walls, if the Nile does not send its waters up over the fields, if the heavens give no rain, if there is an earthquake, if there is a famine or pestilence, straightway the cry is "Away with the Christians to the lion!" (*Apology* 40)

Writing some five decades later, in the middle of the third century, Cyprian, the bishop of Carthage, indicates that Christians are widely blamed for wars, plagues, famines, and droughts: "You have said that all these things are caused by us, and that to us ought to be attributed the misfortunes wherewith the world is now shaken and distressed, because your gods are not worshiped by us" (*Letter to Demetrius* 3).[2]

Cyprian too was eventually martyred for his faith. Remarkably, in his case, we have a transcript of his trial, which appears to be reasonably unadorned and accurate. From it we can see more fully the judicial charges brought against Christians.

Cyprian had been a wealthy and highly educated aristocrat who made his living as a rhetorician. He converted to Christianity as an adult, around 245 CE; within two years he was consecrated bishop of the largest church of North Africa. As a high-profile figure he was under the eye of the local Roman authorities in the persecutions of the 250s (which we will examine later in this chapter). Finally he was arrested on September 1, 258, and put on trial two days later. The magistrate's summary of Cyprian's capital offense is worth citing in full:

> You have long persisted in your sacrilegious views, and you have joined to yourself many other vicious men in a conspiracy. You have set yourself up as an enemy of the gods of Rome and of our religious practices; and the pious and venerable emperors Valerian and Gallienus Augusti and Valerian the most noble of Caesars have not been able to bring you back to the observance of their sacred rites. Thus, since you have been caught as the instigator and leader of a most atrocious crime, you will be an example for all those whom in your wickedness you have gathered to yourself. Discipline shall have its sanction in your blood. . . . Thascius Cyprian is sentenced to die by the sword.[3]

The sentence was carried out immediately. Cyprian was beheaded. His crime: refusing to worship the gods of Rome.

CHRISTIAN FLAGRANT IMMORALITY

We have seen that Pliny suspected the Christians of unethical and even criminal activities in their weekly meetings. Secret societies were always suspect, and the rumors about the Bacchanalia in an earlier age no doubt occasionally affected how people thought about Christians. Recall how Livy had reported that in those Bacchic feasts "all sorts of corruption began to be practiced, since each person had ready to hand the chance of gratifying the particular desire to which he was naturally inclined." These nocturnal festivities involved not

only licentious sexual activities but also the ritual murder of innocent and helpless victims: "No cries for help could be heard against
the shriekings, the banging of drums, and the clashing of cymbals
in the scene of debauchery and bloodshed" (Livy, *History of Rome*
39.10).

We find Christians accused of similar outrageous behavior. Both
Justin around 150 CE and Tertullian some fifty years later refer to the
charges. In rather graphic terms, Tertullian indicates the allegations
had even been ratcheted up a notch for the Christians to include
not just murder but cannibalism: "Monsters of wickedness, we are
accused of observing a holy rite in which we kill a little child and
then eat it; in which, after the feast, we practice incest, the dogs—our
pimps, forsooth, overturning the lights and getting us the shameless-
ness of darkness for our impious lusts. . . . This is what is constantly
laid to our charge" (*Apology* 7).

An even more detailed and shocking exposition of the charges is
set forth in the defense of the faith written by Tertullian's younger
contemporary Minucius Felix, who, according to tradition, had earlier been a lawyer in Rome. His only surviving work is called *Octavius*, named after its main character, who engages in a conversation
with a pagan named Caecilian over the merits of the Christian faith,
with Minucius Felix himself serving as the mediator between the
two. The account is allegedly autobiographical, but if not made up
wholesale, the back and forth has been heavily edited in Octavius's
favor. His speech promoting Christianity takes up twice the space as
Caecilian's attack on it, and at the end of the speech the pagan is utterly convinced. Without further ado, he converts on the spot.[4]

Despite its fictitious features, there can be no doubt that the dialogue contains historically valid information, including the charges
that Caecilian levels against the Christians. These reflect both the
suspicions of Pliny from a century earlier and the statements of other
writers, such as Tertullian later, even if they are unmatched in their
gruesome vividness. Minucius Felix intimates that the charges derive
from the writings of Marcus Cornelius Fronto, the famous rhetorician and onetime tutor of the great emperor Marcus Aurelius.

Caecilian's emphatic castigation of the Christian religion comes in his description of their salacious nocturnal rituals:

> They recognize each other by secret marks and signs; hardly have they met when they love each other, throughout the world uniting in the practice of a veritable religion of lusts. Indiscriminately they call each other brother and sister, thus turning even ordinary fornication into incest. (*Octavius* 9)

The Christians take a remarkable approach to these periodic love feasts, with an inventive way of turning out the lights to encourage anonymous and random sex:

> On a special day they gather for a feast with all their children, sisters, mothers—all sexes and ages. There, flushed with the banquet after such feasting and drinking, they begin to burn with incestuous passions. They provoke a dog tied to the lampstand to leap and bound towards a scrap of food which they have tossed outside the reach of his chain. By this means the light is overturned and extinguished, and with it common knowledge of their actions; in the shameless dark with unspeakable lust they copulate in random unions, all equally being guilty of incest, some by deed, but everyone by complicity.

It is not simply the sexual congress of consenting adults and children that offends Caecilius's ethics. Christians have a gruesome and criminal initiation ritual for new members:

> The notoriety of the stories told of the initiation of new recruits is matched by their ghastly horror. A young babe is covered over with flour, the object being to deceive the unwary. It is then served before the person to be admitted into their rites. The recruit is urged to inflict blows onto it—they appear to be harmless because of the covering of flour. Thus the baby is killed with wounds that remain unseen and concealed. It is the blood of this

infant—I shudder to mention it—it is this blood that they lick with thirsty lips; these are the limbs they distribute eagerly; this is the victim by which they seal their covenant; it is by complicity in this crime that they are pledged to mutual silence; these are their rites, more foul than all sacrileges combined.

So this is what it means to be Christian! Modern readers may find it incredible that anyone could take such scurrilous reports seriously. But they must have done so. Otherwise we would not have such a consistent allusion to them. Still, how could anyone credit them?

It is important to remember that Christian meetings were private and secret. The Christian church was not the building on the street corner. It was a gathering of believers in a private home or a secluded outdoor setting. These meetings usually occurred at night or before sunrise, in the dark. There was a very good reason for that: almost everyone had to work for a living, and in this world there were no weekends. Any meeting would have to take place outside of working hours. But who knew what those people were doing in the dark?

Scholars have had a field day suggesting additional explanations for why the outrageous activities mentioned by Justin, Tertullian, Minucius Felix, and others came to be associated with Christian meetings in particular.[5] Some have pointed out that charges of incest make sense for a sect in which "brothers" and "sisters" regularly engaged in the "holy kiss" as far back as New Testament times. Siblings kissing in the dark? What is that? As to the charge that Christians were killing babies and eating them, surely it was known that Christians had a special meal every week where they ate the flesh and drank the blood of the Son (of God). They were eating a child?

Other scholars have expressed doubt that charges of profligate activities stemmed from an imperfect knowledge of Christians and their periodic meetings.[6] Charges of sexual licentiousness, infanticide, and cannibalism were standard fare in ancient polemics of all sorts. Anyone wanting to malign their enemies could, and often would, say the most scandalous things imaginable to impugn their morals. There was nothing more scandalous than energetically engaging in incest, murdering children, and consuming their flesh and blood. So, while it is possible that imperfect knowledge influenced the charges occasionally leveled against the Christians, these may also simply be standard charges leveled against an unknown but hated group, attacked not only in court but also in scurrilous public opinion.

EARLY ACCOUNTS OF THE MARTYRS

Actual judicial charges against Christians do not appear to have been related to sexual improprieties or other flagrant forms of immorality. This much is clear from the accounts of Christian prosecution, conviction, and execution that have survived antiquity. Unfortunately, trial records are few and far between. As Candida Moss, a historian of early Christianity, has recently argued, we have only six martyrdom accounts handed down to us from before 250 CE, and two or three of these may be forgeries.[7] One or two of the others, however, appear to be based on actual eyewitness testimony, and all of them contain historical information that can be gleaned from a close reading.[8]

In particular, they support what we have seen from Pliny: the "crime" committed by the followers of Jesus was simply their refusal to renounce the name "Christian," since this entailed a refusal to worship gods other than their own. Pagans on the whole had no difficulty with Christians worshiping whichever god they chose, so long as they did not oppose or resist worshiping other divinities as well. That is what everyone else in the world did, except Jews, who for centuries had been the exception. Christians were not an exception. They were non-Jews who spurned traditional religions. That was a punishable offense.

One of the oldest surviving accounts of a Christian martyrdom involves the arrest and execution of Polycarp, a mid-second-century bishop of the city of Smyrna in Asia Minor and an important figure in early Christianity. The *Martyrdom of Polycarp* was long believed to be an eyewitness report produced not long after the event itself, often dated to 155 or 156 CE. Recent scholarship, however, has argued that the narrative is a forgery produced sometime in the early third century.[9] Whatever its precise date, the account reveals how Christians understood the charges leveled against them and shows that Roman magistrates responsible for issuing a sentence often did so only with great reluctance, compelled principally by the urgings of the mob.

The account is allegedly a letter sent by the Christians of Smyrna to those of Philomelium in what is now central Turkey. At the outset the anonymous author indicates his intentions: "We are writing you, brothers, about those who were martyred, along with the blessed Polycarp, who put an end to the persecution by, as it were, setting a seal on it through his death as martyr. For nearly everything leading up to his death occurred so that the Lord might show us from above a martyrdom in conformity with the gospel" (*Martyrdom of Polycarp* 1.1).[10]

We clearly do not have a disinterested report here. The author's guiding purpose is to show that Polycarp's death mirrored that of Jesus, so that it was "in conformity with the gospel." He attains this end through a number of literary touches: like Jesus as portrayed in the Gospels, Polycarp does not turn himself in but waits to be betrayed; he predicts to his followers his coming execution and its specific method; he prays intensely before being arrested, asking that God's will be done; the official in charge of his arrest is named Herod; and Polycarp rides into town on a donkey.

Moreover, like Jesus, the martyr Polycarp is calm and fearless in the face of death. The author foreshadows this divinely inspired bravery by providing a brief narrative of other Christians subjected to torture during the violent persecution:

> For they endured even when their skin was ripped to shreds by whips, revealing the very anatomy of their flesh, down to the inner veins and arteries, while bystanders felt pity and wailed. But they displayed such nobility that none of them either grumbled or moaned, clearly showing us all that in that hour, while under torture, the martyrs of Christ has journeyed far away from

the flesh, or rather, that the Lord was standing by, speaking to them. (*Martyrdom of Polycarp* 2.2)

The crowd, not sated by these gory deaths, calls for the arrest of their leader: "Away with the atheists! Find Polycarp!" (*Martyrdom of Polycarp* 3.1). Following a long account of his search and arrest, Polycarp, once in custody, is urged by the arresting party simply to do what he is being asked: "Why is it so wrong to save yourself by saying 'Caesar is Lord,' making a sacrifice, and so on?" (*Martyrdom of Polycarp* 8.2). Polycarp steadfastly refuses.

When he appears in a makeshift trial in a packed stadium, the governor himself urges Polycarp to repent and say, "Away with the atheists"—that is, to condemn the sacrilegious Christians. In a nice but not overly subtle use of irony, Polycarp looks at the crowd gathered for the festivities, gestures to them with his hand, sighs, and addresses heaven: "Away with the atheists."

The governor repeatedly attempts to get Polycarp off the hook. He urges Polycarp to convince the crowds he does not deserve to die. He threatens to throw him to the beasts unless he recants. He warns he will be sent to the flames. Nothing avails. The governor finally caves in and sends his herald into the center of the arena to announce that Polycarp "has confessed himself to be a Christian" (*Martyrdom of Polycarp* 12.1). The incensed mob cries out against him: "This is the teacher of impiety, the father of the Christians, the destroyer of our own gods, the one who teaches many not to sacrifice or worship the gods" (*Martyrdom of Polycarp* 12.2).

The governor orders him burned at the stake. But a divine intervention prevents the fire from touching the saint's body, and so the executioner takes the dagger to him. Even then there are miracles to behold: so much blood gushes from his side that it douses the entire conflagration, and a dove emerges from the wound and flies up to heaven. Polycarp's spirit has ascended.

Despite such theologically driven details, the account reveals the principal cause of occasional animosity toward the Christians and the corresponding judicial charge leveled against them. Again, it was their steadfast refusal to worship the traditional gods. Equally important, the narrative shows that ruling magistrates were not out for blood. They wanted to keep the peace and much preferred for Christians to come to their senses and perform simple cultic acts. Almost no one else in their known universe had qualms about doing so. Why should the Christians? Throughout our early martyrdom accounts it becomes clear that the Christians' persecutors were not opposed to religion. Quite the contrary: they were often highly religious people who opposed the Christian faith for religious reasons. The Christians—nonsensically—refused to worship any god but their own.

A second account of martyrdom corroborates these conclusions. This one does indeed appear to be based on an eyewitness report, possibly an actual trial transcript. The date was July 17, 180, and the place was Carthage in North Africa. The governor was a pagan named Publius Vigellius Saturninus. On trial before him were a Christian named Speratus and eleven others from the nearby town of Scillium. Unlike the *Martyrdom of Polycarp*, the *Acts of the Scillitan Martyrs* is spare and seemingly unbiased. It is all the more revealing.

Most notable is the repeated insistence of the governor Saturninus that the twelve Christians repent and accept the traditional religious practices of the empire: "If you return to your senses, you can obtain the pardon of our lord the emperor."[11] The Christians insist they have done nothing wrong and will not stray from their religious commitments. Saturninus indicates that he also stands within a religious tradition: "We too are a religious people, and our religion is a simple one: we swear by the genius of our lord the emperor and we offer prayers for his heath, as you also ought to do." Speratus offers to explain the "mystery of simplicity" of his own religion, but Saturninus warns him: "If you begin to malign our sacred rites, I shall not listen to you. But swear rather by the genius of our lord the emperor."

The Christians will hear nothing of it. Saturninus repeatedly tries to persuade them: "Cease to be of this persuasion." "Have no part in this folly." "Do you persist?" "You wish for no time for consideration?" Finally, out of desperation, he grants them a reprieve of thirty days to think it over. They do not want it. They are Christians and will not deny it. And so Saturninus orders their execution. They are beheaded on the spot.

These accounts of martyrdom we have just considered—those under Pliny in Bithynia-Pontus, the martyrdom of Polycarp in Smyrna, and the trial of the Scillitan Christians in Carthage—all concern local conditions and local magistrates. None of them involves an empire-wide persecution ordered from the upper reaches of government. There were times, however, when emperors became involved with the persecution of Christians. At first even these were local affairs. Beginning in the middle of the third century, they became empire-wide. The changes in scope and intensity are almost certainly related to the fact that, as time went on, the church grew. It went from being a minor local irritation to becoming an imperial problem.

PERSECUTIONS SPONSORED BY EMPERORS

We have seen that Christian numbers were relatively minuscule in the first century. But it was not long before Christians became known at the highest level of government, just three decades after the religion had its first converts. The emperor Nero had heard of the Christians, and that led to disaster for the church, at least in the city of Rome.

Nero (Ruled 54–68 CE)

Our principal source of information for Nero's involvement with the Christians comes not from a Christian source but from the writings of the Roman historian Tacitus. His *Annals of Rome* narrates imperial history during the reigns of Tiberius, Caligula, Claudius, and Nero. It is in book fifteen that he describes the disastrous fire in Rome in 64 CE.

The fire started in the Roman circus, spread to surrounding neighborhoods, and soon took over major sections of the city, destroying houses and businesses and killing large numbers of people.

Nero at the time was away from Rome in the town of Antium, but he returned as the fire was approaching one of his mansions. It eventually destroyed his palace on the Palatine Hill. The fire raged for six days before being stamped out, but it then revived. In the end, ten of the fourteen districts in Rome were affected, three completely leveled and seven "reduced to a few scorched and mangled ruins."[12]

No one knew for sure how the fire had started. The leading question was whether it had been a disastrous accident or if Nero himself was behind it. Tacitus himself is not sure: "Whether it was accidental or caused by a criminal act on the part of the emperor is uncertain—both versions have supporters." He seems, however, to lean toward imperial arson, since he reports that in some places gangs prevented anyone from fighting the fire and some were throwing torches into buildings to keep it going—all, they said, "under orders."

Nero did not do much during the conflagration itself to calm suspicions, at least as rumor would have it: "While the city was burning, Nero had gone on his private stage and, comparing modern calamities with ancient, had sung of the destruction of Troy." Fiddling while Rome burns. And why? "People believed that Nero was ambitious to found a new city to be called after himself." If Nero had architectural designs for a new Rome, he could scarcely implement them while old Rome was still standing. Or so it was said.

In any event, Nero needed to shift the blame from himself, and so, Tacitus indicates, he "fabricated scapegoats" by arresting and charging "the notoriously depraved Christians." This group, Tacitus notes, originated with "Christ [who] had been executed in Tiberius' reign by the governor of Judea, Pontius Pilatus." But despite Christ's execution "the deadly superstition had broken out afresh, not only in Judea (where the mischief had started) but even in Rome," where "all degraded and shameful practices collect and flourish."

The Christians were the perfect solution to Nero's problem. Infamous for their "hatred of the human race," they could be expected to find but few supporters. From around the city Nero had them rounded up and subjected to grisly public executions. Some he had wrapped in wild animal skins before letting ravenous dogs loose on them. Others he had crucified. And others he had rolled in pitch and set aflame to serve as human torches for his gardens and in the circus.

This is the first instance on record of a Roman emperor persecuting Christians. Several points need to be made about the event. First, nothing in the account suggests that Nero declared Christianity illegal. On the contrary, as we have seen in our discussion of Pliny and Trajan from nearly fifty years later, no such law was known. Second, and even more important, Nero did not, technically speaking, prosecute Christians for being Christian. He executed them for committing arson. True, they probably were not guilty, but that was the charge. Being a Christian was not punishable, but setting fire to Rome was.[13] Third and finally, Nero's persecution was localized. It involved only the city of Rome. Nothing indicates that Christians elsewhere in the empire suffered any consequences.

Even more significant, it appears that none of Nero's successors down to Trajan (ruled 98–117 CE) persecuted Christians. Later Christian legend asserted that the emperor Domitian did so at the end of the first century, but no convincing evidence supports the claim. It is important to recall that Christians were a barely noticeable portion of the population in the first two centuries. They did not demand attention and rarely received any. Between Nero in 64 CE and Marcus Aurelius in 177 CE, the only mention of an emperor's intervention in Christian affairs, apart from the episode involving Trajan found in Pliny's letters, is a letter from the emperor Hadrian that gives instructions to a local governor to conduct his trials against the Christians fairly.[14]

Marcus Aurelius (Ruled 161–80 CE)

We would not know of Marcus Aurelius's involvement in a persecution of Christians were it not for one brief reference to him in a Christian source later quoted by the fourth-century church historian Eusebius. Even there the emperor is not called by name. The source is one of the most gripping accounts of Christian martyrdom on record, the Letter of Lyons and Viennes, usually dated to 177 CE. This is an actual letter—assuming its authenticity—written by Christians of these two cities of Gaul, modern France, to describe their escalated tensions with the pagan population, culminating in horrific torments imposed on them in an attempt to force them to recant their faith. The heroes of the narrative never do so, even after days of brutal treatment.[15]

The zeal of the pagans leaps off the pages of the account. Again, these were not irreligious people who wanted to torture others for sheer sadistic pleasure. On the contrary, "they imagined in this way they would avenge their gods" by forcing the Christians to worship pagan cult statues. And so "they subjected them to every horror and inflicted every punishment in turn, attempting again and again to make them swear." In most cases, if the account is to be believed, these efforts were doomed to failure. The Christians, we are told, were "reminded by the brief chastisement of the eternal punishment of hell." Better to suffer for a horrible week than for all eternity.

The persecution was carried out under the authority of the regional governor. But at one point in the proceedings he communicated with the emperor concerning how to proceed and received instructions back: "Caesar [i.e., Marcus Aurelius] had issued a command that they should be tortured to death, but any who still denied Christ should be released." Some clearly did so, but for obvious reasons the account focuses on the torments of the valiant faithful rather than on the failings of the apostates.

We have no reliable reports of another emperor's involvement in persecution for another eighty years. By that time Christianity had started to explode in numbers, and emperors started to express concern.

Decius (Ruled 249–51 CE)

The first emperor to issue empire-wide legislation that affected the Christian movement was Decius in 249 CE, shortly after he assumed power. It came in the form of a universal decree requiring everyone in the empire to perform a sacrifice to the gods, taste the sacrificial meat, and swear they had always done so, all in the presence of an official who was to sign a document scholars call a *libellus* certifying it had happened. The only people exempt were the Jews.[16]

We know of this extraordinary measure from several sources: three Christian contemporaries who spoke of persecutions that erupted when followers of Christ refused to comply, and a group of the actual *libelli*, forty-five altogether, discovered by archaeologists.

Traditionally it was thought that Decius enacted the decree specifically to institute an empire-wide persecution of the Christians. Recent historians have persuasively argued this was not the case.[17] Instead, the decree was almost certainly designed to show a commitment to the gods throughout the entire empire in a time of imperial crisis. The middle half of the third century was a notorious period of real upheaval, with economic crises, barbarian invasions, and imperial assassinations, one after the other. The proper worship of the gods was called for as never before.

For modern minds it is interesting how Decius did so. It was not by dictating a certain range of religious beliefs; it was not by insisting on a national day of prayer; and it was not even by naming specific Roman deities who were to be worshiped. It was instead by requiring everyone to perform the cultic act of sacrifice. For Decius and pagans like him, this was the central feature of true religion. It did not matter which of the gods was honored through the sacrifice. The empire had to participate.

It is possible that Decius issued this edict precisely because he knew of the growing numbers of Christians and he wanted to force their hands. James Rives argues, however, that he may not have had only Christians in mind. There were other "foreign" cults that deemphasized sacrifice or neglected it altogether. Decius may have detected an alarming trend and sought to put an end to it.

His edict carried enormous implications. For Roman history prior to 249 CE, religious activities had always been local affairs. Worship was conducted by the individual, in the family, or as part of a local community. At most it was a matter of the province. That was true even of the Roman imperial cult: emperors may have been worshiped throughout the empire, but the specific practices were not controlled by a centralized authority. They were devised and carried out following local customs.

With Decius's edict an official type of religion appeared for the entire empire, a sanctioned and even mandatory cultic act required in every place. This had profound effects on Christian-Empire relations. As Rives puts it: "It is thus not surprising that before Decius' decree on universal sacrifice, there had been no centrally organized persecutions of Christians: it was only when a 'religion of the Empire' had been defined and its boundaries set that there could be a systematic persecution of people who transgressed those boundaries."[18]

As one might imagine, there were certainly ways for Christians—especially those who were wealthy—to get around the requirements of the decree. They could take flight and keep on the move under the radar; they could bribe officials; they could purchase fake *libelli*. But we know from later Christian accounts that even though the reign of Decius was brief—he was killed in battle in 251 CE—serious consequences attended those who refused to sacrifice: exile, confiscation of property, torture, and death. It is impossible, however, to know the extent of the persecutions.

Valerian (Ruled 253–60 CE)

Two years after Decius, Valerian assumed the mantle of office. He was the first emperor to issue decrees specifically directed against the Christians and thus the first to sponsor an empire-wide persecution.[19] The initial decree appeared in 257 CE, requiring church leaders to participate in pagan rituals and banning Christians from meeting en masse in cemeteries. More significant was a rescript the next year ordering the execution of all Christian bishops, presbyters, and deacons in the city of Rome itself. Christians at the rank of senator and equestrian were to be deprived of their status and worldly goods. If they refused to recant their faith, they too were to be executed. Matrons of senatorial rank were to have their property confiscated and be exiled. Members of the imperial household were also to have their goods confiscated and they were to be conscripted to work on imperial estates. This was an aggressive and very serious policy.

During the persecution, the Roman bishop Sixtus and four of his deacons were executed at the Catacombs of Saint Callixtus. Days later the deacon Laurence was executed. The cult revering Saint Laurence was to become a major feature of Roman Christian worship. Also during the persecution came one of the quickest judicial trials on record, set forth in a book called the *Acts of Fructuosus*. A bishop was brought up on charges, and his trial before the magistrate required four words: *"Episcopus es?"* *"Sum."* *"Fuisti."* Literally: "Are you a bishop?" "I am." "You were."[20]

With Valerian's decrees, imperial powers took on the business of stamping out the growing Christian religion. However, the emperor himself was captured by the Persians during his attempt to defend the eastern borders in 260 CE; he was the first Roman emperor ever taken captive by the enemy. His son Gallienus assumed the highest office and did nothing to rescue his humiliated father. He did, however, rescind the persecution of Christians. As a result, the church enjoyed a forty-three year peace as it grew by leaps and bounds at the end of the third century. But after that the worst of times arrived with the Great Persecution under the emperor Diocletian.

Diocletian (Ruled 284–305 CE)

Diocletian was one of the truly great emperors of Roman history. He has nonetheless suffered a sullied reputation because of events that transpired near the end of his reign. Diocletian was highly religious and saw in the rise of Christian "atheism" a threat to the empire. He may have been spurred into action by the vitriolic polemic of the neo-Platonic philosopher Porphyry, whose book *Against the Christians* was seen by later Christian intellectuals to be the best-informed and most serious assault on the faith ever issued from a pagan pen. Diocletian knew Porphyry and had heard him lecture in Nicomedia, where he kept his official residence.[21] On the administrative level, it is often thought that the real driving forces behind the persecution were Diocletian's virulently anti-Christian junior Caesar Galerius and Galerius's later replacement, Maximin Daia. But it was Diocletian who ordered it. This was a state-sponsored attempt to wipe out the Christian church, a persecution that dwarfed anything the empire had ever seen. It was to last on and off for a decade.

Diocletian issued a first edict on February 24, 303.[22] All Christian meetings were declared illegal; Christian places of worship were to be destroyed; Christian Scriptures were to be confiscated; Christians of high social status were to lose their rank; Christian freedmen in the imperial service were to be re-enslaved.

It was one thing, however, for Roman officials, even emperors, to issue an edict and another thing to enforce it. No imperial police force existed to carry out the requirements of Diocletian's decree. Enforcement was a regional or even municipal affair. Apart from a few church building destructions, the decree had little effect in the western part of the empire, and enforcement in the East was spotty. Still, those could be very hot spots indeed.

Months later the imperial palace in Nicomedia caught fire. Twice. Christians were accused and a second decree appeared in the summer of 303 ordering the arrest of all Christian clergy. November of that year saw a third decree, indicating that the imprisoned clergy would be set free only if they sacrificed to the gods.

Some months later, in spring 304, the fourth, final, and most severe decree was issued. It required everyone in the empire to gather in public spaces and participate in sacrifices. Some Christians escaped the requirement by bribing authorities; others apostatized; others refused and faced punishment in the form of imprisonment, torture, and death.

In the western part of the empire, only the first decree appears to have been propagated, and enforcement of even that one was brought to a complete halt with the accessions of Constantine and Maxentius in 306 CE. In the East the persecution continued sporadically, first under Galerius and then, especially, under Maximin Daia, up until the so-called Edict of Milan was issued in 313 CE by the victorious Constantine and his co-emperor Licinius. Still, it was long remembered by Christians as a horrific period of suffering, when the forces of evil strove to overthrow the true worship of God and destroy those who practiced it. We simply do not know how many Christians suffered imprisonment or died at the hands of the authorities: possibly hundreds of people, although almost certainly not many thousands. We do know that, in the end, the Christians came out on top. Constantine converted, and with one brief exception all the emperors to follow were Christian. There would never again be an official Roman persecution of the Christians.

Throughout these early centuries of on-again, off-again opposition, Christians were not always bullied, beaten, tortured, and executed. Most of the time, in most places, they were simply left in peace. Many Christians went from cradle to grave without facing any public ridicule, opposition, or persecution. We do not hear much about these Christians for an obvious reason: peace and quiet rarely make it into the history books.

It also bears noting that when Christians were attacked, either verbally or physically, they did not always accept it passively "like lambs led to the slaughter." They often fought back, if not with swords then at least with words. There is a long and distinguished history of Christian intellectuals defending the claims of their faith and attacking the religious practices of their pagan opponents. Some of these literary works still survive, in a corpus produced by the Christians apologists.

THE CHRISTIAN APOLOGISTS

The Greek term *apologia* does not mean "I'm sorry." It means a defense. When used of a literary genre, it refers to a reasoned defense of one's personal, philosophical, or religious views. The *Apology of Socrates* was Plato's account of the legal defense that Socrates made at his trial in Athens. The speech itself is one of the great classics of ancient literature. They executed him anyway.

Later generations often look back at such unsuccessful defenses and judge them to be irrefutable. That has proved to be the case with many of the Christian apologies. When transposed into a modern Christian context, they seem to be filled with such commonsensical and persuasive arguments that it is a wonder the pagans did not simply agree en masse.

The Christian apologies of the second and third centuries, however, were not meant for or read by outsiders. They were insider literature, written by Christians for other Christians in order to provide moral support and intellectual reasons for the faith. It is true that in almost all instances these apologies are actually addressed to pagans, normally to the emperors themselves. But it defies all sense to think they were actually hand-delivered to the ultimate ruler or that he would take the time to plow through their sometimes convoluted argumentation. Emperors, as you might imagine, were rather busy people.

Some scholars have thought that the apologies were published as "open letters" to the emperors such as you might find today in a daily newspaper. That is possible, of course, but it seems more likely that they were simply placed in circulation within the church communities themselves, just as the writings of modern Christian apologists are almost always read by Christians who want to be armed in their assault on the views of nonbelievers and in the defense of their own, rather than by nonbelievers, who, as a rule, are not all that interested in the intellectual justifications popular among the insiders.

So far as we can tell, early Christians almost always thought they should be able to defend themselves against charges leveled against them, and they were sometimes instructed to do so. Already in the New Testament we have the injunction of 1 Peter: "Always be ready to make a defense [Greek: *apologia*] to everyone who asks for a reason for the hope that is in you" (1 Peter 3:15). No doubt, in the early decades, Christians spoke among themselves about why they believed, why their beliefs were superior to those of the pagan and Jewish worlds in which they otherwise found themselves, and how they could defend themselves verbally when under attack from those on the outside. It is not until the middle of the second century, however, that we begin to get actual written defenses of the faith, produced over the next two hundred years (and a bit beyond) by the very small cadre of intellectuals who had joined the ranks of the faithful.

Their writings were circulated, read, mastered, and utilized, and some of them have come down to us today from such authors as Justin Martyr in Rome, Athenagoras in Athens, Tertullian in Carthage, Minucius Felix in North Africa, and Origen in Alexandria, Egypt. Some of the apologists (Tertullian, Origen) are familiar names because of their other extensive surviving writings; others (Justin, Minucius Felix) are known only from their apologetic works. One of our very earliest apologies, the *Letter to Diognetus*, is never mentioned in any other ancient source. It is named after its recipient, since its author did not identify himself and we have no clue who he was.

Together these apologists provide us with an entire arsenal of arguments used both in the defense of the Christian faith and in the assault on the views of pagans and, to a much lesser extent, Jews. Among other things, the apologists addressed the very strange legal position of the Christians during their court proceedings. As we have seen, Christians were put on trial not for having committed a crime but for committing one in the present, by being Christian. That seemed nonsensical to the apologists, for two reasons. One is that a name is not a crime. Crimes are acts committed against others, such as murder, theft, adultery, and treason. By identifying themselves as Christian, the members of this religious group had not done anything but name themselves. That should be no crime. Even more, the legal proceedings made no sense because Christians were not being asked to confess a crime they had committed—the normal procedure in a criminal court of law—but to deny who they were. They were to forswear their Christian faith and take an oath to the pagan gods. And they were being tortured to do so. The judicial action, therefore, was designed not to uncover a criminal act but to force them to stop committing one. As Tertullian put the irony: "In the case of others denying, you apply the torture to make them confess; Christians alone you torture to make them deny" (*Apology* 2).

Needless to say, such pleas based on logical inconsistencies fell on deaf ears. As did all the other arguments of the apologists, however sensible they may seem to modern readers. As one might expect, most of their defenses addressed the suspicions raised and allegations leveled against Christians that we have already seen: atheism, sexual immorality, infanticide, and cannibalism.

CHRISTIAN ATHEISM

In defending themselves against charges that they were "without gods," the apologists acknowledged they did not worship the pagan divinities. But they certainly worshiped the one creator God over all, the ultimate divine being. And not just him alone: they also worshiped the Son of God and the Spirit of God. Moreover, they acknowledged there were other divine beings in the world—angels, archangels, and so on—who, since they were not at the pinnacle of divinity, did not deserve the adoration due to the one true God but who were recognized for their greatness. And so Christians obviously were not atheists.

Moreover, every nation, every city, every family, had its own gods. The major deities of Britain, Spain, Gaul, Italy, Asia Minor, Syria, and Egypt all differed from one another. Romans did not intervene to force people in Spain or Egypt to worship gods other than the ones they chose. Why should they force the Christians? Suppose the Christian views were wrong, that their god was not the ultimate divine being alone worthy of worship. That would make Christians mistaken and possibly even foolish, but it would not make them criminal. Persecution on these grounds was senseless.

In response to the pagan view that the gods resented not being worshiped and could bring disaster on a people, or an entire empire, that ignored them, Christians pointed out that the gods were *always* being neglected. Since there were so many gods in so many places, anytime pagans worshiped one god they were neglecting to worship hundreds of others. Were these hundreds upset about that? Did they bring disasters on the empire every time someone chose to worship a different god? If not, why would they do so when the Christians chose to worship their god?

Moreover, what evidence was there that gods brought drought, floods, earthquakes, famine, epidemics, or any other calamities because they were not worshiped by the Christians? If that were true, why did such catastrophes occur with equal frequency before the reign of the emperor Tiberius, when Christianity first appeared? Moreover, when such calamities struck in the present, they did not affect just the allegedly guilty parties, the Christian culprits alone. If the gods wanted to punish Christians for their refusal to worship, why would disasters strike pagans as well?

Apologists not only defended themselves against the charge of atheism; they also attacked the pagan gods, pulling out every tool of mockery and sardonic irony in their arsenal. Myths found in the works of Homer, Hesiod, Ovid, Virgil, and others showed that the pagan deities were jealous, mean-spirited, vain, and ridiculous. They had love affairs, they fought and wounded one another, they committed rape; they were thieves, adulterers, liars, and murderers. Can anyone seriously imagine these are gods that deserve worship?

Moreover, the apologists accused pagans of imagining that their idols, made of wood, stone, and metal, were actually gods. For Christians, this was obviously absurd. A statue cannot be a divine being. As Tertullian indicates, they are "simply pieces of matter akin to the vessels and utensils in common use among us" (*Apology* 12). The pagan author Celsus points out that Christians will sometimes stand next to a statue of a god and shout, "See here: I blaspheme it and strike it but it is powerless against me for I am a Christian."[23] Celsus himself considered the charge absurd, since the statue was not the divinity but simply a physical representation of it. But Christians for centuries found the argument persuasive: pagans create material objects and then worship them as gods.

Or worse, they actually worship demons. One major strand of the Christian tradition insisted the pagan gods were fallen angels, evil demons who possessed the idols and demanded worship. Numerous Christian stories showed their exorcists casting demons out of cult statues and subjugating them to the true divine will. As the third-century bishop of Carthage Cyprian claims:

> If you are there, you will see that we are entreated by those whom you entreat, that we are feared by those whom you fear, whom you adore. You will see that under our hands they stand bound and tremble as captives, whom you look up to and venerate as lords. Assuredly even thus you might be confounded in those errors of yours, when you see and hear your gods, at once upon our interrogation betraying what they are, and even in your presence unable to conceal those deceits and trickeries of theirs. (*Letter to Demetrius* 15)

CHRISTIANS AS MORAL REPROBATES

Christians had to defend themselves not only against the legal charge of refusing to worship the gods but also against the widely circulated accusations of rampant sexual immorality, similar to suspicions aroused by the devotees of Bacchus in the second century BCE and by yet other secretive cults in the empire. Apologists were particularly incensed by such charges and claimed that pagan opponents had reversed the issue, charging Christians with activities pursued by their own gods: pagan deities, not the Christians, committed incest, rape, and flagrant adultery. Christians committed themselves to extraordinary ethical standards and were very proud of themselves for it. They were so far removed from sexual impropriety, claimed the apologists, that they spurned not only adultery but also illicit sexual desire, proscribing not just extramarital sex but even lust. This was a uniquely high moral standard.

Some Christians insisted that even marital sex was to be harshly restricted. As Athenagoras insists: "The farmer sows his seed in the ground and waits for the harvest, not troubling to sow his land again the while. For us, too, the begetting of children is the limit of our indulging our passions" (*Plea* 33). Indeed some Christians went even further, intentionally remaining virgins for their entire lives. Even those who marry, claimed the apologists, considered a second marriage, after the death of a spouse, to be adultery. When it came to sex, they averred, the Christians were the most morally upright people on earth.

Although they also occasionally defended themselves against the charges of infanticide and cannibalism, most apologists simply considered them absurd. They pointed out once again that Christian morality far exceeded even what was widely sanctioned in the pagan world. Pagans enjoyed urban spectacles that included such niceties as gladiators fighting to the death in the arena and unarmed criminals being thrown to ravenous wild beasts. Christians opposed the taking of any life, since it was a gift from God.

As far as infants are concerned, the apologists insisted that Christians protected the newborns with unheard-of scruples. Christians alone refused to practice abortion or the exposure of unwanted newborns to the elements or human traffickers. Moreover, since Christians believed there would be a future resurrection of the dead, they absolutely would not allow their own bodies to become the tombs of ingested others.

PROOFS OF CHRISTIAN TRUTH

Christian apologists not only defended themselves against pagan accusations but also mounted positive proof for the superiority of their own religion. It was not superior simply because the others were ridiculous—although for the apologists they certainly were that. It was superior on its own merits.

For most early Christians, the superiority of Christianity was obvious; otherwise they would not have converted in the first place. As we have seen, what convinced most people appears to have been Christian claims about the miraculous. Empowered by their god, Christians could perform amazing acts of healing and spectacular exorcisms of demons. The Christian god was more powerful than anything paganism had to offer, and this was a persuasive apologetic argument.

Some of the apologists—especially Justin—developed a related proof: the life of Jesus and the history of the Christian movement had been predicted with extraordinary accuracy centuries earlier by the ancient Hebrew prophets.

Justin wrote two surviving apologies and a third book that is called the *Dialogue with Trypho*. The apologies are ostensibly directed toward a pagan audience to show the superiority of the Christian faith. The *Dialogue* is meant to show Christianity's superiority to Judaism, even though it too may have been meant to provide arguments convincing to pagans. In it Justin claims to present an actual debate he held with a learned Jewish teacher, Trypho, in which they argue back and forth over the meaning of numerous passages of Jewish Scripture. In every case, Justin maintains the Scriptures contain predictions or foreshadowing of Jesus and the Christian religion. Trypho argues against these Christian interpretations. Since it is Justin who reports the debate, it comes as no surprise to see who appears to have the stronger argument.

Justin and other apologists, in any event, were firmly convinced that details from Jesus's life had been predicted by the prophets of Scripture centuries before he was born. The prophets predicted the messiah would be born to a virgin in Bethlehem; he would be a great miracle worker; he would be rejected by his own people, betrayed by one of his closest followers, condemned to execution, crucified, and raised from the dead; and he would ascend to heaven. All that had happened, just as prophesied. The Scriptures also predicted the Jewish people on the whole would reject Jesus as their messiah; gentiles then would become the people of God; God in his anger would destroy the Jewish capital city of Jerusalem; and on and on. Since these century-old predictions came to fulfillment, we have in Scripture a different kind of miracle. Christianity is a divinely inspired religion.

Although apologists other than Justin do not argue the case at equal length, they all would agree with the corollary, which relates in particular to pagan persecutions of Christians for not following ancient traditions. Everyone in the ancient world placed a high premium on antiquity. Ancient customs were followed because they were tried-and-true. They had worked for centuries. What was not valued was invention or novelty. If a practice or perspective was "new," it was suspect. That is the principal reason pagans did not object to Jews practicing their religion. Jews might be superstitious, strange, and even ridiculous. But their religion had the stamp of antiquity, and so they were allowed to go their own way.

Christians, on the other hand, had a real problem when it came to justifying their views to a pagan audience. Their religion did not go back into hoary antiquity. It was a new thing. Jesus had lived recently. He was a teacher from Judea active during the reign of the emperor Tiberius. Any religion founded in his name was a novelty. It could not possibly be true. If it were true—indeed, the only true religion—what are we to think of the history of the entire human race *prior* to the death of Jesus? Was everyone who ever lived simply and hopelessly wrong? For many pagans, Christianity could not be true because it was not ancient.

The apologists had an argument against this view. They maintained that in fact Christianity was not a new invention arising in the time of Tiberius. It was old. Very old. How old? It was the fulfillment of the entire Hebrew Scriptures, books produced centuries earlier by inspired writers who anticipated, foreshadowed, and predicted Jesus and his church. Christianity was the true and correct interpretation of Judaism. And Judaism goes back to the very beginning—back to the creation itself, since it is the Jewish god who made all things.

That is one reason Christians were, in turn, so virulent in their opposition to the Judaism of their day. If Jews were right about their interpretations of the Scriptures, then Christians were wrong and they could not claim to be an ancient religion. Christians therefore insisted that Jews were a hardheaded and recalcitrant people who had always been disobedient to their god and who had never understood their own Bible. The Jewish Scriptures in fact were Christian. God had rejected the Jews and adopted the Christians. For that reason, the Bible was theirs.

And the Bible contained writings far more ancient than anything on offer in paganism. Moses lived eight hundred years before Plato and four years before Homer.[24] He was centuries older than any author of any pagan writing. Moses predicted Jesus. Jesus was the fulfillment of everything Moses looked forward to. The Christian faith was not an invention of yesterday. It was the most ancient religion on the face of the earth.

CHRISTIAN PERSECUTION AND DEFENSE: IN SUM

Americans are so accustomed to the idea of the separation of church and state that it is hard for many to understand politics and religion any other way. The state should not have power over what or how one worships, and the church should not run the government. Nonetheless, in the broader picture of human history and culture, this view is an anomaly. Before the Enlightenment almost no one argued that the state should stay out of the business of religion. The most notable exceptions were the early Christian apologists.

The apologists wanted the Roman state to leave them alone. It was not right that either local magistrates or senior imperial authorities should oppose a religious cult so long as it was not a social danger or a threat to public morals. Christianity was not dangerous and it advanced an unusually high code of ethics. Leave it alone. Let Christians worship their god as they see fit and do not try to force them to violate their religious consciences.

Even though these arguments may make inherent sense to modern Americans, to ancient pagans they would have been utter nonsense. The gods were very much involved with affairs of state and so naturally the state needed to support the worship of gods. Only certain Christians thought otherwise, and for obvious reasons. They wanted the state to stop opposing them.

Thus they devised the notion of the separation of church and state. This was a view that made considerable sense to Christians of all types so far as we can tell—until the Roman emperor became Christian. Then suddenly the idea seemed to vanish. After Constantine began showering favors on the church, the political views of the apologists were taken off the table. Now it made obvious sense to

Christians for the emperor and all his underlings to support, promote, and advance the cause of religion. As we will see, this imperial shift—not in policy but in allegiance—had a devastating effect on the pagan world. The tables had turned. Now it was Christians, with their exclusivist views about true religion, who were in charge. The persecutors became the persecuted.

Chapter 8

The First Christian Emperor

T he fourth century saw cataclysmic changes in church-state relations, all of them hinging on the conversion of the emperor Constantine. Over the course of a mere eighty years, Christianity went from being under siege, to being tolerated, to becoming officially the state religion of Rome. Rarely has the world seen such a radical shift of opinion and policy in such a short time. By the end of the fourth century, approximately half of the empire claimed allegiance to the Christian faith.

FROM THE GREAT PERSECUTION TO FULL RELIGIOUS TOLERANCE

In exploring the role of Constantine in this shift, we should recall that he was serving as a junior officer in Diocletian's court when persecution began. Constantine was completely disingenuous—in fact, he was telling a bald-faced lie—when he claimed, some twenty years later, that he had watched Diocletian come to his fateful decision to persecute only when he himself was "still a boy."[1] He was no mere boy. This was in 303 CE. Constantine was born in 272 or 273. He was a thirty-year-old holding an important position in the emperor's administration. He may not have been personally complicit in the opening years of the Great Persecution, but nothing indicates he expressed any disapproval either.

Soon afterward he served under Galerius, who was known to our Christian sources as particularly energetic in enforcing the decrees of persecution and possibly the one who urged their instigation in the first place. Galerius administered the eastern part of the empire, but in the West there was almost no enthusiasm for the edicts. Constantine's father, Constantius, was the first western Caesar in the Tetrarchy and was himself probably a henotheist, although almost certainly a devotee of Sol Invictus, the Unconquered Sun, rather than the god of the Christians. He was not interested, in any event, in persecuting the Christian church.

Constantine joined his father in Gaul in 305 CE before being acclaimed Augustus himself on his father's death in 306. The senior emperor of the West at his accession, Severus, was soon thereafter captured in his assault on Maxentius in Rome, and was replaced in the imperial college by a military man named Licinius, who was to play an important role in Constantine's life for the next sixteen years.

The Great Persecution continued sporadically, mainly in the East, until the death of Galerius in 311. Immediately prior to his demise, Galerius—to everyone's great surprise—issued the Edict of Toleration, in which he officially called the persecution to a halt. A copy of this edict has been preserved for us by the Christian historian Eusebius in his lengthy *Church History*. It is an intriguing document, in no small measure because it shows so clearly that Galerius pursued persecution not as a hater of religion but, quite the contrary, as an avid supporter of the gods.

In the document, Galerius argues that he had advocated persecution "for the advantage and benefit of the nation," because "the Christians . . . had abandoned the convictions of their own forefathers and . . . refused to follow the path trodden by earlier generations." The persecution was designed to compel the Christians "to go back to the practices established by the ancients." But opposition to the religion had not had the desired effect. Christians "persisted in the same folly" and were not "paying to the gods in heaven the worship that is their due." So the emperor chose to rescind the persecution: "In view of our benevolence and the established custom by which we invariably grant pardon to all people, we have thought proper in this matter also to extend our clemency most gladly, so that Christians may again exist and rebuild the houses in which they used to meet, on condition that they do nothing contrary to public order" (*Church History* 8, 17).

This was no deathbed conversion. But it was as close as one could get to admitting he was wrong. Galerius died soon thereafter, but his successor, Maximin Daia, resumed persecution with a vengeance for another two years before being defeated in battle by Licinius not long after the conversion of Constantine and the battle at the Milvian Bridge.

With all that upheaval in the imperial college, the Tetrarchy was no more. Maximinus, Severus, Galerius, Maxentius (never admitted into the college), and Maximin Daia were all dead. That left Constantine in the West and Licinius in the East. These two decided to broker a peace and met in Milan to cement their relationship. To create a family bond, Constantine arranged for Licinius to marry his half sister Constantia. More significant for our interests here, the rulers jointly agreed to bring the Great Persecution to a definitive and final end.

What emerged from the meeting was the so-called Edict of Milan. This was not an edict but a letter addressed to provincial governors in the East. It was not written from Milan but from Bithynia, after the imperial meeting. Moreover, it was published not by Constantine but by Licinius, even though it appeared under both their names.

The letter is significant for two particular reasons: it declared an official state policy of tolerance for all religions whatsoever—not just Christianity—and it stated the reason for the policy: to ensure that "whatsoever divine and heavenly powers exist might be enabled to show favor to us and to all who live under our authority." In other words, prosperity in the human realm required peace with the divine. Precisely this view, of course, drove the persecutions of the Christians in the first place. Both current emperors, the Christian

Constantine and the pagan Licinius, agreed that, for the empire to thrive, God, or the gods, needed to look favorably upon it. That required toleration of difference, to ensure that "respect and reverence for the Deity [be] secured."[2]

Thus, the edict explicitly states a policy of complete tolerance for all:

> We have given the said Christians free and absolute permission to practice their own form of worship. When you observe that this permission has been granted by us absolutely, [you] will understand that permission has been given to any others who may wish to follow their own observance or form of worship—a privilege obviously consonant with the tranquility of our times— so that everyone may have permission to choose and practice whatever religion he wishes. This we have done to make it plain that we are not belittling any rite or form of worship. (*Church History* 10.5)

This is a remarkable statement, unlike any seen before. In the words of Constantine scholar Harold Drake, it was "the first official government document in the Western world to recognize the principle of freedom of belief."[3] It is not that the Christians had now assumed control of the empire and were turning the tables on the pagans; it is simply that Christianity was being recognized as completely legitimate. So too were all the traditional religions of Rome. There was to be equality and toleration all around, a policy of complete noncoercion.

Some modern Christian scholars have thought that if Constantine refused to compel his pagan subjects to convert to his new faith, he must not have been a "real" Christian, except on the surface. That is a wrong reading of the so-called Edict of Milan and of the rest of Constantine's reign. Throughout history there have been millions and millions of sincere Christians who have adopted a live-and-let-live policy toward people of other faiths. Constantine was one of them, even if he did happen to be the most powerful figure in the early history of the religion.[4]

It is also important to emphasize that when Constantine arrived at the conference in Milan in 313 he was a newly minted Christian. He had converted just months before. One cannot expect him to have had a full awareness of everything—or even anything—involved in his newly acquired faith. Learning an entirely new religion takes time. For Constantine it may have been a steep learning curve. But it did not take long for him to embark on his Christian education. He was forced to jump feetfirst into ecclesiastical life, almost immediately.

CONSTANTINE'S INVOLVEMENT IN CHURCH AFFAIRS

It may seem peculiar to modern minds that Constantine, a recent convert, should impose himself on affairs of the church right after he himself had joined its ranks. It is important to remember, however, that he, like most rulers before him, was deeply committed to religious ideology: social and political success—not just for him personally but for the entire empire—required divine support. And divinity required proper worship. Anything that affected divine worship was therefore important for the well-being of the state. Apart from the earlier Christian apologists, whom Constantine almost certainly had never read, no one was arguing for a separation of church and state.

The Donatist Controversy

Constantine himself certainly conceived of no separation of powers. In the very year he agreed on an empire-wide policy of toleration with Licinius, he became embroiled in a dispute threatening to tear the church apart, especially in the important region of North Africa. The Donatist controversy was Constantine's first foray into ecclesiastical matters, and it is safe to say he had absolutely no idea what he was getting himself into. Unity of the empire was one of his chief ambitions, and a unified church could contribute to the cause. The church, however, was anything but unified. Constantine intervened in hopes of settling the controversy. As it happened, it would drag on for more than a century.[5]

The first decree of Diocletian in 303 CE—just ten years earlier—had required Christian clergy to hand over copies of the Scriptures for destruction. Most Christians saw this not only as an awful policy of the persecutors but also as an act of sacrilege for anyone who complied. The clergy who had done so were labeled *traditores* ("those who handed over") and were not just castigated verbally but were dismissed from office. Their dismissal raised a crucial question of polity: what does their unsuitability for sacred position say about the efficacy of their earlier official actions? In the church at the time, Christian leaders conducted numerous ritual activities: performing baptism, administering the Eucharist, ordaining new members of the clergy, and so on. These were not actions just any Christian could perform. There was a sanctity inherent in the clergy that conferred the divine power associated with these sacramental rites. But *traditores* had obviously rescinded their sanctified status. Were the rites they performed while still in office legitimate?

The issue mattered a good deal. What if someone had been baptized by a *traditor*? Was the baptism still valid, or did it need to be performed a second time? What if a bishop had been ordained by the laying on of hands of a *traditor*? Was that person actually consecrated as a bishop?

The largest church of North Africa, Carthage, debated the issue with particular vigor. Some leaders of the church insisted that the sacraments were valid no matter who had performed them, whether *traditor* or not. The efficacy of the sacraments came from the power of God, not the worthiness of the one who administered them. But there was virulent—even violent—opposition to this view. The most vocal opponent was a man named Donatus, who had a large number of followers. In particular, Donatus argued that the bishop of Carthage, Caecilian, had not received a valid ordination. He could not be regarded as a true bishop. The church needed a different leader.

It is a long and complicated story that eventually involved such fifth-century stalwarts as the great Augustine. Constantine probably thought the solution was simple: he would have an established ecclesiastical authority judge the issue, he would sanction the answer, the church would accept it, and life would move on. But it was not to be.

His involvement began with a request for assistance from the Donatists themselves. Constantine turned the case over to the bishop of Rome, who appointed a kind of ecclesiastical court to rule on the matter. The Donatists lost the case, and Caecilian was exonerated. But the Donatists refused to accept defeat and appealed a second time to the emperor, who decided to take matters more directly into his own hands. He called for an entire council of bishops to meet in the city of Arles in 314 CE. Quite obviously this was the first time an emperor had called a council of bishops, and it set a precedent for things to come.

The bishops at the Council of Arles ruled decisively against the Donatists. Constantine himself had at first been somewhat inclined to their position, probably for practical reasons rather than because of any theological sophistication he could have brought to the table: he was certainly not well-read in the intricacies of sacramental theology. But when the Donatists refused the verdict of the council and appealed to him yet a third time, he saw them as obstructionists and set himself against them. Constantine was not particularly interested in the nuances of Christian theology or even of church polity. He was interested in unity. The Donatists were interfering with it. So he took the other side.

The other side could be seen as anti-rigorist. The Donatists took a hard line and were unforgiving of difference. That too did not sit well with Constantine. As Drake has observed, "Rigorists clearly were not the type of Christian he favored."[6] Moreover, this early dispute reveals that, all things being equal, in deciding a church issue Constantine preferred reasoned argument and considered opinion to the use of imperial force. Let the bishop of Rome make a sensible decision. If that does not work, have an entire council of bishops decide. Constantine was not interested in sending in the armies to bring the Donatists in line.

This was a position he continued to take throughout his lengthy reign, even when it came to the much more weighty matter of whether to compel nonbelievers to adopt the Christian faith. A decade later, after he had established himself as sole ruler of the empire, he sent a letter to his subjects in the East in which he stated unequivocally, "It is one thing to take on willingly the contest for immortality, quite another to enforce it with sanctions."[7]

The Arian Controversy

A year after Constantine wrote this letter in 324 CE, another ecclesiastical crisis came to a head. This one involved a dispute of theological importance. At least, it seemed important to the participants at the time, as it has to theologians in the centuries since. But to Constantine—and many others till today who have stood outside the ranks of the professional theologian—it seemed picayune and immaterial. This was the famous Arian controversy, a dispute that had arisen in Alexandria, Egypt, between a priest in the church named Arius and his bishop, Alexander.

There had been heated debates for generations among Christian theologians over the true nature of Christ. From almost the beginning, Christians had maintained that Christ was not just a human (even though, for most theologians, he was certainly that) but also the Son of God. In fact, already in our earliest Christian author, Paul, Christ was understood to be a divine being who existed in the heavenly realm prior to his birth (Philippians 2:6–8). In some sense he was God. But in what sense?

This was an issue that had never been satisfactorily resolved, in no small part because most Christians had always wanted to affirm with vigor four different propositions that, at least on the surface, appear to create a contradiction: Christ is God. God the Father is God. Christ is not God the Father. And there is only one God. So if Christ is God and God is God, how is it that Christians can say there is only one God? In short, how can Christians be monotheists?

It all hinges on what it means to say that there is only "one" God, and on how the Son of God is understood to relate to the Father. It is on these issues that Arius disagreed with his bishop, Alexander. Arius held a view in wide circulation among Christians for a long time, even if no one had articulated it with the same clarity and force. Christ, for him, was certainly a divine being, the Logos (the Greek word for "word") of God, and he certainly existed before he came into the world as Jesus Christ. Moreover, he was the agent of all creation. As the Gospel of John affirms: it was through the Logos that God created the heavens and the earth (John 1:1–3). So he was divine, but he was separate from God. Then how do the two relate to each other?

Arius maintained that Christ, the Logos, could not be equal with God the Father. The Father himself is almighty. There cannot be two beings who are both almighty, since then neither of them is "all" mighty. For Arius, only God the Father is almighty. Originally, in eternity past, God existed alone, by himself. He then, prior to the creation of the universe, begot a Son, a second divine being, who, since he was begotten of God, was secondary and subservient to him, as a son is to a father. This was the Logos, through whom the world was made and who much later took on human form and came into the world in order to bring salvation. The Logos, then, is a subordinate divinity who was brought into being at some point: he had not always existed. God the Father is superior to God the Son by an "infinity of glories."

Arius's bishop, Alexander, could not disagree more. He took a hard line that Christ was not subservient to God the Father as a subordinate being. Christ himself had said, "I and the Father are One" and "If you have seen me you have seen the Father" (John 10:30; 14:9). The two are equal. They are not identical, to be sure: the Son is a separate being from the Father. But they are equally omnipotent and have both existed forever. There never was a time that the Logos did not exist.

Those taking Alexander's side in the debate could point out that, by definition, if something is perfect it can never change. If something changes, necessarily it becomes either better or worse from the change. But if it becomes better, it was not perfect before; and if it becomes worse, it is not perfect after. Since God is perfect, he can never change. That means he could not *become* the Father by begetting a Son, since this would involve a change in his status from not-Father to Father. Necessarily, then, God had always been the Father. If he was always the Father, then the Son must always have existed.

Thus, Alexander's side of the debate maintained that the Son was coeternal with the Father and all-powerful along with him. He was not merely "like" the Father, of a "similar" kind of divine substance. He was "equal" with the Father, of the "same" substance. In the Greek terms used in these debates, the idea of being of the "same substance" is expressed by the word *homoousias*. By contrast, the word for "similar substance" is *homoiousias*. As you can see, they are very similar words, different only with the letter *i*, or in Greek, the iota, in the middle. Some observers have noted that the theological controversy threatening to fracture the church was a debate over an iota.

That is certainly what Constantine personally thought. Because the dispute was causing such turbulence, he felt compelled to intervene, and did so first by writing the two principals a letter. In it he clearly states his ultimate concern, which had never been about theological niceties but about unity: "My first concern was that the attitude towards the Divinity of all the provinces should be united in one consistent view."[8] Constantine did not care which view emerged from the debate. He simply wanted one side to concede to the other and thereby effect unity. Personally, he indicated that he considered the matter "extremely trivial and quite unworthy of so much controversy." For him, these were "small and utterly unimportant matters," involving a "very silly question." He urged Alexander and Arius to settle the matter between themselves.

They were unable to do so. It was not simply that they were at odds with each other. Both sides had numerous supporters who engaged in vitriolic attacks on the theological ignorance of the other. The debate was racking the church. Constantine decided to intervene in a major way by calling for the first worldwide, or ecumenical, council of bishops to meet and resolve the issue. This was the famous Council of Nicaea of 325 CE, named after the city in Asia Minor where the meeting was held. Later records indicate that some 318 bishops from around the world came to participate, most of them from the eastern provinces. (As we have seen, the church was not nearly as well established in the West[9]).

Constantine himself attended the meeting. He gave the opening address and participated in the discussions. At the end the bishops took a vote. Arius lost. The council devised a creed, a statement of faith that expressed its understanding of the nature of both the Father and the Son and related important theological matters. Included in the creed were a number of "anathemas," or "curses," on anyone who took a contrary position. That creed ultimately came to form the basis of the Nicene Creed, still recited in many churches today. At the council, only twenty participants ended up on the Arian side. Constantine pressured the naysayers to concede the case and convinced nearly all of them to do so. The only two recalcitrant bishops—along with Arius himself—were sent into exile.

As was true of the Donatist controversy, the council called by Constantine did not finally resolve the matter. Arians continued to press their case and made converts to their cause. Emperors after Constantine—including his own offspring—adopted the Arian view and exercised their authority to cement its stature in the church, even though, as we will see, it eventually lost. Our concern here, however, is with Constantine himself and his relation to the Christian faith. By 325 CE he had learned more about the intricacies of Christian theological discourse than he ever expected. He wanted unity, but he was not willing to impose it by sending troops to de-convert the Arians by the sword. When it came to matters of the church, he believed in persuasion.

In terms of civil governance, on the other hand, he remained very much a military man, quite willing to lead the armed and dangerous forces himself when it was to his political advantage.

CONSTANTINE'S MILITARY AND POLITICAL ACTIVITIES

By 313 CE, Constantine and Licinius had reached a temporarily amicable decision to co-rule the empire. Diocletian's brainchild, the

Tetrarchy, was a thing of the past. One might think the two-emperor solution imposed by the resolution of the civil wars would prove practicable. Constantine could rule the West and Licinius the East. It was not to work out that way in the long run, however, in no small measure because Constantine was a man never satisfied. He knew how to wait for what he wanted, but ultimately he was driven by massive ambition. From early he had set his sights on being the sole ruler, the first since the early days of Diocletian's reign some four decades earlier.

The next decade saw the rise of antagonism with Licinius and occasional military flare-ups as relations frayed. According to Eusebius, the final straw came in 324 CE with Licinius's decision to renew the persecution of Christians in the East. This was all the excuse Constantine needed—in fact, some modern scholars think it is an excuse he himself manufactured for the occasion. Constantine chose to move against his co-emperor and "rescue" his co-religionists. He defeated Licinius in a major battle, sent him to retirement in Thessalonica, and eventually ordered his death. Constantine was now in complete control.

Not everyone was joyful at the prospect. When Constantine traveled to Rome to celebrate his twentieth anniversary as emperor in 326 CE, he chose not to follow the centuries-old custom of making a token sacrifice to Jupiter upon entering the city as conqueror. That decision has always made perfect sense to Christian commentators, but it proved disastrous for imperial public relations, incensing pagan members of the Roman senate. Constantine's ties with the ruling elite soured. He had already by this time begun building a new capital city for the empire, a kind of "New Rome" that he named after himself, "Constantinople"—that is, "Constantine's City"—now modern Istanbul. He was to spend much of his final years in residence there, never again even visiting Rome.

For the new capital he chose a strategically important location, something that Rome itself, obviously, never had: the city of Byzantium on the Bosphorus strait. From there it would be much easier to oversee troop movements both east and west, and the site itself was relatively easy to defend and difficult to assault. Constantine had Byzantium destroyed and then he carried out a carefully conceived architectural plan for its replacement.

He built his capital as an explicitly Christian city.[10] There were to be no temples to pagan divinities and no sacred idols, with one exception: in order to adorn his city with statuary, a typical feature of the ancient urban environment, Constantine had sacred sites from around his empire pillaged, with bronze statues brought back and installed in public spaces throughout the city. This decision had a triple function: it deprived pagan religions of their revered cult images, it desacralized the statues and made them "secular" objects of art, and it raised the aesthetic appeal of his new capital. In the process, it gave the opportunity for Christians, whether resident or visiting, to mock the religious views of pagans. In Eusebius's *Life of Constantine* we are told that the emperor "used these very toys"—that is, the pagan playthings, their idols—"for the laughter and amusement of the spectators" (*Life of Constantine* 3.54). If Eusebius is right, we can assume the despoiled pagans were not amused. Acts such as this, and the attendant mockery, foreshadowed much worse things yet in store for devotees of traditional pagan religions.

This was not the end of the mischief, however. Constantine also stripped the doors and roofs off temples throughout the empire. He had other uses for the fine metal. So too with cult statues plated with gold. He sent several members of his inner circle on a destructive campaign "to every province" of his reign, to go "city by city, country by country" and order "the consecrated officials themselves to bring out their gods with much mockery and contempt from their dark recesses into daylight." They then had the gold plate stripped off and melted down for other uses. After denuding the statues, they left the "superfluous and useless" remnants to "the superstitious to keep as a souvenir of their shame" (*Life of Constantine* 3.54).

How the tide had turned. Now it was not the Christians who were superstitious; it was the pagans. It was not the Christians who embraced a religion open to public mockery; it was the pagans. It was not the Christians who suffered from the imperially sponsored violence; it was the pagans. The tide would continue to turn against the pagans in years to come, and it would never turn back, except for one brief moment under the reign of the emperor Julian.

Constantine thus built his city and adorned it with the spoils of the pagan empire. It was a city built to last. It remained the capital of Christendom for over a millennium, until the assault of the Ottoman Turks in 1453.

CONSTANTINE AS AN ADVOCATE FOR THE FAITH

There should no longer be any doubt about the sincerity of Constantine's devotion to the god of the Christians, despite the incredulity of some scholars over the years.[11] Of course, it is technically possible that it was all a front. But his deep and personal commitment to Christian causes, if nothing else, should lay all suspicions to rest. As should his own words, found repeatedly throughout the sources, as in a letter he sent to those living in Palestine: "Indeed my whole soul and whatever breath I draw, and whatever goes on in the depths of the mind, that, I am firmly convinced, is owed by us wholly to the greatest God" (*Life of Constantine* 2.29).

Not only did Constantine take a vital interest in internal Christian affairs; he also took considerable steps to improve the lot of the church and the clergy who ran it. Most of the staffing and funding of ancient urban societies came from local aristocracies, not through high taxes but through enormous demands placed on their time, energy, and resources. Public office was an oft-noted burden for the wealthy, involving considerable outlays of cash—not just expected but demanded—for public buildings and public services. These official positions did provide real status for its occupants, but the large outlays of personal resources could obviously have been put to other, more personal uses.

Constantine issued legislation that absolved Christian clergy—who by this time tended to be among the local aristocracies—from having to serve in civic capacities, relieving them of such duties and financial obligations. Moreover, he provided them with extensive funds out of the imperial treasury for use in their congregations. Most famously, Constantine himself arranged for the building of major churches throughout his empire, including the Lateran in Rome.

In some instances he had these churches constructed on sites that had previously boasted famous and important pagan shrines. That required, of course, the destruction of temples. As Eusebius reports with approbation in his *Life of Constantine*, Constantine took shrines that pagan priests had "splendidly adorned" and stripped them bare, so that he "completely destroyed" temples that had been "most highly prized by the superstitious" (*Life of Constantine* 3.1).

It has sometimes been thought, based on this passage, that Constantine went on an empire-wide rampage, but Eusebius can specify only five sites that suffered this fate, three of them involving the worship of Aphrodite, one connected with the famous opponent of Jesus, Apollonius of Tyana, and another on the sacred site of Mamre, a place that was to be revered because it was connected with the Jewish patriarch Abraham in the Old Testament (see Genesis 18). One of the temples of Aphrodite was also located on holy ground: the place of Jesus's passion. The temples of Aphrodite were suspected as places of sacred prostitution, providing Constantine all the excuse he needed to send in the wrecking crews. Thus, Constantine may have had good reasons for these particular destructions. They do not, however, indicate a trend. As one recent scholar has observed, "There is no reason to generalize from these cases to an empire-wide policy of temple destruction."[12] Still, once more we see a foreshadowing of things to come.

The religious zeal behind these demolition and building projects can be seen in Eusebius's account of the Church of the Holy Sepulcher in Jerusalem. It is sometimes thought that Constantine's mother, Helena, herself very Christian by this time, instigated the building of the church, but that is almost certainly not the case. Eusebius indicates that Constantine himself "decided that he ought to make universally famous and revered the most blessed site in Jerusalem of the Savior's resurrection" (*Life of Constantine* 3.25). Unfortunately, there was already a shrine on the spot. And not just any shrine, but an unholy, vile, pagan shrine built by "wicked men" who had been driven by demons to cover over the place where Jesus had been buried. They had brought in dirt from elsewhere and "covered up the whole place, then levelled it, paved it, and so hid the divine cave somewhere down beneath a great quantity of soil." Above it, they had built a terrible "tomb" of their own for "dead idols." It was a "gloomy sanctuary to the impure demon of Aphrodite." There they "offered foul sacrifices . . . upon defiled and polluted altars." Constantine's solution? A demolition and refurbishing of the site. The shrine was torn down and destroyed, the place dug up, and the cave where Jesus had been buried uncovered. On the spot Constantine had built a magnificent structure in honor of the savior, at the site still visited by millions of pilgrims and tourists to this day.

Helena is not said to have had any hand in the affair. But she was active as a Christian ambassador in other ways. She is indeed most famous for her pious journey as a septuagenarian to the Holy Land, back in the days when it had never occurred to the faithful of Christendom to "walk where Jesus walked." But she did so, and brought with her funding from the imperial treasury to recapture the place for Christ.[13] It is not true that Helena claimed to have discovered the wood of the True Cross. That is the stuff of later legend. Eusebius, who discusses key events of her visit, says nothing of the sort. But Helena did choose two auspicious sites for special church buildings: one, the Church of the Nativity, in Bethlehem, where Jesus was believed to have been born; the other, the Church of the Ascension, just outside Jerusalem, on the Mount of Olives, the site of his being taken up into heaven after his resurrection. In these projects, needless to say, Helena had the full backing of her avid Christian son.

In contrast to those scholars who have argued that if Constantine were a "real" Christian he would have been even more avid, some modern experts have argued that Constantine was so thoroughly committed to the Christian cause that his ultimate goal was to convert the entire empire.[14] However, that is almost certainly not the case. Even if he himself was firmly committed to the Christian god, Constantine had imperial reasons for not forcing the issue or compelling his subjects. He had seen well enough what would come of coercion. He had lived through the Great Persecution, observing it up close as a member of the courts of both Diocletian and Galerius. It did not work. Constantine obviously was heavy-handed when he felt a need to be, as with the bishops at Nicaea. He was not, however, inclined to compel the religious preferences, or even practices, of his predominantly pagan empire.[15]

In the next chapter we will see that some of Constantine's successors did not share his commitment to tolerance: by the end of the fourth century serious legislation issued from the imperial throne banning pagan practices altogether on pain of severe judicial penalty. One particularly thorny historical question involves Constantine's tolerance of traditional cultic practices, or his lack of it. Did he try to shut down pagan religious activities by criminalizing animal sacrifice? There is no doubt about his personal views. He despised animal sacrifice: the blood, the gore, the stench, and, in fact, the entire practice. He repeatedly said so. The historical issue is whether this is one instance in which he forced his views on all others by disallowing sacrifice throughout his empire.[16]

Some prominent experts have claimed he did, and in support they can cite some important evidence. For one thing, this is explicitly what his biographer Eusebius states. According to the *Life of Constantine*, after defeating Licinius in 324 CE, Constantine passed a law that "restricted the pollutions of idolatry which had for a long time been practiced in every city and country district, so that no one should presume to set up cult objects, or practice divination or other occult arts, or even to sacrifice at all" (*Life of Constantine* 2.45). Later Eusebius indicates again that by imperial injunction "for all those under Roman rule, both civilian and military, access was universally blocked to every form of idolatry, and every form of sacrifice banned." Moreover, "in successive laws and ordinances he prohibited everyone from sacrificing to idols, from practicing divination, and from having cult-figures erected" (*Life of Constantine* 4.23, 25).

One cannot underestimate how significant such legislation would be. If the rates of growth and figures provided in chapter 6 are relatively correct, by 325 CE there would have been something like five million Christians in the empire. If there were also some four million Jews, we might round up and say that of the sixty million inhabitants of the empire, fifty million were still pagans practicing their traditional cults. Did Constantine bring the worship of five-sixths of his empire to a crashing halt? If so, would other sources have failed to mention some such little incident?

One other reference does seem to confirm the act. It comes in a law passed in 341 CE, four years after Constantine's death, by his emperor son Contantius, who clearly did indeed attempt to abolish pagan sacrificial practices. Here is what the law said, according to the later compilation of legal injunctions made early in the fifth century known as the Theodosian Code:

> Superstition shall cease; the madness of sacrifices shall be abolished. For if anyone in violation of the law of the sainted Emperor, Our Father, and in violation of this command of Our Clemency, should dare to perform sacrifices, he shall suffer the infliction of a suitable punishment and the effect of an immediate sentence. (Theodosian Code 16.10.2)[17]

We have already seen that it was far easier in the Roman Empire to issue legislation than to enforce it, and the enforcement even of this explicit condemnation of pagan sacrifice appears to have been lax indeed—virtually nonexistent. It was another fifty years—and millions more Christian conversions later—before anti-pagan legislation took any serious hold. But for our purposes, the important point is that Constantius II in 341 CE indicates that his father had already ordered a cessation of sacrifice. That coincides with what Eusebius claimed just two years earlier in the publication of his *Life of Constantine*. Are these two Christian sources, one an imperial biographer and the other an actual emperor, to be trusted?

It has proved to be one of the most hotly debated issues of Constantine's religious activities. On one hand this is because there is no hard evidence of any such law. Eusebius, who claims it existed, never cites it, either in his *Life of Constantine* or in his *Church History*, in both of which he was more than a little eager to celebrate the triumph of the church over the evils of paganism, and especially to trumpet the victories of the faith over the powers of darkness achieved by the emperor Constantine. Why would he not cite the actual law if he had something to cite?

Moreover, there is no such law in the Theodosian Code. This was a collection of legislation made by legal scholars under the reign of Theodosius II, published in 438 CE. It is a very large book containing laws passed by emperors starting with Constantine himself in 313 CE and continuing for the next 125 years. The laws are arranged topically and represent, to be sure, only a selection of legislation: the compilers had to choose what to include and what not to. But the final book of the code is devoted to important laws connected with religion—almost exclusively related in one way or another to Christianity, of course—and there is a section of the book that focuses on legislation against pagan practices. No law of Constantine is cited forbidding sacrifice.

The case against such legislation is even stronger than that: we have the direct testimony of the famous Roman rhetorician Libanius, a major figure in Roman imperial life toward the end of the fourth century. Libanius was an avid pagan and advocate of traditional religions. Living during the reign of the über-Christian Theodosius I, he felt the pressure from the empire on his personal commitments and issued a plea for religious tolerance in the face of imperial legislation against pagan practices. In the course of his eloquent oration, Libanius urges the precedent of Constantine himself for toleration, reminding the emperor that Constantine "made absolutely no alteration in the traditional forms of worship" (*Oration* 30.6).[18]

That would have been a very foolish argument to make if there was any solid evidence that in fact Constantine had shut down, or tried to shut down, the entire apparatus of pagan worship. How, then, can we explain all the evidence, some that says he did (or attempted to) outlaw sacrifice, and other that indicates he did not?

Numerous solutions have been proposed over the years, including attempts to reconcile the statements in various sources, so that both

Eusebius is right that Constantine passed such a law and Libanius is right that he did not.[19] Most of these reconciliations are a bit forced, however, and possibly it is best to adjudicate the matter by considering what Constantine himself says about it in a letter that he directed to inhabitants of the eastern provinces in 324 CE. Here Constantine states directly that the "doctrines of the divine word"—that is, the tenets of the Christian faith—are held firmly by "those who think aright and who are concerned with genuine merit." It simply cannot be helped, he indicates, if non-Christians refuse to come to the truth for salvation: "If any prevents himself from being cured, let him not blame it on someone else, for the healing power of medicines is set out, spread openly to all."

Here Constantine intimates a doctrine of tolerance for those foolish enough to refuse the healing salve provided by Christ. But he goes on to insist explicitly on toleration for those who choose to continue practicing pagan cults:

> Let no one use what he has received by inner conviction as a means to harm his neighbor. What each has seen and understood, he must use, if possible, to help the other; but if that is impossible, the matter should be dropped. It is one thing to take on willingly the contest for immortality, quite another to enforce it with sanctions. (*Life of Constantine* 2.6)

Constantine clearly and directly opposes the use of sanctions to enforce religious practices on those who are unwilling, or to disallow practices. His own comments show that Harold Drake, a leading expert on the reign of Constantine, is probably right: Constantine opted for persuasion, not coercion.

CONSTANTINE THE IMPERIOUS EMPEROR

That should not be taken to mean that Constantine was soft in his rule of the empire. Roman social historian Ramsay MacMullen has raised the question of what practical difference it made to the empire that the emperor became Christian.[20] Working through the legislation found in the Theodosian Code, one finds penalties enacted by Constantine that reveal clearly his "judicial savagery." It is true that most of these laws were meant to promote social decency and to advance basic principles of morality. But the punishments! Imperial bureaucrats who accepted bribes were to have their hands cut off (Theodosian Code 1.16.7); ineffective guardians of girls who had been seduced were to have molten lead poured down their throats (Theodosian Code 9.24.1); tax collectors who treated women tax delinquents rudely were to "be done to death with exquisite tortures"; anyone who served as an informer was to be strangled and "the tongue of envy cut off from its roots plucked out (Theodosian Code 10.10.2); slaves who informed on their masters were to be crucified (Theodosian Code 9.5.1.1); anyone guilty of parricide "shall not be subjected to the sword or to fire or to any other customary penalty, but he shall be sewed in a leather sack, and, confined within its deadly closeness, he shall share the companionship of serpents" and then thrown into a river or ocean "so that while still alive he may begin to lose the enjoyment of all the elements" (Theodosian Code 9.15.1).

How is one to account for such judicial cruelty from a Christian emperor? MacMullen suggests that by the fourth century Christianity was revealing an increasingly cruel streak. He notes in particular the heightened popularity of the Christian literature we previously considered that delights in recounting in graphic detail the torments of hell for those who refuse to do God's will.[21] Possibly what applied to heaven applied to earth: If this is how God handles sin, then who are we to act differently? As MacMullen puts it: "Religious beliefs may have made judicial punishment specially aggressive, harsh, and ruthless."[22]

In a similar vein MacMullen also stressed one of the key differences between Christianity and traditional pagan religions that we too have already seen: the centrality of religious ethics. True, pagans were as a rule no more or less ethical than Christians. But in pagan circles ethical teachings fell under the province of philosophy, not religion, with rare exceptions, such as cases of parricide. For that reason pagan cults did not take a stand on matters of daily behavior or misbehavior. Not so Christianity. And that, MacMullen asserts, meant that strong Christian commitments among imperial powers led to harsher punishments for ethical misbehavior. In his words: "For pagans, only correct cult mattered. Christian zeal in contrast was directed over all of daily life. Hence, threats and torture, the stake and the block, spread over many new categories of offense."[23]

Constantine's harsh judgments did not fall only on anonymous inhabitants of his empire. They were felt by his own kin. We have already seen how, upon his accession to power, he had his ten-year-old nephew, the son of his rival Galerius, executed. More shocking still, and the source of considerable puzzlement, were the deaths, possibly on his orders, of his eldest son, Crispus, and his wife, Fausta.

Constantine had four sons, the first, Crispus, with Minervina (possibly his concubine), and the other three with his wife, Fausta, daughter of the emperor Maximian, whom he had married in 307 CE. As a young man—we are not certain of the year of his birth—Crispus was made a junior emperor, or Caesar. This was in 317 CE. He became an entrusted officer in Constantine's military and played a key role in several armed conflicts, most notably as a leader of the naval forces in the defeat of Licinius in 324 CE. But two years later, in July 326, both he and his stepmother died under mysterious circumstances, one after the other. Their deaths were obviously connected. Crispus was either murdered or executed on order of the emperor; soon thereafter Fausta suffered a grisly fate, cooked to death in a steam bath overheated for the occasion.[24]

Attempts to explain the two deaths go back to ancient times. The sixth-century pagan historian Zosimus and the twelfth-century Zonaras both provide salacious details. In the fuller version, Fausta attempted to seduce her stepson, only to be repudiated. In her fury she accused him of attempted rape, and Constantine had him executed. When he later found the accusation was false, he ordered for her a particularly gruesome execution.

Many modern historians doubt the story. But Noel Lenski points out that Constantine did have a highly moralistic streak (see the legislation above) and that he was especially averse to adultery. So Lenski supposes that "there may then be a kernel of truth in this pagan version."[25]

On the other hand, Timothy Barnes, one of the most prolific and controversial modern scholars of Constantine, has worked out an alternative scenario, less sexy, equally speculative, but entirely plausible. He begins by arguing that Crispus was indeed executed on order of the emperor. But since none of our sources reveals the charges, Barnes concludes there must not have been a public trial. It was a private affair carried out by Constantine himself, "with only his most trusted advisers present." Fausta, on the other hand, could not have been executed. Emperors, including Constantine, never resorted to massively overheated steam baths for their executions. What, then?

Barnes considers but rejects the various options, including an even more titillating theory that Crispus and Fausta had in fact consummated a tryst. When she unintentionally became pregnant, he was executed and she attempted to facilitate an abortion through the excessive heat of a steam room, inadvertently dying in the process.[26] But Barnes is not convinced. There is no real evidence for sexual misconduct, and there are other plausible and far more common reasons for an emperor to execute a son who was the future claimant to the throne. Barnes thinks Fausta told Constantine that Crispus was planning a coup, inventing the story so as to remove the heir to the throne and make way for one of her own sons. Constantine responded as tyrants do: he had his son executed. But then Constantine's mother, Helena, informed him of Fausta's insidious plot. Rather than face what would surely be a gruesome execution, Fausta committed suicide in a steam bath. It may not have been the most sensible choice, but frantic people are not always rational.

We will never know what really happened or why. It is one of the many puzzling episodes of Constantine's relatively well-documented reign.

THE DEATH OF CONSTANTINE

For some historians of antiquity, the most telling aspect of Constantine's final days is his decision to wait until the last minute to be baptized. Would he have done so if he had really been a Christian for twenty-five years? As we have already seen, however, not only would Christians conceivably delay baptism; they often did so. Constantine's own son, the vigorously Christian Constantius II, who was theologically Arian, did the same thing. The afterlife was much safer for those with no time to commit post-baptismal sins before arriving at the Pearly Gates. And so they both delayed.

Less puzzling is the sequence of events leading up to Constantine's demise. Throughout his long reign, Constantine had to deal with the problems of foreign invasion. In 337 CE, when the Persians began to flex their expansionist muscles in the East, Constantine decided once more to lead his armies to the frontier. Conveniently for his purposes, the march would take him north of Palestine, allowing him to make a detour en route to be baptized in the Jordan River, just like Jesus himself. Constantine knew he was on his last legs. But his legs were not destined to last even that long. Constantine took ill soon after beginning the journey and was forced to stop in Nicomedia, in the western part of what is now Turkey. There he called in the bishop of Nicomedia and was baptized on his deathbed. He died on May 22, 337. His sons were to take over the reins of the empire, and the Constantinian dynasty would last to 363 CE.

THE CHRISTIAN EMPEROR CONSTANTINE: IN SUM

In summing up the rule of Constantine, it is simplest to begin by again emphasizing what Constantine did not do, contrary to what many people have thought and some scholars have argued. He did not make Christianity the official state religion of the Roman Empire. He almost certainly would not have objected to doing so had he been in a position to make it happen, but that was not the case. If our numbers are correct, no more than four million of the empire's sixty million inhabitants shared his religious preference when he himself converted to the Christian faith. He was vastly outnumbered and it probably never occurred to him to legislate Christianity for all his subjects.

On the contrary, Constantine had no mission to convert the masses of pagans who continued to follow traditional religious practices. He remained remarkably open to those of other persuasions, especially to those who, like his father, embraced some kind of pagan henotheism. He was content to practice Christianity himself, to support and promote the activities of the church, to intervene in ecclesiastical affairs when issues of unity arose, to fund the building of churches, and to provide social and economic advantages to Christian clergy. It may have been his duty to be Christian, in some sense, as an emperor, but it was not his duty to proscribe pagan practices, shut down large numbers of temples throughout the empire, or prohibit the practice of sacrifice, even though he personally detested it.[27]

During Constantine's reign, Christianity was certainly a favored religion, and it probably did not require extraordinary intelligence for members of the imperial elite to realize that converting to the faith would not hurt their chances for advancement. This was especially true for elites who were then tabbed for official church service, given the economic privileges enjoyed by the Christian clergy. In any event, most of the pressure Constantine applied came through acts of persuasion, either overt or subtle, but not through force.

This much we can say about what Constantine did not do. Obviously more important is what he did do. He certainly converted to worship the Christian god alone in 312 CE, in connection with the battle at the Milvian Bridge, even if it took a long time to realize fully what it meant to embrace the Christian faith. Still, this was a genuine conversion. At that point Constantine dedicated himself to honoring and obeying the god of the Christians. He did not do so with complete success, if being a faithful Christian means loving your enemies and turning the other cheek. Then again, he was not the sort of figure Jesus would have envisioned while preaching in rural Galilee. Constantine was an emperor with enormous burdens and responsibilities. Harsh legislation and the occasional ruthless act were all part of the job.

Possibly the most important thing Constantine did for the future of the religion is that he saw that his sons were raised in the Christian tradition in preparation for what was to come next. The Tetrarchic experiment of Diocletian had died nearly as soon as its policy of meritorious succession was carried out. Constantine returned to the dynastic principle that emperors had regularly followed, or tried to follow, since the early days of the empire. In his case, that meant succession would come to Christians. With the exception of the nineteen-month reign of Constantine's nephew, Julian, in 361 to 363 CE, every remaining Roman emperor was Christian.

Constantine also set an important precedent in his decision to intervene in ecclesiastical affairs. His intervention makes perfect sense in a Roman imperial context. All of Constantine's predecessors had been the chief priest, the *pontifex maximus*, of the religions of Rome—as was he, despite the fact he was a Christian. The Roman emperor, like the Roman state, was not removed from the religious sphere but was at the very center of it. And so, even though he was a complete neophyte, a theological child, Constantine thrust himself into matters of Christian polity and theology. A unified church was important for a unified empire. And a disunified church—or at least parts of it—obviously failed to carry out the will of the God over all. That could lead to disaster. Constantine entered into the fray with what might look like wild and naïve abandon, but his decision to do so makes sense both politically and theologically.

These interventions may have seemed good and natural at the time, but they were to have a domino effect in the years and decades to come. If emperors actively dictated the direction of religion in the empire, and of the church in particular, what might happen when the Roman world experienced a sea change, when the Christians overtook the pagan majority, and when there was no longer any real fear of massive uprisings or reprisals against the Christian cause? What might happen should emperors more aggressive than Constantine arise—rulers with no qualms about using the power of state to promote the purposes of faith?

It was almost bound to happen. By the end of the fourth century the first Christian emperor's decision to prefer persuasion to coercion had become a thing of the past. Christianity was declared the state religion. Traditional pagan practices were proscribed, temples were leveled, and sacred cult objects and art were destroyed.

Chapter 9

Conversion and Coercion:
The Beginnings of a Christian Empire

T he most significant Christianization of the Roman world occurred throughout the course of the fourth century. The massive conversions over this period—as the church grew from two or three million to something like thirty million—do not mean that the rate of Christian growth increased; on the contrary, it slowed considerably. That is the miracle of an exponential curve: once the raw numbers start to increase, they snowball.

One major reason the rate of growth must have decreased is that new additions to the faith left fewer persons to convert. Still, even as the rate of conversion slowed, the ease of conversion increased. It became easier and easier to become a Christian. With Constantine the persecutions had ended. No longer was conversion dangerous to life and limb. On the contrary, the emperor himself claimed allegiance to the church; more people were joining the Christian ranks daily; church buildings were being constructed; members of the elite were starting to convert.

A shift of religious commitments could be so propitious that we have records of fake conversions. The biographer of Constantine, the church father Eusebius, mentions people who converted in order to take advantage of the benefactions coming to the Christians from the emperor himself (*Life of Constantine* 4.54.2). The pagan orator Libanius maintains that coercive means of conversion led to phantom Christians: "If [the Christians] tell you that some other people have been converted by such [forceful] measures and now share their religious beliefs, do not overlook the fact that they speak of conversions apparent, not real. Their converts have not really been changed—they only say they have" (Oration 30.28). The bishop of Milan, Ambrose, mentions pagans who converted to raise their stock with Christian women with whom they had a love interest.[1]

The bulk of the conversions, however, were certainly real. Most people turned to the Christian faith because they had become convinced of its message and looked forward to the divine benefits that could be provided by the Christian god. Once a family converted, the children would be raised Christian, and at that point, just in familial terms, no conversions were needed. That was true of most of the imperial families who came in the wake of Constantine, beginning with his own sons and heirs. They were Christian from infancy.

Emperors after Constantine—with the one exception of his nephew Julian—publicly declared their commitment to the Christian god, promoted the Christian religion, and with increasing frequency openly opposed traditional pagan cults with their practices of sacrifice. But there was no one moment when the world stopped being pagan to become Christian, no single breaking point. Most of the inhabitants of the empire did not perceive that they were in the midst of a momentous shift or that anything like a life-and-death struggle—a fight to the finish for the soul of paganism—was occurring around them. Most people were pagan up until the end of the fourth century, and many continued to be pagan well beyond that. For the majority of the population, theological questions and religious allegiances were probably not overwhelmingly important, even if they did matter a great deal to a number of people in power, all the way up to the emperor.

Even among these powerful elites one could find a large range of religious commitments, both pagan and Christian. As historian of late antiquity Peter Brown has argued, even into the 390s "polytheism, in fact, remained prevalent on all levels of East Roman society."[2] Indeed, if pagans kept to themselves, they were for the most part left alone, unmolested, despite the legislation issued against their practices and the occasional acts of violence that occurred. But legislation did appear and violence did sometimes raise its ugly head as the shift from pagan to Christian occurred, especially in the high reaches of government, with the emergence of Christian emperors far more vocal and forceful in their religious views than Constantine had been.

THE SONS OF CONSTANTINE

Constantine's father, Constantius, became Caesar of the West in 293 CE and then senior Augustus in the imperial college with the abdication of Maximian in 305 CE. His dynasty was to last seventy years, until the death of Constantine's nephew Julian in 363 CE.[3]

It was not a peaceful and closely knit family, as seen nowhere more clearly than in the vicious bloodbath that occurred after Constantine's death on May 22, 337, with the event known as "the massacre of the princes." Constantine's three remaining sons—Constantius II, Constans, and Constantine II (the eldest Crispus having been executed earlier)—were to divide his empire among themselves, but there were eleven other male relatives who could, in theory, have a stake in the succession and for that reason could be seen as a threat to those already in power. Almost immediately upon the emperor's death, nine of these were summarily murdered in cold blood—all except two young boys, Gallus and Julian, Constantine's nephews.

Later in life, Julian named Constantius II as the culprit for the slaughter, and he was probably right. Constantius II was the first son to arrive in Constantinople after Constantine's death and he had command of the military who carried out the executions. With no rivals, the three sons then divided the empire among themselves, with Constans ruling over Italy, North Africa, and Illyricum; Constantine II over Gaul, Spain, and Britain; and Constantius II over Thrace and the eastern provinces.

The three did not rule harmoniously. In 340 CE, Constantine II attempted to wrest Italy from the control of his younger brother Constans, but died in battle. A decade later, in 350 CE, Constans himself was murdered by a usurper. After putting down the usurper, Constantius II then survived as sole ruler. Four years earlier Constantius II had elevated his cousin Gallus to the rank of Caesar, but in 354 he had him executed because of a suspected coup. And so, just seventeen years after Constantine's death, of the fourteen male relatives alive at the time, only two remained: the emperor and his young cousin Julian.

All this lust for power and loss of life may make the post-Constantinian imperial court look somewhat less than Christian. But imperial support for the church grew as the blood flowed. Constantius II himself became an outspoken and even vehement proponent of the Christian tradition. Unlike his father, he was committed to the theological views of the Arians that had been denounced at the Council of Nicaea. Numerous internecine Christian controversies occurred during his reign, but more important for our purposes is the heightened anti-paganism. Constantius II ordered pagan temples closed and sacrificial practices stopped.

We have already seen a law issued in 341 CE: "Superstition shall cease; the madness of sacrifices shall be abolished" in accordance with "the law of the sainted Emperor, Our father." Anyone "who performs sacrifices . . . shall suffer the infliction of a suitable punishment and the effect of an immediate sentence" (Theodosian Code 16.10.2). In a law of 346 CE, the penalties are specified: Temples "in all places and in all cities" are to be "immediately closed" and "access to them forbidden." No one may perform a sacrifice. Anyone who does "shall be struck down with the avenging sword" and his "property shall be confiscated." Any governor who fails to avenge such crimes "shall be similarly punished" (Theodosian Code 16.10.4); and perhaps more drastically, later in Constantius's reign, in 356: "Anyone who sacrifices or worships images shall be executed" (Theodosian Code 16.10.6).

These laws were directed to specific locales, not empire-wide, and there existed no state apparatus to ensure they were carried out.

As a result, they had but little effect: paganism continued, unchecked in most places. But the laws do show the will of the emperor, and this would not have gone unnoticed. Conversions away from paganism continued apace. There was, however, one major hiccup in the triumphal march of the Christian church. It came after Constantius's death with the brief rule of his cousin Julian.

THE LAST PAGAN EMPEROR

Julian probably escaped the massacre of the princes because he was just a six-year-old at the time.[4] Constantius II appears to have seen him as a potential successor to the throne and made him his ward. For the next eighteen years Constantius II kept him out of public view, under careful scrutiny but at arm's length. Much of Julian's young life and virtually all of his education were in isolation.

By 355 CE, barbarian invasions into Gaul had become a major problem, but Constantius II himself was occupied in the East, defending the borders from the Persians. So he appointed the completely inexperienced Julian as Caesar to deal with problems in the West. In his later writings Julian claimed he was granted no real power along with his title, but that appears not to be true. On the contrary, even though completely lacking in military field experience, he did have a good bit of textbook knowledge. Remarkably enough, it appears to have stood him in good stead. Julian had studied the commentaries of Julius Caesar in his military endeavors, and used what he learned to significant effect.

By the end of 358 CE, Julian's military prowess was evident to all, including the suspicious Constantius II, who kept a close watch lest his cousin's success in the field should translate into political ambition. The breakdown in relations occurred in 360 CE. Constantius II was experiencing increasing problems with the Persians, while the situation in the West had significantly calmed. He directed his cousin to transfer to him a massive number of troops, over a third or possibly even a half of Julian's entire army. Those western troops, many of them from Gaul, were not happy with the order, and responded by declaring their own commander Augustus. It is not clear whether this was a spontaneous and unexpected act, as Julian himself later claimed, or whether he himself had orchestrated it. In either event, since the acclamation became known to Constantius II, the two stood at irreconcilable odds. Civil war was the only option. Julian marched to confront his cousin, but as fate would have it, Constantius II died unexpectedly before he arrived, at the age of forty-four.

Julian spent his first six months as emperor in Constantinople, and then nine unhappy and turbulent months in Antioch, before marching against the Persians. He was killed early in the conflict, having ruled the empire for a mere nineteen months. It was an eventful year and a half, however, especially for pagan-Christian relations. Upon ascending to the throne, Julian declared he had converted to paganism years earlier. (The very fact that he could understand paganism as a "religion" to which he could even convert shows just how much had changed by this time.)[5] He made it one of his goals to reinstate traditional pagan sacrificial practices throughout the empire. That required him to suppress the burgeoning Christian movement.

We do not know why, exactly, Julian became such a passionate devotee of pagan traditions. We do know that as a studious young man, in addition to reading Christian literature, he devoured the pagan classics and was drawn to the moral world they portrayed. Moreover, his bad experience with Christians may have made the difference. His ardent Christian cousin Constantius II had arranged for the murder of all his male relatives.

In some ways Julian's passionate devotion to the pagan cause was driven by a now-familiar motivation: he indicates that the gods "say they will give rewards for our labors, if we do not grow slack."[6] He certainly was not slack. At the beginning of his reign he reopened pagan temples, restored pagan rites, and declared universal religious tolerance. More famous than these positive steps to rejuvenate traditional religion were the negative measures he took to strangle Christianity. Julian had no intention of persecuting Christians, imprisoning them, or making them martyrs. He was a good enough student of history to know how badly that would go. But he did rescind many of the benefits afforded Christians by his predecessors and reversed several of their policies.[7]

Some of his actions were subtle. For example, his Arian cousin Constantius II had exiled a number of Christian leaders who did not toe the Arian theological line that he preferred. Julian brought them back from exile. This appears not to have been an act of tolerance; on the contrary, it was almost certainly an attempt to weaken the church by reintroducing vehemently opposed spokespersons back into communities that had earlier been rid of them. A disunified Christian movement posed far fewer problems to a pagan resurgence than a unified front.

Less subtly, Julian eliminated privileges accorded to Christian clergy since the time of his uncle Constantine: no longer were they exempt from participating in civil life or contributing their wealth to municipal causes. This move satisfied two needs: it weakened the elite clergy by draining a good bit of their resources, and it strengthened the governance of the cities. It also, of course, brought funds from the church into the municipal coffers.

Julian sometimes refused to provide justice for Christian leaders. In December 361 an Arian bishop named George was murdered by a pagan mob in Alexandria, Egypt. When Christians howled their objections, Julian chose not to penalize the culprits and explained why: he considered George "an enemy of the gods."[8] Julian would not order the deaths of Christian leaders, but he would not object to them either.

Possibly most insidious of all was an edict Julian published on June 17, 362, proscribing Christian instructors from teaching the pagan classics to schoolboys. Julian's logic was that no one should teach what they did not believe; moreover, Christians were unqualified to teach the classics because they were themselves morally deficient. Christian teachers were given a choice: they could either acknowledge the gods or resign their positions. This policy may seem relatively benign but in fact it was unusually clever. No longer could Christians teach the principal subjects of instruction: grammar, rhetoric, and philosophy. That meant the next generation of elites would be trained exclusively by pagans. As ancient historian

Glen Bowersock points out: "Julian knew perfectly well what he was doing. Within little more than a generation the educated elite of the empire would be pagan."[9]

In trying to devise steps to increase the attractiveness of the pagan traditions, Julian strove to make changes, particularly in light of what he considered to be the greatest appeal of the Christian tradition—its social programs: "Do we not observe that what has most of all fostered the growth of atheism [i.e., Christianity] is humanity towards strangers, forethought in regard to the burial of the dead, and an affectation of dignity in one's life? Each of these ought, in my opinion, to be cultivated genuinely by us."[10] To provide pagan counterparts, Julian set up guesthouses in cities and free distribution of wheat and wine to the poor. Clearly these policies were not simply driven by a good-hearted nature. They were an attempt to attract converts back into paganism and thus decimate the ranks of the Christians.

Among the many pieces of ancient literature that we greatly regret no longer having is a book, or possibly a series of books, that Julian himself wrote to attack Christianity. The work is commonly called *Against the Galileans*, and unfortunately it survives only in fragments quoted by a later Christian author, Cyril of Alexandria, in an effort to refute it. Julian was particularly well positioned to attack Christians, their theology, and their Scriptures. He had been raised a Christian himself and had been an active participant in the Christian churches even during the years when he was, for political reasons, disguising the fact that in his heart he was a pagan. Yet even as a pagan emperor he knew it was better to attack the Christian movement through words and arguments than through harsh measures of persecution. From his uncle Constantine he had learned to promote his views through persuasion rather than coercion. Many of his successors took a different view.

CHRISTIANITY AS THE STATE RELIGION

When Julian was killed in a poorly conceived and even more poorly executed battle with the Persians on June 26, 363, he was succeeded by Jovian, one of his military commanders. Jovian and every Roman emperor who followed him were Christian. Many of these successors were quite vehement in the public affirmation of their Christian commitments and their resistance to traditional pagan religions. Arguably the most forceful in his views was Theodosius I, also known as "the Great," who ruled from 379 to 395 CE and who was responsible for making Christianity, for all intents and purposes, the official state religion of the Roman Empire.

Theodosius was born to a military commander, also named Theodosius, who served under the emperor Valentinian I but was executed in 376 CE, apparently for crimes against the state. Two years later Theodosius was elevated to one of the top military positions in the army, and in 379 CE made Augustus. As with other emperors, much of his reign involved military exploits, but what matters more for our purposes is his passionate commitment to the cause of Christianity. By the time he assumed the highest office, Christianity had grown massively, with converts arriving in droves. Theodosius sought to continue the trend. Early in his reign he provided a major disincentive for anyone inclined to revert to paganism: an apostate from Christianity would not be allowed to make a will. That is to say, anyone who de-converted could not pass on any worldly property to heirs. Moreover any apostate who already had a will was to have it nullified (Theodosian Code, 16.7.1; passed in 381 CE).

Theodosius issued legislation that proscribed sacrifices, divination, and the use of temples to those ends (Theodosian Code 16.10.7; passed in 381 CE). In the most comprehensive law to date, he directed that "no person shall pollute himself with sacrificial animals; no person shall slaughter an innocent victim; no person shall approach the shrines, shall wander through the temples, or revere the images formed by mortal labor, lest he become guilty by divine and human laws" (Theodosian Code 16.10.10; passed in 391 CE). The law further stipulated that any judge who participated in worship in a pagan temple would be fined fifteen pounds of gold; governors of consular rank and their staff members who did so would be fined six pounds of gold. Nearly two years later came a law prohibiting pagan cults of any kind, even in the privacy of one's home: "No person at all, or any class or order whatsoever . . . shall sacrifice an innocent victim to senseless images in any place at all or in any city. He shall not, by more secret wickedness, venerate his Lar with fire, his genius with wine, his Penates with fragrant odors; he shall not burn lights to them, place incense before them, or suspend wreaths for them." The penalties were stiff—confiscation of property and large fines—as were the penalties for judges who connived in cases of violation: they would be fined thirty pounds of gold (Theodosian Code 16.10.12).

Equally important for the question of religion in the empire is the particular kind of Christianity that Theodosius promoted. Unlike some of his predecessors, he virulently opposed Arian Christians and vehemently advocated the kind of orthodox Christianity that had emerged from the Council of Nicaea. Thus we have a law issued early in his reign: "It is Our will that all the peoples who are ruled by the administration of Our Clemency shall practice that religion which the divine Peter the Apostle transmitted to the Romans. . . . That is, according to the apostolic discipline and the evangelic doctrine, we shall believe in the single Deity of the Father, the Son, and the Holy Spirit, under the concept of equal majesty and of the Holy Trinity" (Theodosian Code 16.1.2). Nicene orthodox was to be the law of the land. That did not bode well for pagans.

It might seem that such legislation would settle the matter once and for all. The empire was now Christian. Nicene Christian. In one sense that may have been true, but the reality on the ground was much different. We have repeatedly seen that Roman law was not like laws of modern developed countries, where national legislation applies to everyone, with set penalties enforced in more or less the same way everywhere. The empire was enormous and each region, each province, each city, each smaller locality, ran its affairs as well as it could. There were no national agencies that publicized, enacted, and enforced laws issued from the emperor. Many laws were never enforced at all, and many others were enforced with remarkable infrequency, depending on the time and place.

Moreover, as both pagan and Christian authors point out on various occasions, there was simply no way that a law could ensure personal religious convictions. In the days of Theodosius, most of the inhabitants of the empire were still pagan. Pagans continued their traditional practices as the occasion arose. No evidence suggests pagans were being forced to convert en masse. That raises the question that Christian leaders had to address: Should coercion at least be attempted? It is interesting to see how different Christians answered this question, depending on the context within which they lived. Early in the fourth century, Christians were almost uniformly in favor of complete freedom of religion and, like the apologists before them, opposed efforts by the pagan state to force them to recant their faith. Toward the end of the century we find outspoken representatives opposing freedom of religion and arguing that the state should exercise its powers to force pagans to convert to Christianity against their will. It would not be the last time a group recently come to power flipped its position on an important issue.

CHRISTIAN COERCION

The Christian scholar Lactantius, one of our primary sources for the Great Persecution under Diocletian, was an early-fourth-century proponent of freedom of religion. Lactantius was raised pagan and trained in the classics. He became a well-known rhetorician and was appointed to be a professor of Latin rhetoric by Diocletian. Sometime after he converted to Christianity in 300 CE, Lactantius was deprived of his position; late in life he was appointed by Constantine to be the tutor of his son Crispus.

One of Lactantius's most famous literary works is called the *Divine Institutes*. This was written during the Great Persecution for Christianity's cultured despisers, who, among other things, cast aspersions on the inferior literary quality of the Christian Scriptures. Lactantius's defense of the faith was the most learned apology produced by a Christian to date, and included not only reasoned arguments for the superiority of the religion but also a plea for administrative tolerance.

Lactantius argues that "there is no need of force and injury, because religion cannot be forced. It is a matter that must be managed by words rather than by blows, so that it may be voluntary." Moreover, religious violence has only the opposite of its desired effect; echoing the claims of Tertullian from over a century earlier, Lactantius insists that "the religion of God is increased the more it is oppressed." Christians, Lactantius maintains, never try to compel anyone to accept their religion against their will. That is because "truth cannot be joined with force nor justice with cruelty." For that reason, "those who destroy religions ought to be punished."[11]

That Christian tune was soon to change in some circles—not all, obviously. A stark contrast to Lactantius's appeal for tolerance comes in an equally passionate plea for forced conversions in the writings of a Christian scholar named Firmicus Maternus produced just some thirty-five years later, no longer under the rule of the pagan Diocletian but under the joint rule of the Christian sons of Constantine, Constantius II and Constans.[12]

Like Lactantius, Firmicus was a convert from paganism. Two of his books have come down to us, one a work on astrology written while he was still a pagan (around 335 CE), the other a forceful Christian apology from ten or fifteen years later. In the apology he condemns the traditional religions he once practiced, demonizing them and asking Constantius II and Constans to do everything in their power to suppress them. His final plea to the emperors is chilling in its violent urgency: "But on you also, Most Holy Emperors, devolves the imperative necessity to castigate and punish this evil [pagan religion], and the law of the Supreme Deity enjoins on you that your severity should be visited in every way on the crime of idolatry."[13]

He goes on to explain that Scripture itself demands the forceful destruction of pagan worship, quoting Deuteronomy 13:6–10, which says:

> If anyone secretly entices you—even if it is your brother, your father's son or your mother's son, or your own son or daughter, or the wife you embrace, or your most intimate friend—saying, "Let us go worship other gods," whom neither you nor your ancestors have known, any of the gods of the peoples that are around you . . . you must not yield or heed, any such person. Show them no pity or compassion and do not shield them. But you shall surely kill them; your own hand shall be first against them to execute them, and afterwards the hand of all the people. Stone them to death for trying to turn you away from the Lord your God.

Pitiless words that provide no exception clause. God directs his faithful to murder anyone who promotes the worship of other gods, even their own sons, daughters, or spouses. And not just relatives but whole populations. Quoting another passage in Deuteronomy, Firmicus stresses: "Even for whole cities, if they are caught in this crime, destruction is decreed: 'Killing you shall slay all who are in the city with the death of the sword, and shall burn the city with fire.'" Because God himself directs rulers to slaughter those opposed to him, Firmicus makes a final terse injunction: "Therefore do what he bids, fulfill what he commands" (*Error of the Pagan Religions* 29). In other words, he tells the emperors: Kill the pagans.

This level of violent intolerance is not found everywhere in the Christian tradition of the mid- to late fourth century, any more than in the pagan tradition decades earlier, before the conversion of Constantine. In both periods sincerely devout people, both pagan and Christian, lowly citizens and powerful governmental officials, supported religious nonviolence, freedom of religion, and tolerance. Thus, one of the leading Christian theologians of the fourth century, Gregory of Nazianzus, bishop of Constantinople, writing somewhat after Firmicus's day, said quite plainly: "I do not consider it good practice to coerce people instead of persuading them."[14]

THE TERMS OF THE DISCUSSION

It is impossible to know which side of the tolerance-intolerance divide most Christians occupied. We simply have no record of the views of 99.9 percent of the Christian world at the time. Even so, the intolerant strain within Christianity took on a new cast when Christian leaders appeared with political power at their disposal and the will to use it in order to impose their religious preferences on others.

It should be clear from everything I have said that religious intolerance is not the same thing as exclusivity. Exclusivity involves the commitment to adhere to only one particular set of religious beliefs and practices. Throughout history, large numbers of people have held exclusive views and commitments without insisting they had the one and only path to truth. In Roman antiquity most Jews were both exclusivist when it came to themselves and tolerant of those outside their Jewish community.

Intolerance is a different matter. It is the principled rejection of other beliefs and practices as wrong, dangerous, or both. One might unreflectively consider intolerance merely a particularly virulent offshoot of strict exclusivity, but it patently is not that, for the simple reason that adherents of more inclusive traditions such as Roman paganism were also sometimes intolerant, as the worshipers of Bacchus and the followers of Christ both discovered with exquisite clarity.

In those cases the intolerance involved violent suppression. But there is no reason that intolerance needs to produce violence: it can just as well involve a purely mental state. However, when it does turn violent, and when that violence is designed not only to penalize but also to convert—that is, to change the victim's religious views and practices by force—that would be coercion. Both pagans and Christians were guilty of attempted coercion in antiquity, with some late-fourth-century Christians engaging in acts of violent intolerance that their parents in the faith would have abhorred just decades earlier.

ACTS OF CHRISTIAN INTOLERANCE

When enacting religious violence, Christians could claim to be following the injunctions of Scripture, as Firmicus Maternus and others pointed out, including the terse command of Exodus 34:13–14: "You shall tear down their altars, break their pillars, and cut down their sacred poles, for you shall worship no other god, because the LORD, whose name is Jealous, is a jealous God." Luckily for pagans, only rarely were the requirements of Deuteronomy 17:2–5 followed and idolaters executed by the community. But pagan practices were disrupted, temples closed, and cult statues destroyed. Not everywhere, and possibly not in most places. But in some times and some places. Acts of violence occasionally came through state officials but more frequently on the local level as Christians exercised their newly won power in full awareness of the religious proclivities of the ultimate authorities.

In an enlightening if sometimes disheartening recent study, Troels Myrup Kristensen recounts numerous instances of Christian violence against pagan sites and objects.[15] A particularly intriguing example comes from an archaeological discovery made in 1904 in the city of Ephesus, an inscription on the base of a statue of the city protectress, the goddess Artemis. The inscription reads: "Having destroyed a deceitful image of demonic Artemis, Demeas set up this sign of truth, honoring both God, the driver-away of idol, and the cross, that victory-bringing immortal symbol of Christ."[16]

What this otherwise unknown man Demeas had done was destroy the statue of the goddess and replaced it with a (probably wooden) cross, which itself has not survived the ravages of time. Did he expect that by destroying the statue he had robbed the goddess of her power? That he had driven away the demon? Throughout Ephesus, other statues were defaced and the name of Artemis erased from inscriptions. In Kristensen's words: "It would seem that Demeas's response was rather typical of his time, and erasure of images and inscriptions an ordinary method of publicly denouncing paganism and calling forth a new Christian image."[17]

Throughout the empire one can find numerous cult statues not merely destroyed but systematically defaced, subject to bodily mutilation. These mutilations deliver an obvious message. By removing the statue's eyes, ears, mouth, and nose the Christian antagonist showed in graphic terms that the pagan god could not see, hear, speak, or sense in any way. Hands were lopped off to show the god could not do anything; genitals were mutilated to show it could provide no fertility. The ideology behind such mutilations goes back to biblical times. In the Hebrew Bible we read that idols "have mouths, but they speak not; eyes have they, but they see not; they have ears, but they hear not; neither is there any breath in their mouths" (Psalm 135:16–17).

But Christian attacks were not limited to destruction. There was also the matter of replacement. Demeas replaced Artemis with a cross. Sometimes Christians who mutilated a statue then scratched the sign of the cross on its forehead. Now the pagan idol had become a witness to Christ. So too with sacred buildings. Christians built a church within the temple precinct of Artemis in Ephesus, allowing them to usurp "one of the most revered pagan cultic places in Asia Minor."[18]

At other times, statues were simply desacralized, moved from cultic sites and redeployed as objects of art, as seen with Constantine's decoration of his New Rome and as poetically embraced by the Christian author Prudentius (348–413 CE):

Of bloody sacrifices cleansed
The marble altars then will gleam
And statues honored now as gods
Will stand, mere harmless blocks of bronze.[19]

Violence against pagan sacred places and objects became increasingly pronounced during the reign of Theodosius I. Even though the laws he passed against pagan practices and the cultic use of pagan temples lacked empire-wide enforcement clauses, they had their effect because of both imperial action and local acts of violence.

Most famous from the imperial level was the energetic mission of one of Theodosius's most high-ranking officials, the Spaniard Maternus Cynegius, dispatched to the eastern provinces to close temples. Cynegius did not have a systematic plan of attack; he visited important sites and with military backing shut down sacred shrines. In some ways, more important than his sporadic actions was the precedent he set. Some scholars think his incendiary activities promoted the mob violence decried especially by Libanius, the pagan rhetorician we met earlier. If anything, local turbulence proved more destructive than official imperial actions.

This much is suggested in one of Libanius's surviving orations, addressed to Theodosius as a plea to bring a halt to marauding monks who had run wild among pagan religious sites, bringing destruction in their wake. These unruly and uneducated Christians, robed in black, were wreaking vengeance on sacred temples:

> This black-robed tribe, who eat more than elephants and, by the quantities of drink they consume, weary those that accompany their drinking with the singing of hymns . . . hasten to attack the temples with sticks and stones and bars of iron, and in some cases, disdaining these, with hands and feet. Then utter desolation follows, with the stripping of roofs, demolition of walls, the tearing down of statues and the overthrow of altars, and the priests must either keep quiet or die. After demolishing one, they scurry to another, and to a third, and trophy is piled on trophy, in contravention of the law. (Oration 30.8–9)

The monks did more than destroy property: "I forebear to mention the numbers they have murdered in their riotings in utter disregard of the name they share" (Oration 30.20). But the major damage was done to sacred sites: "In estate after estate, shrine after shrine has been wiped out by their insolence, violence, greed, and deliberate lack of self-control" (Oration 3.21). Country shrines "great and small alike, in which the weary used to find repose, have all been demolished" (Oration 30.24).

From other sources we learn that where pillaging monks destroyed, Christian bishops appropriated, taking over pagan holy sites and making them Christian, baptizing them, as it were, into the new faith. In addition to the temple of Artemis in Ephesus were the "Pan-Hellenic temples" in Achaea, called this because they served not merely their own localities but all of Greece. Most of these major sacred sites actively sponsored pagan celebrations at the end of the third century, but two hundred years later, in the words of Amelia Robertson Brown, "every major sanctuary in Achaea contained at least one Christian basilica."[20] Sometimes this appropriation of pagan holy sites for the Christian cause involved other forms of profanation as well, as in the case of the sanctuary of Zeus in Gaza. When the site was destroyed in 402, the Christian bishop Porphyry used blocks from the temple to pave the atrium of the new church, so that they would be walked over not only by Christian worshipers but also by the dogs and swine. In the words of Porphyry's biographer: "This pained the idolaters more than the burning of the temple."[21]

As with Libanius, many of the pained idolaters lodged official protests, but usually to no avail. In the early fifth century, the most prestigious pagan temple in the city of Carthage was converted into a church. Pagans erupted in protest. The imperial officials dealt with the problem by having the place destroyed.

VIOLENCE IN ALEXANDRIA

To wrap up this brief catalog of violent intolerance, I focus on two incidents that occurred in the city of Alexandria, Egypt. Both left a black eye on the Christian cause. The first involved the destruction of one of the great architectural structures of Roman antiquity, the other the murder of one of its great scholars.[22]

The Destruction of the Serapeum

The magnificent temple of the Egyptian god Serapis was known as the Serapeum. Ancient authors likened its glories to the Acropolis of Athens. It took a hundred steps from ground level to reach the site, on which were located lattice gates, enormous columns, stoas (long-roofed colonnades), and storehouses. The roofs of the stoas were made of gold. The capitals of the columns were in bronze and plated with gold. There were two stone obelisks on the site. In the words of one ancient author from the second half of the fourth century, "The beauty surpasses the telling." An anonymous writer of 359 CE maintained: "Nowhere in the world is found such a building or such an arrangement of a temple or such an arrangement of a religion."[23]

Our principal source of information for the destruction of the site is the Christian historian Rufinus, who had spent eight years in Alexandria (373–80 CE). He indicates that inside the temple building itself

> was an image of Serapis, so huge that its right hand was touching one wall, while its left touched another—a monstrous object said to have been made from all sorts of metals and woods. The interior walls of the shrine were covered at first by gold plates, then by silver plates above these, and finally by bronze plates to protect the more precious metals (*Church History* 11.23).[24]

Nothing suggests that either the official activities of Maternus Cygenius or the reckless violence of Christian monks played any role in the destruction of the Serapeum. It was a local affair, resulting from a series of accidents and missteps in 391 CE.[25] During the renovations of a basilica in Alexandria, workmen discovered an underground sanctuary, probably devoted to the god Mithras. Inside were sacred cult objects. The powerful bishop of Alexandria, Theophilus, decided to have these items publicly paraded through the marketplace in order to mock their religious significance and, by implication, the people who might have revered them. Many devout pagans were not amused.

They responded by attacking Christians and retreating into the Serapeum, which functioned as an enormous fortified structure.

From there they occasionally ventured out, taking Christians captive and forcing them to sacrifice on altars. Christians who refused were tortured to death, crucified, or thrown into caverns with their legs broken.

To resolve the standoff, an appeal was made to the emperor Theodosius, who responded by offering amnesty to the pagans holed up in the Serapeum but ordering, as well, the suppression of pagan cults. Out of fear of reprisal, the pagan instigators fled the site and escaped by merging with the crowds. Christian soldiers entered the precincts and decided to wreak damage in retribution. We are told that one went straight to the center of the temple to attack the statue of Serapis. At first he hesitated, aware of prophecies of divine retribution for anyone who dishonored the god. But he took courage, grabbed an axe, and struck the jaw of the statue. No supernatural vengeance ensued, and so the soldiers hacked the statue to pieces and took parts to different areas in the city to be burned. They incinerated the trunk of the statue in the public theater.

The bishop Theophilus converted some of the buildings of the Serapeum complex into churches; two of these were later made to house the alleged relics of John the Baptist and the prophet Elijah. The emperor Theodosius, rather than maligning the violation of the pagans' sacred space, issued an edict further restricting pagan activities: "No person shall be granted the right to perform sacrifices; no person shall go around the temples; no person shall revere the shrines. . . . [I]f any person should attempt to anything with reference to the gods or the sacred rites, contrary to Our prohibition, he shall learn that he will not be exempted from punishment by any special grants of imperial favor."[26]

The penalty clause is strikingly vague, but its intent is clear enough. Pagans were no longer allowed to practice their religions. What followed was a widespread destruction of other images of Serapis throughout the city. The head of the god was paraded around, while, in the words of one ancient Christian source, Christians "mocked the weakness of him to whom they had once bowed the knee."²⁷ As one modern historian has argued, "the violence of 391 proved to be the linchpin that initiated the downfall of public paganism throughout Egypt."²⁸ Usually the ensuing violence was not officially sanctioned, but, as another scholar has pointed out: "Providing that law and order was not unduly compromised, it was understood that the civil authorities would either turn a blind eye to the activities of the bishops, or even go so far as supply them with edicts to fit their requirements."²⁹

Destruction was not carried out systematically. When looked at in hindsight, pagan religions in Alexandria may have been on the defensive and in clear decline, but it was not yet the end. This is evident from the fact that another horrific act of violence occurred there twenty-four years later.

The Murder of Hypatia

Hypatia was that rarity of antiquity, a highly trained, well-known, and revered woman philosopher. Daughter of Theon, the most famous mathematician of the day, Hypatia was an expert in algebra, geometry, and astronomy, and was even more famous as a Neoplatonic philosopher. She remained unmarried and celibate and had a large following in Alexandria as a public intellectual and a teacher who had men as her students.

A sense of her commitment to the views of Plato, as interpreted by other philosophers of her time, can be seen in a rather amusing anecdote handed down to us in a tenth-century encyclopedia known as the *Suda*. There we learn that Hypatia was not only incredibly learned but also unusually beautiful. One of her young male students fell in love with her. She, however, was focused on matters of the mind rather than the body, and she—good Platonist that she was—thought that real beauty could be found only in the truths uncovered through intellectual endeavors, not in sexual attractions. Thus, she tried to repulse her would-be lover's advances, but with little success. As a last-ditch effort she brought out some of her used sanitary napkins, threw them at his feet, and declared, "You love this, O youth, and there is nothing beautiful about it." Platonic reality won the day.[30]

Hypatia's life would prove a fascinating study if only we had extensive sources of information. Regrettably, we are informed most fully about her death.[31] It came at the hands of a Christian mob, at the end of a rather complex set of incidents. The year was 415 CE. The prefect of Egypt—that is, the senior civil authority—was a Christian named Orestes, who had a running political battle with the local Christian bishop, Cyril, successor of Theophilus. Their contretemps came to a head over violence that had erupted between Christians and Jews in the city. The issue, at bottom, involved a contest over authority for handling the crisis, the civil authority appointed by the state or the bishop appointed by the church.

Cyril had a large band of Christian strongmen who supported him, engaged in his charitable work, and carried out even his uncharitable orders. In the midst of the difficulties, these men confronted Orestes in public and accused him of being a pagan. One of their number hurled a stone that bloodied Orestes's head. He responded by ordering the man captured and tortured to death.

Orestes, naturally enough, had his own supporters, and it was widely thought that Hypatia was a particularly close advisor. Cyril's mob decided to make an example of her. They found her in public riding in her chariot. Pulling her down, they dragged her to a church, tore off her clothes, and murdered her with fragments of pottery found at hand. They hauled her body outside the city and burned it on a pile of sticks.

One of the questions historians have always puzzled over is the degree to which Cyril was responsible for Hypatia's death. Our sources give varying accounts. Were his strongmen acting on his orders, or was this simply their own bright idea? Possibly a mediating position is best: that Cyril was not directly or legally responsible for what happened but that he had incited his passionate followers to wreak vengeance on those who sided with Orestes. In either event, the fifth century as a result lost one of its most brilliant intellectuals in the murder of a pagan philosopher at the hands of a Christian mob.

THE REASONS FOR CHRISTIAN INTOLERANCE

Even if such violence was not planned or executed with consistency and rigor, it did happen. Historians have long puzzled over the reason why. Christianity began with the ethical teachings of Jesus: his followers were to love their neighbors as themselves and turn the other cheek—indeed, to love even their enemies. Christians of the fourth century continued to advocate such principles. Yet sometimes Christians at the highest levels of government, leaders of the church, and uneducated Christian mobs practiced intolerance, occasionally leading to violence. How can it be explained?

It is sometimes argued that violent opposition to the "other" is the inevitable outcome when an exclusivist religion becomes dominant and able to enforce its claims with the arm of the law and violence on the streets.[32] There may indeed be some truth in this. Yet it is also important to remember that, as historian Harold Drake in particular has emphasized, even pagans could be intolerant in matters of religion. No exclusivity was needed. Moreover, there were many committed exclusivist Christians, even powerful rulers, bloodied warriors, and ruthless disciplinarians—think Constantine—who tolerated religious differences.[33]

In reflecting on the appearance of violent intolerance in some Christian circles, it may be helpful to consider again a key aspect of religion in antiquity, whether pagan or Christian. Then as now, one principal reason people engaged in religious practices was to please God in order to merit divine benefaction. For pagans, adhering to the ancestral traditions of worship was pleasing to the gods and could lead to the benefits needed to live and, if all went to plan, live well, with good health, plentiful crops, and a loving partner at one's side. Failing to please the gods, on the other hand, could lead to disaster. It was just this logic that led to the some of the Christian persecutions, coming to a head first with Decius and Valerian but then more dramatically under Diocletian. The gods expected sacrifices and anyone who refused to perform them was a danger to the community.

Christians too shared this logic, but for them the stakes were even higher. For one thing, anyone who did not adopt their particular set of beliefs and practices would be in danger of incurring divine anger not only in the present but also in the afterlife. Unrepentant pagans were destined to roast in hell forever. It mattered that they be persuaded to follow the Christian religion. Indeed, it mattered for the whole world, since in the near future the corrupt kingdoms of earth were to be replaced by the earthly Kingdom of God. This world transformation was to be inaugurated by believers in the present. Christians had sacred Scriptures ordering them to oppose all other religious traditions and practices, to convert nonbelievers by force if necessary. Some Christians took these injunctions literally. The options were clear: Were they to do what God commanded or not?

One other unique feature of this Christianity led to the rise of intolerance: its heightened emphasis on true knowledge. Unlike other religions, Christianity was not principally just a set of religious practices such as baptism, the Eucharist, the reading of Scripture, prayer, and worship. It was also a matter of proper belief. Ultimately, eternally, it mattered what people acknowledged to be true. These beliefs were in the process of refinement in their minute details, and according to some Christian leaders the least variation from correct doctrine could lead to eternal damnation. Doctrines had eternal consequences, doctrines involving the question of whether there was once a time before which the Son of God existed or not, whether Christ had a human spirit or a divine spirit, or whether the power of all evil, Satan, would at the end of time be converted to the truth. Christians had various views of such things, but one thing most of the varying views shared was the sense that getting the answers wrong could have eternal consequences.

Because of the enormous significance of "right belief" for eternal life, the intolerant potential of this exclusivist religion came to be fanned into white-hot passion early on, leading to widespread though certainly not universal intolerance. Wrong belief was so dangerous it could not be tolerated. We see Christian intolerance as early as the writings of the New Testament and continuing on down to the fourth century. It was directed against the "other," whomever that was: Jew, pagan, or even Christian.

As with all things Christian, in some sense it started with Jesus himself. In line with other Jews of his day, the historical Jesus was convinced that other interpretations of the Jewish religion were flawed. During his public ministry he could scarcely tolerate some of his enemies among the Pharisees. The hostile comments he directs toward them in Matthew 23 are probably Matthew's own formulations, but they almost certainly reflect Jesus's sense that the Pharisees were both wrong and wrongheaded. That intolerance grew with the passing of time, and the Gospels came to portray a Jesus who was even less forgiving of the views of his enemies. Particularly severe is the polemic in the Gospel of John, where Jesus regularly confronts enemies who are simply categorized as "the Jews" as if including all of them. At one point he declares that "the Jews" are not the children of God but offspring of Satan, murderers and liars (John 8:42–44).

The anti-Judaism grew with the passing of time. The author of the early-second-century letter of Barnabas indicates that Jews never were the people of God because they broke the covenant of God as soon as he made it with them, when, because of Israel's apostasy, an angry Moses smashed the clay tablets containing the Ten Commandments. As a result, Barnabas indicates, Jews never understood their own Scriptures, coming up with ridiculous literalistic interpretations of commandments (such as not eating pork) that were meant to be interpreted figuratively (they were not to behave like pigs). The Old Testament, for Barnabas, was a Christian book, not a Jewish one.

By the end of the second century we have even more vitriolic charges, none more gripping than what is found in a sermon preached by a bishop of Asia Minor named Melito of Sardis, who claimed that since Jesus was God, and the Jews executed him, the

Jews had killed their own god. Jews were not simply Christ killers. They were God killers. By the fourth century, Christians in charge of the empire began acting out this hateful intolerance of Jews, leading to the ugly history of Christian anti-Judaism still seen in parts of the world today.

It is almost certainly because Christianity emerged out of Judaism that the earliest expressions of Christian antagonism were leveled at fellow Jews. But it was not long before hatred of all that was pagan followed suit. The New Testament itself attests to the belief that when Jesus returns in glory for his second coming, he will not come meekly. On the contrary, he will return from heaven with "his mighty angels in flaming fire, inflicting vengeance upon those who do not know God and upon those who do not obey the gospel of the Lord Jesus. They shall suffer the punishment of eternal destruction" (2 Thessalonians 1:7–9). It will not be a pretty sight.

Still, for those who want to see the sight, there is always the book of Revelation. Anyone who insists that "the Old Testament God is a God of wrath, but the New Testament God is a God of mercy" has never read, or at least hearkened to, the final book of the Christian canon. Pagans will spend eternity in a lake of fire for their failure to believe in Jesus, with no hope of redemption.

For anyone who wants more variety in the eternal torments of the damned, the later Apocalypse of Peter, already discussed, provides numerous scenarios described with scarcely disguised excitement. One thinks again of Tertullian's Schadenfreude at seeing his enemies tormented for all eternity, including the persecutors of Christians to be seen eternally "liquefying in fiercer flames than they kindled in their rage against Christians" (*On the Spectacles* 30).

Most striking of all, from the outset Christians despised and rejected members of their own Christian communities who did not toe the theological line. We find a steady dose of intolerance already in our earliest Christian author, Paul, who curses anyone—human or angel—who dares to proclaim a gospel message different from the one he himself preached (Galatians 1:8–9). This is a real divine curse, a declaration of eternal damnation, delivered in this particular case to anyone who thinks that when people believe in Jesus they need also to follow God's commandment to be circumcised.

Such Christian intolerance is not restricted to Paul but is found throughout the pages of the New Testament. Near its chronological end is the first letter of John, written by an unknown author incensed at members of his own community because they think that Christ was so much a divine being that he could not be fully human like the rest of us. It may not seem like an unreasonable view—it is one that lots of Christians have had over the years—but the author condemns it and those who hold it, calling them not only bald-faced liars but "anti-Christs." No salvation for them!

After the New Testament we find one writing after another, in one genre after another, filled with vitriol against those Christians who take a theological view out of line with the author's own. Another apocalyptic vision of the torments of the damned, this one allegedly granted to the apostle Paul, itemizes an entire range of Christians who either misbehaved or misbelieved and so are subject to torments as horrific as anything to be suffered by the rankest pagan. The worst—"seven times greater" than any other torture—is reserved for theologians who propounded an understanding of Christ that the author deemed unorthodox, saying "that the bread and cup of the Eucharist of blessing are not the body and blood of Christ" (*Apocalypse of Paul* 41). Eucharistic theology is more important, apparently, than believing in Christ or being a good person.

THE LOGIC OF LEGISLATION

We have seen that opposition to pagans came to manifest itself in actual state legislation, and so it should be no surprise to find laws passed against Jews as well. Already under Constantine any Jew who attacked one of their own for converting to Christianity was to be burned to death (Theodosian Code 16.8.1). Constantius decreed that any Christian who converted to Judaism was to have his property entirely confiscated (Theodosian Code 16.8.8). Under Theodosius I it was declared that any Christian who married a Jew would be guilty of the crime of adultery. In the early fifth century, Jews were deprived of the right to serve in the imperial service. Later it became illegal for Jews to build or even repair a synagogue.[34]

On the other hand, it should be noted that a number of laws were issued to preserve the rights of Jews in the empire. (See the Theodosian Code 8.8.) That cannot be said of heretics. They were roundly condemned. All heretics of every type—that is, anyone not subscribing to the creed of Nicaea—were proscribed by Theodosius (Theodosian Code 16.5.5). They were forbidden to have any meeting places (Theodosian Code 16.5.6). Eventually they were to be "expelled from the cities and driven forth from the villages" (Theodosian Code 16.5.20). They were to be sought out in all places and forced to return to their countries of origin (Theodosian Code 16.5.12). In sum, anyone who did not subscribe to the "apostolic discipline and the evangelic doctrine" that promoted the theologically correct understanding of the Trinity (this would include Arians of various kinds) was legally pronounced "demented and insane" and was to "be smitten first by divine vengeance and secondly by the retribution of Our own initiative, which We shall assume in accordance with the divine judgment" (Theodosian Code 16.1.2).

To understand the implicit logic behind the violent intolerance of pagans, it is useful to consider the logic made explicit here in the intolerance of heretics. They were enemies of God, and he would judge them. Since he would judge them at the end, it is the duty for Christians in power to judge them in the meantime. Mutatis mutandis, the same applies to pagans. Such is the view set forth in the urgent injunctions of Firmicus Maternus to the emperors Constantius II and Constans: it is God's will that pagans be slaughtered.[35]

This in itself may explain many of the acts of Christian intolerance toward pagans and their religion, but a recent proposal has been put forth by historian Harold Drake to explain the upsurge in violence toward the end of the fourth century, after the attempt of Julian the Apostate to push his apostasy on the rest of the empire. It is to be recalled that Julian refused to martyr Christians for their faith, but he did make life increasingly difficult for them. There is no telling what might have happened had he not made some bad military decisions and been killed in battle just nineteen months into his reign. What if he had ruled for nineteen years instead? Or over thirty, as did his uncle Constantine? Would his anti-Christian measures have become more pronounced? Would they have taken a drastic toll on the Christian church? Would they have reversed the trend and produced a massive return to the traditional religions throughout the empire? Could the empire have again become overwhelmingly pagan?

Drake is less concerned about answering such questions than he is about suggesting that Christians after Julian's death probably asked them. Christianity had been surging rather dramatically, with a series of Christian rulers in Constantine's wake. Then Julian came along, an anti-Christian pagan with ultimate power. Luckily for the church, he died young. Still, what if another pagan emperor were to come along, and then another? According to Drake's theory, the Christians who came after Julian, especially the emperor Theodosius I, were bound and determined not to let that happen. Paganism could not be left alone to die a natural death. It had to be attacked and killed.

As a result, Julian's efforts to promote paganism in the end led to its relatively quick demise. In Drake's words: "Ironically, this analysis means that Julian was the trigger, not for a pagan offensive, but a Christian one."[36]

PLEAS FOR TOLERANCE

Christians who experienced persecution in the years before the conversion of Constantine sometimes pled with their pagan opponents to show toleration. The second- and third-century apologist Tertullian in particular advocated freedom of religion. As he wrote to Scapula, the governor of Carthage: "It is a fundamental human right, a privilege of nature, that everyone should worship according to his own convictions: one person's religion neither harms nor helps another. It is assuredly no part of religion to compel religion. . . . You will render no real service to your gods by compelling us to sacrifice"

(*To Scapula* 2). Elsewhere he urges his pagan opponents not to violate human freedom "by taking away religious liberty, and forbidding free choice of deity. . . . Not even a human being would care to have unwilling homage rendered him" (*Apology* 24).

These pleas fell on deaf ears. Years later, when the tide had turned and Christians were in power, sometimes intent on using that power to coerce pagans into leaving their traditional religions, it was pagan intellectuals who pled for tolerance. The great rhetorician Themistius (317–88 CE) played a prominent role in Roman government for more than thirty years, from the reign of Constantius II into that of Theodosius. In addition to being a trusted advisor to Christian emperors, Themistius was also an outspoken pagan who advocated freedom of religion.

Among Themistius's surviving orations is one delivered on January 1, 364, on the occasion of Jovian's accession to the imperial throne. The empire had just seen its final pagan emperor. Themistius, of course, had no way of knowing that. But he did know that Jovian was a Christian and that anti-pagan measures might well be in the offing. His oration was, in part, designed to forestall any such unhappy event. In it Themistius points out that the new emperor must know "that a king cannot compel his subjects in everything, but that there are some matters which have escaped compulsion and are superior to threat and injunction, for example, the whole question of virtue, and, above all, reverence for the divine" (Oration 5.67b–c).[37] In other words, an emperor cannot expect to legislate either virtue or proper religion.

Themistius argues that everyone has a natural desire to be pious, but it is important to allow "the manner of worship depend on individual inclination" (Oration 5.68a). Torture cannot change a person's views of the divine or of how to worship. Nor is there only one path to truth. Instead, religions are like a race in which various competitors all head toward the judge, but by different routes. By the rules of this hypothetical race, such varieties are allowed, even if some routes are more direct and better than others: "Thus you realize that, while there exists only one Judge, mighty and true, there is not one road leading to him."

This plea for tolerance came to be repeated by other pagans in the years that followed. A particularly important occasion came when the young Christian emperor Gratian removed the altar of the goddess Victory from the Roman senate house in 382 CE. This altar had stood in the senate for more than four centuries, installed there by Caesar Augustus himself early in his reign. Traditionally senators performed a simple sacrifice to Victory upon entering the chamber to assure the success of their endeavors. By the end of the fourth century, Christian senators, of course, would not perform the sacrifice. Under pressure from Christian leaders, Gratian ordered the removal of the altar, much to the consternation of pagan traditionalists who saw this as one more attempt to infringe on their customary religious practices.

Most outspoken was a Roman statesman, orator, and intellectual named Symmachus. After Gratian passed from the scene, Symmachus delivered an address for the new emperor, Valentinian II, pleading that the altar be replaced. Symmachus pointed out that the ancient religious customs of the Romans had long put them in good stead: "This worship subdued the world." Even if others chose a different religious path, there should be freedom of worship, not constriction. All should worship according to the dictates of their own conscience: "It is just that all worship should be considered as one. We look on the same stars, the sky is common, the same world surrounds us. What differences does it make by what pains each seeks the truth? We cannot attain to so great a secret by one road" (*Relatio* 3, par. 10).[38]

Most Christian leaders—both bishops and state officials, all the way up to the emperor—had a different opinion. Their religion had long been built on a solitary notion of truth. One way was right and the other ways were wrong. There was one path to the divine, and it was the one that could be found in the orthodox Christian creeds. Some Christians, of course, did believe that true religion was a personal matter and that there was no reason to force their views on others. Others, however, practiced complete intolerance for any difference, whether found among Jews, pagans, or other Christians. This was not a problem that would quickly go away. Meanwhile the Christian church acquired more and more power, eventually becoming the most powerful institution in the Western world, destined to outlive the Roman Empire itself by many centuries.

THE EFFICACY OF COERCION

Some scholars have argued that Christianity ultimately succeeded in taking over the empire because of its coercive efforts.[39] In this view, pagans converted in droves because they were more or less forced to do so. Exercising their newly won power, Christians imposed their will on the religious world of the time.

Other scholars have maintained that this view is inherently implausible. Coercion rarely succeeds in forcing people to change their minds, even if it compels them to alter their patterns of behavior. Think about pagan attempts under Diocletian to force Christians to recant. Many Christians complied with the imperial decrees, turning over the Scriptures when demanded or performing sacrifices. When the persecution ended, most of these returned to the Christian fold. It surely would not have been different with pagans deprived of their right to follow the cultic traditions of their ancestors. They could be forced to stop sacrificing, but they could not be forced to accept the god of the Christians against their will.

Moreover, and even more important, there is scant evidence that coercion was widely practiced. There were certainly instances, including the ones I have detailed. But there is nothing to indicate that Christians everywhere were cracking pagan heads in an effort to make them convert. That is why a scholar such as Michele Renee Salzman, focusing on the western empire, has argued that "it is hard to accept the interpretation advanced by certain scholars that physical violence, coercion, was a central factor in explaining the spread of Christianity."[40]

THE RISE OF CHRISTIAN INTOLERANCE: IN SUM

No century of Christian history was more transformative than the fourth. In 303 CE, the Roman emperor Diocletian declared war on the Christian church and instigated the most massive persecution it ever endured. In 312 CE, the emperor Constantine himself converted to become a Christian. In 313 CE, Constantine and his co-ruler Licinius issued a declaration of complete toleration for all religions, pagan and Christian. In 325 CE, Constantine ruled over a council of bishops at Nicaea called to resolve the deep but nuanced theological disputes of the day. In 341 CE, the Christian emperor Constantius II issued the first legislation banning pagan cultic practices. In 361 CE, the pagan Julian ascended the imperial throne and spent nineteen months attempting to suppress Christianity and reinstate paganism. In 363 CE, the Christian emperor Jovian replaced him, and from that time on there would never again be a pagan ruler of the empire. In 391 to 392 CE, the vehemently orthodox Christian Theodosius declared all pagan practices illegal and in effect made Christianity the state religion of Rome. It was to remain the state religion for as long as the empire stood—not just the West, which fell in the fifth century, but also the East, which lasted until the fifteenth. Christianity was to become the greatest and most powerful institution Western Civilization has ever seen.

With the growth of Christianity came moments of heightened intolerance. Sometimes this intolerance erupted in ugly acts of violence, suppression, and coercion. Christians were not, of course, the only intolerant people on the planet. They themselves had been the victims of violent coercion early in the century. In addition, it would be a mistake to consider the majority of Christians as intolerant. Most, to be sure, were exclusivist in their religious views. For them, there was only one god and only one set of correct theological beliefs and ritual practices (even if they disagreed among themselves about what those beliefs and practices were supposed to be). Any other paths to truth were excluded. But as with Jews before and alongside them, for many Christians this exclusive religion did not compel intolerance toward others.

By the end of the fourth century about half the empire was Christian. A triumphalist narrative of the march of Christian progress might well celebrate that historical reality as some kind of ultimate victory. Still, it is important to realize that the other half of the empire was not Christian. Jews possibly made up 5 to 7 percent of the empire; pagans the rest. And despite the occasional acts of Christian violence, most of the time, in most places, all these people—Jew, pagan, and Christian—more or less got along. It is wrong to think that the legislation passed by Theodosius, enforced sporadically by officials such as Maternus Cynegius and used occasionally to justify local violence, absolutely crushed paganism and forced all followers of traditional religions into hiding.

On the contrary, as Princeton historian Peter Brown has so elegantly argued in numerous publications, pagans and Christians into the fourth and fifth centuries by and large accommodated one another and generally managed to work, function, and live together. This was certainly the case at the higher reaches of imperial government, which had its own concerns apart from the need to enforce religious conformity. For one thing, it had to keep the empire running. That required raising revenues, quelling internal turmoil, and defending the borders. The leaders of the empire were politicians who recognized the need for compromise in order for government to run efficiently. In Brown's words, when it came to achieving their desired goals, these rulers understood full well "the art of the possible."[41] These were goals largely shared among members of the upper-crust ruling elite, both pagans and Christians. Indeed, Brown and others have shown that the educated and ruling elite Christians had more in common with their pagan counterparts than with lower-class, uneducated fellow Christians.

Still, even without massive coercive efforts, it cannot be ignored that Christianity continued to grow as very large numbers converted. Although there were not armed bands of military police attacking groups of non-Christians at every pagan shrine, there were laws proscribing pagan practices and occasional acts of violent intolerance. Even though such coercion almost certainly had no effect on the widespread practices of traditional religion in the short run, it is easy to see how it might take its toll over the long haul. Unlike Christianity, paganism was never declared "legal" after a short period of persecution. Christian emperor followed Christian emperor. And people continued to convert, in increasingly large numbers.

In some places temples were shut down. Cult statues were destroyed, mutilated, or desacralized and made secular works of art. Most important, public funding to the traditional religions began to be cut. In some instances this was because the Christian government withdrew its support. But even more it was the result of the conversion of the upper classes. Local pagan cults were almost always supported by local pagan aristocrats. As the Roman upper classes increasingly became Christian, naturally their resources were redirected to the church. It was not just in converts but also in cash that traditional religions experienced a massive collapse over time, with the Christian church experiencing a growth that was literally exponential. Paganism did not have to be destroyed by violent acts of Christian intolerance. It could, and did, die a natural death, cut off from resources and abandoned by popular opinion.

Gains and Losses

The idea for this book struck me twenty years ago during my first trip to Athens. I was keen to explore the archaeological wonders of the city, and most especially the Agora and the Acropolis. The Agora was the ancient center of the city and is still filled with monumental buildings: the old Athenian meeting place called the Metroon; the impressively reconstructed South Stoa with its rooms, shops, and areas for people to mingle; and a number of ruined sacred sites—including the single best-preserved Greek temple to come down to us from antiquity, one dedicated to the Greek god Hephaestus, god of volcanoes, fire, and metal working.

Constructed from 449 to 415 BCE during the glory days of Athens, the temple is a large and imposing structure in the northwest part of the Agora. Made completely of marble, it stands on a large platform, 104 by 45 feet. The front and back—east and west sides—are adorned with six massive columns, the two longer sides with thirteen. Along the top are magnificent friezes, one of which depicts the labors of Heracles. Inside the temple, in antiquity, stood bronze statues of Hephaestus and Athena, the patron goddess of Athens. This testament to the architectural skills of ancient Greece stands virtually intact today—including its roof—appearing much as it did to the Athenians twenty-five centuries ago, a glorious temple that would have been observed in person by Euripides and Sophocles, by Socrates and Plato.

High above the Agora, to the southeast, stands the Acropolis, home to numerous archaeological wonders, including the glorious Temple of Athena Nike; the temple known as the Erechtheion with its six enormous female statues, the Caryatids; and of course, chiefly, the Parthenon, perhaps the most magnificent ruin of any kind to come down to us from classical antiquity. Although much larger than the Temple of Hephaestus, the Parthenon took less time to complete, just fifteen years. The temple is dedicated to Athena, the *parthenos*—that, is the virgin. But the building was not a cultic site devoted to her worship. It was instead used as a treasury for the city of Athens.

The building is simply enormous. It stands on a base measuring 228 by 101 feet, on which stand eight giant columns on both front and back, seventeen on each side. Their construction is an architectural marvel. If all the columns had been straight and exactly the same size, the building would appear curved to the naked eye. And so the architects designed the columns to lean slightly toward the interior of the building and enlarged them slightly in the middle. Moreover, the floor of the temple is imperceptibly higher in the center than at the sides. Altogether these carefully plotted design features make the building appear completely straight and symmetrical.

In antiquity a statue of Athena stood inside the structure, measuring twelve meters high and constructed of fine ivory and gold around a wooden core. It was made by Phidias, the most famous sculptor of classical antiquity. Numerous other sculptures adorned the temple, including those known today as the Elgin Marbles, named after the man who pilfered them in the early nineteenth century, Thomas Bruce, seventh earl of Elgin and British ambassador to the Ottoman Empire. The marbles can still be seen in all their relocated glory in the British Museum.

The temple of Hephaestus and the Parthenon were high on my agenda during my visit, as were the surrounding archaeological remains. But I was especially intent on climbing an otherwise unimpressive rock outcropping that, as a historian of early Christianity, I had known about since my youth. This is called the Areopagus, or Mars Hill. It is where the apostle Paul allegedly delivered a speech to Epicurean and Stoic philosophers upon first arriving in Athens during his storied travels.

The Areopagus today looks much as it did in Paul's time, a stony crag overlooking the city, boasting no ruins of any kind. Its only distinctive features are a plaque embedded in the rock below, encapsulating the text of the speech Paul delivered, and a set of slippery steps leading up to the top. It is a spectacular location, not because of any inherent merit or archaeological ruins, but because on both sides can be seen the vestiges of one of the most spectacular civilizations the world has ever known, the magnificent remains of the Agora below and the even more magnificent remains of the Acropolis above. This is Athens, the home of some of the greatest philosophers, dramatists, artists, architects, and political thinkers of classical antiquity, captured in a gaze downward and upward.

Paul visited the spot on his second missionary journey (Acts 17). He had come to Athens to preach about Jesus and his resurrection. Some of his original audience wanted to hear more from him. So, as requested, he ascended the Areopagus to speak to a group of philosophers who regularly gathered there. He started his speech by mentioning he had seen a large number of temples and idols in their city, but was particularly struck by an altar dedicated to "An Unknown God."

Scholars of early Christianity have long debated how to make sense of such an altar. Possibly it was erected as a backup measure by a group of pagans nervous about leaving a god out of their collective worship—in case there was one god who had been left unmentioned, unnamed, and unattended in the city. This altar was in that one's honor.

Paul uses this altar to an Unknown God as a launchpad for the rest of his address. The Athenians may not know who this god is, but Paul does. He in fact is the one God over all, the ultimate divine being, the God who created the heavens and the earth. As the creator of all things, he has no need for any physical representation or earthly temple. This is the God who is soon to judge the world and everyone on it through the second coming of his son, Jesus, whom God had raised from the dead.

Paul's words did not find a welcome acceptance on the Areopagus. It is not that the philosophers there were shocked, dismayed, or challenged. They were simply amused. Paul was relatively uneducated—in comparison to them, at least—and was speaking nonsense about a physical resurrection of the dead. Most of them mocked, although some wanted to hear more later. Paul did make one or two converts.

While standing on the site twenty years ago, I thought about Paul, his sermon, and his surroundings. Paul was a lower-class artisan and itinerant preacher. From an external, material perspective, nothing stood in his favor. He was widely maligned and mistreated, frequently beaten, sometimes within an inch of his life, and lacking any worldly power or prestige. In many ways he stood on precisely the opposite end of the spectrum from the great cultural heroes of Athens, the heart of Greek civilization.

Then the realization struck me. In the end, Paul won.

What Paul preached that day on the Areopagus eventually triumphed over everything that stood below me in the Agora and above me on the Acropolis. It overwhelmed both the Temple of Hephaestus and the Parthenon. No one except, probably, Paul himself would have predicted it. Yet it happened: Christianity eventually took over Western Civilization.

In this book I have tried to explain the triumph of Christianity without making it a triumphalist narrative. As a historian, I do not think the Christianization of the Roman Empire was inevitable and I do not celebrate it either as a victory for the human race and a sign of cultural progress on the one hand, or a major sociopolitical setback and cultural disaster on the other. I think it is impossible to say whether the world would have been a worse place or a better one had it not happened. Something else would have happened in its stead. But what?

What would have happened if the emperor Julian had ruled for forty years instead of nineteen months? Would he have managed to achieve his goal of marginalizing and then eliminating Christianity? Would the glories of Greece and Rome have lived on? Would what we think of as Western Civilization ever have occurred? What would have happened if the emperor Constantine had not won the Battle at the Milvian Bridge but instead died in the conflict? Would Christianity have sputtered and died? Or would the movement have continued to grow at an exponential rate? Would one of his emperor sons have later converted? Or would persecution have continued and succeeded in quashing the faith? If so, what would have happened then? Even more, what difference would it have made to the world if Paul had not "seen the light"? Would someone else have arisen to take the Gospel to the gentiles, making possible the conversion of the entire pagan world? Or would the religion have remained a sect of Judaism, with the historical importance of, say, the Jewish Essenes?

We do not know and we cannot know.

We do know that Christianity won over the empire and in doing so considered their historical movement a triumph. If about half the empire was Christian by the year 400 CE, the great majority was Christian by 500 CE. This Christianization brought massive benefits to the church. It went from being legalized under Constantine, to being legislated under Theodosius, to being the dominant religion of the West in the centuries to follow. Once emperors became Christian, masses came in and, of particular importance, the path was open for the aristocracy to follow. The leaders of the churches shifted from being simply local believers who happened to be literate to embodying the most highly educated, well-connected, politically astute, wealthy, and revered elements of society.

The wealth and the power of the church itself became enormous. The wealth was evident not simply in magnificent church structures or their spectacular accoutrements but in vast tracts of land and the holdings of the bishops. So too the power was not simply over the personal religious lives of the faithful; it was also social and political power. After the West saw its last Roman emperor with Romulus Augustulus in 476 CE, the church itself only grew in strength, as it did in the East as well.[1]

In fact, eventually, the Roman popes claimed to rule the West. In the eighth century or, as one recent study has argued, in the ninth, there appeared a document known as the Donation of Constantine, in which the first Christian emperor allegedly bestowed the rule of all western provinces on the bishop of Rome. This is what Constantine is said to have written:

> As a return gift to the most blessed bishop, our father Silvester, the universal pope, we decree that our palace . . . as well as the city of Rome and all the provinces, places, and cities of Italy and the western regions must be distributed to his power and the administration of his successor bishops. Through a firm imperial judgment [and] by means of this divine, sacred, and lawful constitution we allow everything to remain under the jurisdiction of the holy Roman church.[2]

The document was not revealed to be a forgery until the middle of the fifteenth century. Before that it was taken to authorize papal control of Western Europe. The thirteenth-century pope Gregory IX (pope from 1227 to 1241) used the document to confront Frederick II, king of Sicily, arguing that "Constantine had given to the bishop of Rome the imperial insignia and scepter, the city with its entire duchy, and also the empire with perpetual oversight." More explicitly Pope Boniface VIII (pope from 1294 to 1303) declared: "I am Caesar; I am the emperor."[3] How much more powerful could a leader of the church be? For him, the takeover of the empire was complete. This was a triumph indeed.

But not, obviously, for everyone else. If victory for one means defeat for others, we might consider what was lost with the Christianization of the empire.

On one level, it is impossible to say that Christianity *caused* the disappearance of so much that was lost. What we can say is that much that was alien to Christianity did indeed disappear. A great deal of pagan culture was eventually destroyed or, at least, never renewed. We have seen the beginnings of the destruction in the fourth century, with temples, shrines, and cult statues taken down and mutilated. Some, of course, remain, adorning many of the great museums of the world or left, in some instances, intact at archaeological sites on their places of origin. But most went away forever, destroyed by fervent bishops or marauding monks.

Other artifacts that were not made of marble and stone disappeared out of neglect. All sorts of literature, gone forever, thousands of books known and suspected to have once existed: plays, novels, poems, histories, philosophical works, scientific treatises, essays, name your genre. It is not that these were necessarily burned by zealous Christians opposed to the classics, although that sometimes did happen. Instead, they simply were never recopied for posterity. And for a simple reason: copyists throughout the Middle Ages were almost invariably Christian monks working in monasteries. They were far more interested in producing copies of the letters of Paul than the plays of Plautus. Such pagan works may have been lost anyway, of course, without the Christianization of the empire. We can never say.

Apart from artifacts of broader culture, there were losses sustained within the realm of religion itself. The triumph of Christianity meant a new kind of religiosity, and it is worthwhile thinking about the significance of the change. The Christianity that Theodosius and his successors promoted, sometimes with vigorous legislation and imperial force, was strictly Nicene orthodoxy. This form of Christianity was doctrinaire, insisting on certain theological views as the only right basis for all religious belief. Variation—even in seemingly minute details of theological niceties—came to be disallowed. There was one form of truth, and eternal life depended on knowing what it was.

One thing lost in this triumph was all the massive and glorious diversity of religious expression found everywhere throughout the pagan world. We can never lose sight of just how varied the thousands of pagan cults were. They did share common features—sacrifice and prayer, for example. But they involved the worship of different gods, known from different myths, adored through different practices, cults devoted to Zeus, to Athena, to Apollo, to Hephaestus, to gods of forests and streams and meadows, to gods of the household and gods of the family. As a rule this enormous diversity brought with it a widespread tolerance of difference, a sense that varying paths to the divine were not only acceptable and allowed but also desirable. Tolerance was to be encouraged. Freedom of religion was to be embraced. One of the greatest aspects of ancient paganism, taken as a whole, was the widespread willingness to accommodate and even revel in diversity. That was lost with the triumph of Christianity.[4]

But changed as well was a world that separated religion, ethics, philosophy, and myth into distinct spheres of human thought and life. Now with the triumph of Christianity there appeared on the scene a "totalizing" discourse about religion that encapsulated the totality of the lives of those who adhered to it, affecting not just their cultic practices but also the moral precepts they followed, the stories they told about the divine, and the views they embraced not just about God but about reality itself. Christianity not only took over an empire, it radically altered the lives of those living in it. It opened the door to public policies and institutions to tend to the poor, the weak, the sick, and the outcast as deserving members of society. It was a revolution that affected government practices, legislation, art, literature, music, philosophy, and—on the even more fundamental level—the very understanding of billions of people about what it means to be human. However one evaluates the merits of the case, whether the Christianization of the West was a triumph to be treasured or a defeat to be lamented, no one can deny it was the most monumental cultural transformation our world has ever seen.

Appendix

THE RATE OF CHRISTIAN GROWTH

In 1996, Rodney Stark published a book for general audiences called *The Rise of Christianity*.[1] In it he explained sociological factors that, in his judgment, led to the triumph of Christianity in the Roman world. The book was not well received by experts in the field of early Christian studies, who noted numerous flaws in Stark's reasoning and, especially, in his uncritical use of ancient sources.[2] But even though Stark is not a historian of ancient Christianity, he is a sociologist. As a sociologist, he knows how to calculate population growth. Far and away the most significant and intriguing part of his book are his calculations.

Stark did something no one before him had tried. He actually did the math. Suppose, he says, Christianity had 1,000 adherents in the year 40 CE. How quickly would it need to grow in order to reach 10 percent of the empire—6 million people—by the year 300? Would the rate of growth need to be miraculous? Or would there need to be massive conversions for three centuries? No, on both scores. There would need to be a steady rate of growth. And an absolutely plausible one. To get from 1,000 Christians to 6 million 260 years later, the church would need to grow at a rate of about 40 percent per decade.

That's actually not that much. It is 3.4 percent per year. If this year there are 100 Christians, next year there need to be 103 or 104. In other words, in any group of 100 Christians, only 3 or 4 of them need to make a single convert each over the course of the entire year, or one of them needs to convert just one small family unit.

A steady rate of growth involves an exponential curve. At first not many people are converting. But at the same exact rate later, when there are lots more converts, the numbers suddenly become enormous. Those 3 or 4 converts that you win when there are only 100 of you become 30,000 or 40,000 (in one year!) when you number 1 million. It is like compound interest. At one point you have trouble believing it is happening, but it is and you are making money hand over fist. It does not require substantial rates of growth. In fact, Stark revels in the fact that we have a clear historical analogy. One of his main areas of expertise is the Mormon Church. As it turns out, Mormonism had grown by 43 percent per decade from its founding to the time Stark was writing in the mid-1990s. There is nothing implausible at all about the early Christian church growing at a similar rate.

Stark himself realized his calculations for early Christianity are very rough. In fact, as stated they do not work very well. One point Stark did not consider adequately is his opening figure: 1,000 Christians in the year 40 CE. That would be just a decade after Christianity started. For the following twenty-six decades Stark shows that the church would need to grow at a rate of 40 percent. But how do we get to the number 1,000? If the New Testament is right—and there is no reason to doubt it, since it is hard to figure out, in this particular respect, how it can be wrong—Christianity began with a small group of Jesus's followers, men and women, something like 20 people. That would be in the year 30. If those 20 people had grown to be 1,000 by the year 40, it would be a growth rate of 4,900 percent for that decade. Are we supposed to think that for the first ten years Christianity grew at a rate of 4,900 percent but then for the next 26 decades at 40 percent? Obviously not.

Moreover, the numbers do not work too well at the other end.

Suppose Christianity grew at a relatively steady rate of 40 percent per decade for three centuries and that it comprised 6 million adherents by the year 300. What happened next? If the church continued to grow at 40 percent per decade over the next century, then by the year 400 it would have numbered 170 million. But there were only 60 million inhabitants in the empire, so that can't be right.

Obviously Christianity was not growing at a steady rate, and Stark, more than anyone, knows this. It is true that there must have been a rapid rate of growth early on in the movement, even if seems unrealistic to suppose a rate of 4,900 percent per decade. But clearly, in the early years, it had to grow faster than 40 percent. That can easily be shown. If Christianity started with 20 people in 30 CE and grew at 40 percent per decade, there would have been only 55 Christians in the entire world when Paul wrote his letter to the Romans around 60 CE. But he greeted 26 people by name in just this one letter and mentioned several Christian assemblies there. This was in a church that he did not found himself—one, in fact, he had never even visited. Surely he would not have known most of the people in the church, and it was just one church. What about all the other Christians in all the other churches that we know about, in Jerusalem, Damascus, Antioch, Ephesus, Philippi, Thessalonica, Corinth, throughout the region of Galatia, and on and on? There must have been hundreds or thousands of Christians at the time, not 55. There may not have been tens of thousands, but surely there are many hundreds.

Thus, we need to figure out how to get from 20 Christians in 30 CE to some hundreds in 60 CE. The rates of growth will be relatively high early on.

Moreover, the rates will almost certainly need to be lower at the tail end of the period. Suppose we are right (in what I argue in chapter 6) that there might be as many as 3 million Christians in the year 300 CE but around 30 million in 400 CE. For that to happen we need a growth rate of only 25.9 percent per decade. Even if there are just 2 million at the outset of the fourth century, to get to 30 million by the end we need a growth rate of just 31.1 percent. It's not a statistically huge difference: just under 0.5 percent more per year—that is, for a group of 100 people, one additional convert every two years.

REVISING THE RATE OF GROWTH

As a result of these considerations, I want to suggest some minor tweaks in the way we understand the rate of Christian growth. It is important to emphasize that there could never have been anything like a steady rate. Populations ebb and flow for all sorts of reasons. For the growth of the Christian church there are a large number of imponderables. How quickly were Christians dying in relation to the rest of the population? Did they have more births? Were persecutions occasionally cutting into their numbers? Or did the bravery of martyrs actually increase their numbers?

Some scholars, including Stark, have tried to take such matters into consideration, but in fact probably none of them is significant. Christians were born and died at about the rate of others, despite elite Christian authors claiming that Christians never practiced abortion or infanticide. These claims have been shown to be propagandistic and cannot be accepted naïvely as factual.[3] Nor, as we have seen, did improved Christian health care probably lead to better mortality rates. In addition, not enough people were actually martyred to decrease the Christian population significantly.[4]

As a result, for our purposes, we will not take into account special features of Christianity that one might unreflectively suppose led to a difference. I will base my calculations on two fixed numbers. It does appear to be right that the religion started with about 20 people in the year 30, and that by the year 400 it was about half the empire—so, say, 30 million. And so the question is, how much would Christianity have to grow to get from 20 persons to 30 million in 370 years?

Paul, as indicated, provides us with solid evidence that the initial rates of growth were sizable, especially in relation to what came later. Most of his letters are addressed to churches he had personally founded. In them he greets people by name and refers to churches in other places, but not in order to prove a point about how successful he has been or to provide statistical data for inquiring minds of the twenty-first century. He is simply writing letters to people, not realizing how these letters might be used later.

Paul himself founded churches in the regions of Macedonia, Achaia, Asia Minor, and elsewhere. We know of his churches in Corinth, Thessalonica, Philippi, Ephesus, throughout the region of Galatia, probably in Syria and Cilicia, and possibly in the Nabataean kingdom called Arabia in the New Testament. (See, for example, Galatians 1:15–21.) He also refers to other churches he did not found: for example, in Jerusalem, Damascus, Antioch, Colossae, and Rome. Altogether sixty-five communities are mentioned in the Pauline letters (not including the Pastoral epistles of 1 and 2 Timothy and Titus). An additional thirteen are mentioned in the book of Acts.

Moreover, there are indications that these churches each comprised more than two or three people. We have seen that Paul's modus operandi entailed staying in a city until he had made enough converts to establish a viable community that could then begin to propagate itself. The letters themselves intimate communities that surely number in the dozens. The Christians in Thessalonica, for example, are upset that some of their number have died and Paul writes to reassure them that this will not be the fate of everyone else (1 Thessalonians 4:13–18). The clear impression is that several people within a large community have passed away.

Or consider the church in Corinth. Paul's first letter to the church indicates numerous problems experienced by numerous people. There are factions in the church with different members following different spiritual leaders; Paul mentions four of the factions (1 Corinthians 1:12). There are men in the church who have been visiting prostitutes and bragging about it (1 Corinthians 6). Other men have been told, in a quite different vein, that they are not supposed to have sex with anyone, even their own wives (1 Corinthians 7). There are other instances of sexual immorality (1 Corinthians 5). Some people are arguing that Christians should not eat meat from sacrifices to pagan gods and others who argue that it is perfectly acceptable (1 Corinthians 8 and 10). Some of the women are coming to church without head coverings (1 Corinthians 11). The wealthy people are coming to weekly meals and gorging themselves when others, the slaves and day laborers, have to come late and there is nothing left to eat (1 Corinthians 11). Worship services have turned chaotic as people try to show spiritual one-upmanship by speaking in unknown tongues more than anyone else (1 Corinthians 12 and 14). People are not using their various spiritual gifts for the uplifting of the community (1 Corinthians 12 and 13). Some Christians claim that they have already experienced a spiritual resurrection and have enjoyed the full benefits of salvation (1 Corinthians 15). Surely this enormous mass of problems presupposes a community of dozens and dozens of people. And this is just twenty-five years after the death of Jesus, in just one location. There could not be merely fifty-five Christians in the entire world.

Thus it appears that the beginning of the Christian movement saw a veritable avalanche of conversions.[5] Possibly many of these are the direct result of the missionary activities of Paul. But there may have been other missionaries like him who were also successful. So let's simply pick a sensible rate of growth, and say that for the first forty years, up to the time when Paul wrote his last surviving letter, the church grew at a rate of 300 percent per decade. If the religion started with 20 people in 30 CE, that would mean there were some 1,280 by the year 60. That is not at all implausible as a guess, but it is way too precise—so let's just say 1,000 to 1,500 Christians. But growth cannot continue at that rate. If it did, a century later, in the year 160, there would be well over 1 billion Christians in the world.

So we can probably assume there was a burst of initial enthusiasm generated by the new faith, both among people who had heard Jesus preach during his public ministry and among those evangelized through the extraordinary missionary work of Paul and possibly others like him. After Paul's death there was almost certainly a rapid decline. The change would not be immediate or steady, but we are dealing with ballpark figures here. Say it went down on average to 60 percent per decade for the next forty years up to the end of the first century. There would still be a lot of energy and enthusiasm among those who thought not only that Jesus saved them from their sins but also that he was coming back very soon, creating a kind of urgency for their message. This would be a rate of growth just under 5 percent per year. Every year each group of 20 people needs to make just one convert. At a rate like that there would then be something like 8,389 Christians in the world in the year 100 CE. That sounds about right, but again, it is impossibly precise. So let's just say 7,000 to 10,000.

There is no point—and no way—to do a breakdown decade after decade. Clearly growth cannot be sustained at 60 percent, since that would give us over 100 million Christians in the year 300 when we think that there might have been 2 or 3 million. To get to 2 million there would need to be a growth rate of 31.5 percent per decade of those two hundred years; for 3 million there would need to be not much more, just 34.2 percent per decade. Just as our earlier numbers were far too precise, so too are these rates of growth, but the matter is complicated by the obvious fact that very small differences in percentage lead to unrealistic numbers of conversion. So, for broad illustration, we can simply suggest a rate of growth between 100 and 300 CE as between 30 and 35 percent per decade on average, with huge fluctuations over time, in different places, all based on external and internal circumstances.

In the fourth century, when massive conversions occur in part because of Constantine and the favors he showered on the church, the rates of growth must have slowed down. Otherwise, again, by the end of the century there would be more Christians than inhabitants of the empire, in a time when we know for a fact there were still a large number of pagans, as both pagan and Christian authors attest. It may seem counterintuitive that we would get a *slower* rate of growth after the conversion of Constantine. Wasn't that the event that changed everything? Well, not exactly. One reason the rate of growth declined (this may seem ironic) is because the numbers of converts increased. The more people who converted to become Christian, the fewer non-Christians there were to convert. And so they could not convert at the same rate simply because there were not as many of them.

Suppose, then, that the rate slows to something like 25 percent to around 30 percent. If there were 2 million by 300 CE, a rate of 31.1 percent per decade would get to 30 million by 400 CE; if there were 3 million by 300 CE, then a rate of 25.9 percent would get us there.

Obviously all this is simply tweaking the rates given by Stark in order to provide a bit more reality to the situation, in light of what we know about (a) the starting number of Christians in the world, (b) the necessarily rapid (but not unimaginable) rate of growth early on, and (c) the slowing rate of conversion as the number of converts rises. Anyone can tweak the numbers further—indefinitely, in fact, for one who really likes to play the numbers game. But the reality is that at a certain point the educated guessing simply becomes wildly speculative guessing. So, based on some educated guessing, we have ballpark figures. Nonetheless, they are striking. Given the precise rate adjustments I'm using—starting in 30 CE (300 percent); in the year 60 CE (down from 300 percent to 60 percent), 100 CE (down to 34 percent), and 300 CE (down to 26 percent)—here is how the numbers of Christians would break down over time (rounded up to the nearest 1,000 starting with 150 CE):

30 CE—20 Christians

60 CE—1,280 Christians; say 1,000 to 1,500

100 CE—8,389 Christians; say 7,000 to 10,000

150 CE—36,000 Christians; say 30,000 to 40,000

200 CE—157,000 Christians; say 140,000 to 170,000

250 CE—676,000 Christians; say 600,000 to 700,000

300 CE—2,923,000 Christians; say 2,500,000 to 3,500,000

312 CE—3,857,000 Christians; say 3,500,000 to 4,000,000

400 CE—29,478,000 Christians; say 25,000,000 to 35,000,000

Notes

INTRODUCTION

1 For information about the temple, its excavation, and the historical background to its destruction, see the report of Barbara Gassowska, "Maternus Cynegius, Praefectus Praetorio Orientis and the Destruction of the Allat Temple in Palmyra," *Archaeologia* 33 (1982), 107–127.

2 Ibid., 113.

3 For a fuller statement, see Troels Myrup Kristensen, *Making and Breaking the Gods: Christian Responses to Pagan Sculpture in Late Antiquity* (Aarhus, Denmark: Aarhus University Press, 2013), 89–106.

4 Gassowska, "Maternus Cynegius," 119.

5 Eberhard Sauer, *The Archaeology of Religious Hatred in the Roman and Early Medieval World* (Stroud, UK: History Press, 2009), 157.

6 I will explore the issues of gain and loss more explicitly in the Afterword.

CHAPTER 1

1 There are numerous authoritative biographies of Constantine. Among the most hard-hitting accounts written by scholars for

scholars are the following: Timothy D. Barnes, *Constantine and Eusebius* (Cambridge, MA: Harvard University, 1981); Timothy Barnes, *Constantine: Dynasty, Religion and Power in the Later Roman Empire* (Chichester, UK: Wiley Blackwell, 2014); and Harold A. Drake, *Constantine and the Bishops: The Politics of Intolerance* (Baltimore: Johns Hopkins, 2000). Somewhat more accessible to the general reader but fully authoritative are Noel Lenski, ed., *The Cambridge Companion to the Age of Constantine* (New York: Cambridge University Press, 2006) and David Potter, *Constantine the Emperor* (New York: Oxford University, 2013). See also the interesting account of Paul Stephenson, *Constantine: Unconquered Emperor, Christian Victor* (London: Quercus, 2009).

2 See, for example, Lewis R. Rambo and Charles E. Farhadian, *The Oxford Handbook of Religious Conversion* (New York: Oxford University Press, 2014).

3 I am not using the term "pagan" in a derogatory sense but simply to refer to the broad array of non-monotheistic religions embraced by virtually everyone except Jews (and then Christians) in antiquity. See further my discussion on pp. 76–78.

4 We will be discussing pagan religions more fully in chapter 3. For general overviews, see the brief treatment of A. D. Lee, "Traditional Religions," in Lenski, ed., *The Age of Constantine*, 159–79. For a particularly useful book-length discussion, see James B. Rives, *Religion in the Roman Empire* (Oxford, UK: Blackwell, 2007). A terse but helpful overview is Ramsay MacMullen, *Paganism in the Roman Empire* (New Haven, CT: Yale University Press, 1981). Now classic is the elegant book by Robin Lane Fox, *Pagans and Christians* (New York: Knopf, 1987). A valuable full assessment can be found in the two-volume collection of sources and analysis of Mary Beard, John North, and Simon Price, *Religions of Rome* (Cambridge, UK: Cambridge University Press, 1998). For my comments about paganism as an "ism," see also James B. Rives, "Christian Expansion and Christian Ideology," in W. V. Harris, ed., *The Spread of Christianity in the First Four Centuries: Essays in Explanation* (Leiden, Netherlands: Brill, 2005), 15–41.

5 Among the many authoritative accounts of the period, see the useful and detailed studies in Alan Bowman, Avril Cameron, and Peter Garnsey, *Cambridge Ancient History, The Crisis of Empire: 193–337*, 2nd ed., vol. 12 (Cambridge, UK: Cambridge University Press, 2005).

6 There have been scholarly controversies over how, precisely, the system was supposed to work. I am following the reconstruction of Barnes, *Constantine: Dynasty, Religion, and Power*, 63.

7 See the works cited in note 1 for this chapter.

8 Not only was the opposing army commanded by Maximian, the highly experienced father of Maxentius, but so too had been most of Severus's own troops several years earlier. They appear to have continued to have felt close loyalties to their previous general, and so deserted to him when the opportunity arose.

9 Galerius had never been to Rome and apparently did not realize just how large it was. He did not bring enough troops for a siege.

10 See the references given in note 1 for this chapter. The two main primary sources from Eusebius are his *Church History*—see Eusebius, *The History of the Church from Christ to Constantine*, trans. G. A. Williamson, revised and edited by Andrew Louth (London: Penguin, 1965)—and a biography of Constantine (the only one of him to survive from antiquity) called *The Life of Constantine*: see Eusebius, *Life of Constantine*, trans. Averil Cameron and Stuart G. Hall (Oxford, UK: Clarendon Press, 1999). Quotations are taken from this translation.

11 See Lee, "Traditional Religions."

12 Eusebius, *Life of Constantine*, chapters 13–18, 27.

13 A translation of the panegyric, along with the others delivered to Constantine during his career, can be found in C. E. V. Nixon and Barbara Saylor Rogers, *In Praise of Later Roman Emperors: The Panegyrici Latini* (Berkeley: University of California Press, 1995).

14 See the references in note 1 for this chapter. The account is found in Eusebius, *Life of Constantine*, 1.27–32.

15 In his comments Eusebius seems to intimate that this was based on a private audience with the emperor, but more likely it was a public event, probably a dinner of the bishops who had attended

the Council of Nicaea (discussed in chapter 8) after the completion of their work in 325 CE. This means, of course, that Constantine's recollections of his vision were revealed to Eusebius and the others some thirteen years after the event itself.

16 Eusebius, *In Praise of Constantine* 8.1; see also Eusebius, *Life of Constantine* 1.47. The most recent and the fullest discussion of Constantine's visions is Raymond van Dam, *Remembering Constantine at the Milvian Bridge* (New York: Cambridge University Press, 2011). Van Dam applies recent developments in the studies of memory to argue that it is really impossible, at the end of the day, to know what, if anything, actually happened. The accounts of the visions are hopelessly at odds with one another, and even if we just stick with one or the other, there are enormous problems. The fullest version of Eusebius, for example, presents Eusebius's biased reporting of what he claimed he heard Constantine say many years after the fact. But Constantine had reasons of his own (i.e., biases) for shaping his story the way he did. Moreover, he was remembering the past in light of all of his thinking and experiences in the meantime, so that his recollections of the past may not be an accurate reflection of what happened, or what he thought happened, at the time.

17 See the discussions in Rambo and Farhadian, *The Oxford Handbook of Religious Conversion*.

18 See note 16 for this chapter. As to what Constantine actually saw (if anything), there have been numerous suggestions over the years, none as tantalizing or widely discussed as one made by a German scholar named Peter Weiss, who argued that Constantine may have seen a "solar halo." Solar halos are an unusual but completely normal optical phenomenon in which the light of the sun is refracted by millions of ice crystals suspended in the atmosphere. The sun is surrounded by a bright halo—you can see many instances online—and sometimes appears to have rays shooting out in a few or in many directions. You can imagine seeing the phenomenon and thinking that the sun looks like a laurel wreath, or even a cross. Sometimes the phenomenon lasts as long

as two hours, appearing suddenly and disappearing as quickly. Did Constantine and the soldiers with him have such a vision? Some scholars have maintained it is at least possible. Others have argued there is no way to verify any such "naturalistic" explanations of allegedly "supernatural" occurrences and pointed out that all such explanations are hopelessly speculative. Weiss's article was first published in German in 1993. The article was translated by A. R. Birley, with some revisions by Weiss, as "The Vision of Constantine," *Journal of Roman Archaeology* 16 (2003), 237–59.

19 See, for example, Potter, *Constantine the Emperor*: "In 312, Constantine's God was both the Sun and the Christian God. It may not have been hard to make this leap, for in some Christian communities the sun god was already equated with Christ" (pp. 158–59).

20 Eusebius suggests that Maxentius had designed the bridge to collapse under stress and planned to draw Constantine and his forces onto it as a trap. But the plan backfired when his troops were routed and needed to make a hasty retreat back to the city. It is an intriguing claim but rather difficult to credit.

21 In addition to Drake, *Constantine and the Bishops*, see H. A. Drake, "Constantine and Consensus," *Church History* 64 (1995), 1–15.

22 Rather than being an imperial edict issued from Milan, it was a letter from Licinius based on an agreement he and Constantine had reached at a meeting they had held earlier in Milan.

23 See the fuller discussion in chapter 8.

24 English edition in Mark Edwards, *Constantine and Christendom* (Liverpool: Liverpool University Press, 2003).

25 See note 21 for this chapter.

CHAPTER 2

1 Biographies and studies of Paul are legion. For a fuller account of my perspective, see Bart D. Ehrman, *Peter, Paul, and Mary Magdalene* (New York: Oxford University Press, 2006). A classic in the field, approaching Paul from the perspective of social

history rather than theology, is Wayne A. Meeks, *The First Urban Christians: The Social World of the Apostle Paul*, 2nd ed. (New Haven, CT: Yale University Press, 2003). A helpful but very brief book-length treatment is E. P. Sanders, *Paul: A Short Introduction* (New York: Oxford University Press, 2001). Longer (massive) and more recent is E. P. Sanders, *Paul: The Apostle's Life, Letters, and Thought* (Philadelphia: Fortress, 2015). Another recent and informed contribution is Albert Harrill, *Paul the Apostle: His Life and Legacy* (Cambridge, UK: Cambridge University Press, 2012).

2 The seven undisputed letters: Romans, 1 and 2 Corinthians, Galatians, Philippians, 1 Thessalonians, and Philemon. On the issues of forgery in antiquity, the matter of terminology (is it appropriate to call such works forgeries?), and the dubious authorship of the Pauline letters, see Bart D. Ehrman, *Forged: Writing in the Name of God—Why the Bible's Authors Are Not Who We Think They Are* (San Francisco: HarperOne, 2012).

3 See my discussion in *Forged*, 202–209.

4 For a dating of the book in the early second century, some six decades after Paul's death, see Richard Pervo, *Dating Acts: Between the Evangelists and the Apologists* (Santa Rosa, CA: Polebridge Press, 2006).

5 For overviews of Judaism in the time of Paul, see Shaye Cohen, *From the Maccabees to the Mishnah*, 3rd ed. (Louisville, KY: Westminster John Knox, 2014) and E. P. Sanders, *Judaism: Practice and Belief, 63 BCE to 66 CE* (Philadelphia: Trinity Press International, 1992).

6 This has long been the contention of E. P. Sanders, a premier scholar of both Paul and ancient Judaism. See his books cited in notes 1 and 5 for this chapter. His classic statement of this view is in his scholarly monograph *Paul and Palestinian Judaism* (Philadelphia: Fortress Press, 1977).

7 See the discussions of Cohen and Sanders in the books cited in note 5 for this chapter.

8 See my book *Jesus: Apocalyptic Prophet of the New Millennium* (New York: Oxford University Press, 1999).

9 There are numerous book-length treatments just on the chronology of Paul's life and ministry. One widely used treatment is Gerd Luedemann, *Paul, Apostle to the Gentiles: Studies in Chronology* (Philadelphia: Fortress Press, 1984).

10 A number of scholars object to calling the early followers of Jesus "Christians," since many of the distinctive features of Christianity—especially its cardinal doctrines—had not yet developed. On the other hand, the same could be said for centuries, and yet no one hesitates using the term "Christian" for followers of Jesus in, say, the year 250. My view is that the very basic notions that made the Jewish followers of Jesus distinct among other Jews were already in place by the time Paul converted. These were the beliefs that Jesus's death had somehow brought about salvation with God and that God had then raised Jesus from the dead and taken him up to heaven to "sit at his right hand." Such views were known to Paul even before he himself became a follower of Jesus, and I think there is no harm in calling anyone who subscribed to them a Christian (without denying, of course, that the person could also be a Jew). The term "Christian" first appears in the New Testament in Acts 11:26 and 1 Peter 4:16.

11 For an account of Jewish messianic expectations at the time, see John Collins, *The Scepter and the Star: The Messiahs of the Dead Sea Scrolls and Other Ancient Literature* (New York: Doubleday, 1995).

12 See my discussion in Bart D. Ehrman, *How Jesus Became God: The Exaltation of a Jewish Preacher from Galilee* (San Francisco: HarperOne, 2014).

13 The Greek could also be translated "revealed his son *in* me." If that is the proper translation, it would mean that the revelation of God occurred within Paul—that is, it was a personal insight that he received, in his own mind.

14 I do not mean to imply that his thoughts occurred in a vacuum. Since Paul had been persecuting the Christians, he already knew, of course, that they claimed Jesus was the one favored by God who had been raised from the dead. The thought processes that

I describe here are how he figured out for himself how this was possible and what it all meant.

15 Harrill, *Paul the Apostle*, 26.

16 One particularly helpful study of Paul's mission is Terence L. Donaldson, "'The Field God Has Assigned': Geography and Mission in Paul," in *Religious Rivalries in the Early Roman Empire and the Rise of Christianity*, ed. Leif E. Vaage (Waterloo, ON: Wilfrid Laurier University Press, 2006), 109–37.

17 See the full discussion of Meeks, *The First Urban Christians*.

18 Ronald F. Hock, *The Social Context of Paul's Ministry: Tentmaking and Apostleship* (Philadelphia: Fortress, 1980), 27.

19 Johannes Munck, *Paul and the Salvation of Mankind* (London: SCM Press, 1959), 49.

20 See especially Hock, *The Social Context of Paul's Ministry*, and Meeks, *The First Urban Christians*.

21 Hock, *The Social Context of Paul's Ministry*.

22 Examples taken from Meeks, *The First Urban Christians*, 28, and Ramsay MacMullen, *Roman Social Relations: 50 B.C. to A.D. 284* (New Haven CT: Yale University Press, 1974), 63.

23 See pp. 75–76.

CHAPTER 3

1 Apart from the apostle Peter in the book of Acts, in stories that I will be arguing later are legendary. See pp. 139–44.

2 Others whom Paul names are often identified as Jews based on their appearance in other sources, including most notably Prisca and Aquila, who are clearly mentioned as Jews in the book of Acts. Paul himself does not indicate one way or the other.

3 On the gentile origins of Matthew, see my discussion in Bart D. Ehrman, *The New Testament: A Historical Introduction to the Early Christian Writings*, 6th ed. (New York: Oxford University Press, 2016), 143.

4 For a fuller discussion, see David C. Sim, "How Many Jews Became Christians in the First Century? The Failure of the Christian

Mission to the Jews," *Harvard Theological Studies* 1 and 2 (2005), 417–40.

5 For a very useful discussion of the broader phenomenon of Roman paganism, see James B. Rives, *Religion in the Roman Empire* (Oxford, UK: Blackwell, 2007). A terse but helpful overview is Ramsay MacMullen, *Paganism in the Roman Empire* (New Haven, CT: Yale University Press, 1981). A particularly valuable full assessment can be found in the two-volume collection of sources and analysis of Mary Beard, John North, and Simon Price, *Religions of Rome* (Cambridge, UK: Cambridge University Press, 1998). A classic is the elegant discussion of Robin Lane Fox, *Pagans and Christians* (New York: Knopf, 1987). For a more detailed, shorter study that is particularly insightful and on which I have relied heavily, see James B. Rives, "Religious Choice and Religious Change in Classical and Late Antiquity: Models and Questions," *Antigüedad, Religiones y Sociedades* 9 (2011), 265–80.

6 Among many discussions of the term, see Pierre Chuvin, *A Chronicle of the Last Pagans*, trans. B. A. Archer (Cambridge, MA: Harvard University Press, 1990), 7–13; Christopher Jones, *Between Pagan and Christian* (Cambridge, MA: Harvard University Press, 2014), 5–8; and James J. O'Donnell, *Pagans: The End of Traditional Religion and the Rise of Christianity* (New York: Ecco, 2015), 159–64.

7 See the works of Rives cited in note 5 for this chapter.

8 Among other things, there is the problem of terminology. Scholars not only debate what the term "pagan" may have originally meant; they dispute whether it should be used at all. A strong argument can be made that creating an "ism" out of these widely variant practices skews the world of ancient religious thought and practice. Moreover, some scholars do continue to be wary of the negative connotations often associated with the terms "pagan" and "paganism" among those who are not historians of the period.

On the other hand, none of the proposed alternatives is any better. A number of scholars have suggested that we talk instead about ancient "polytheism," since, as we have seen, one common feature of this widely diverse set of religions is that they all assumed the existence of numerous gods. The difficulty is that even within that polytheistic world there were people—and not just Jews—who insisted on the primacy of one ultimate divine being. Some non-Jews even refused to worship any god beside this one. For that reason, "polytheist" does not capture the whole religious spectrum.

Other scholars have suggested, somewhat more plausibly, that it is simplest to refer to ancient "traditional religions." There is a clear benefit in this term, as there is nothing negative about it, and it seems to be reasonably accurate for the phenomenon we are examining. It does have several downsides, however. For one thing, the term simply employs one later designation that ancient people would not have recognized ("religion") instead of another ("paganism"). Moreover, "traditional religions" cannot conveniently be converted into a collective noun analogous to the word "pagans." Finally, we should be wary of differentiating *completely* between the varied cultic practices found throughout the Roman world: they differed significantly among themselves, but they were not different "religions" in the way that, say, Christianity, Islam, Buddhism, and Hinduism would be seen as distinct religions by most people today. On one hand, they lack the coherent systems of belief and practice we normally associate with religion; on the other hand, even though ancient cults were not standardized, they did share some features based on commonly held assumptions and broadly defined practices.

For these reasons, in my discussion I will follow widespread practice and continue to speak of "traditional religions," "pagan religions," and "paganism" interchangeably (with no negative connotations). My position is that it does indeed help to see not only what made each of these cultic systems distinct but also what all (or most) of them had in common, at least when seen from the outside, many centuries later.

9 I have taken these examples from MacMullen, *Paganism*, 1.

10 For that reason I prefer calling the worship of just one god within the realm of Roman paganism "henotheism" (the worship of one god) rather than "monotheism" (the belief that there is only one god). For scholars who do use the term "monotheism," see, for example, Stephen Mitchell and Peter Van Nuffelen, *One God: Pagan Monotheism in the Roman Empire* (Cambridge, UK: Cambridge University Press, 2010).

11 See especially Rives, *Religion in the Roman Empire*, 23–28.

12 This is a thesis of Robin Lane Fox, *Pagans and Christians*.

13 Translation by T. R. Glover, *Tertullian: Apology; De Spetaculis*, Loeb Classical Library 250 (Cambridge, MA: Harvard University Press, 1931).

14 Translation by Beard, North, and Price, *Religions of Rome*, vol. 2, 152.

15 MacMullen, *Paganism*, 49.

16 *The History of Rome*, book 39, chapters 8 to 22. I will be citing the translation by Henry Bettenson, *Livy: Rome and the Mediterranean* (London: Penguin, 1976).

17 See, however, my discussion on pp. 160–61.

18 Recall that in the pagan world, daimones were not necessarily malevolent divine beings that possessed human bodies, making them engage in hurtful activities, as they later came to be for Christians; they were simply lower-level divinities, some good and some harmful.

19 For a classic statement, see James George Frazier, *The Golden Bough: A Study of Magic and Religion* (first published 1890; reprinted many times since).

20 Rives, *Religion in the Roman Empire*, 183.

21 For a helpful historical overview, see Dale Martin, *Inventing Superstition* (Cambridge, MA: Harvard University Press, 2004).

22 For a hilarious caricature of "The Superstitious Person," see the brilliant sketch in the ancient book *The Characters of Theophrastus*, trans. and ed. J. M. Edmonds (London: William Heinemann Ltd., 1929).

23 Plutarch, "On Superstition." I am using the translation by Frank Cole Babbitt, *Plutarch's Moralia II*, Loeb Classical Library 222 (Cambridge, MA: Harvard University Press, 1971).

24 Ibid.

25 Ibid.

26 Cited in Edward J. Watts, *The Final Pagan Generation* (Berkeley: University of California Press, 2015), 18, 2n.

27 Watts, *The Final Pagan Generation*, 23.

28 In addition to the works cited in note 5 for this chapter, see Hugh Bowden, *Mystery Cults of the Ancient World* (Princeton, NJ: Princeton University Press, 2010) and Marvin Meyer, *The Ancient Mysteries: A Sourcebook of Ancient Texts*, 2nd ed. (Philadelphia: University of Pennsylvania Press, 1999).

29 The basic meaning of the word "mystery" is simply "initiated."

30 On Mithraism, see especially Roger Beck, *The Religion of the Mithras Cult in the Roman Empire*, 2nd ed. (New York: Oxford University Press, 2007).

31 There is less reason to think that mystery religions typically involved a deity who died and then rose again. See especially Jonathan Z. Smith, *Drudgery Divine: On the Comparison of Early Christianities and the Religions of Late Antiquity* (Chicago: University of Chicago, 1990).

32 References taken from Beard, North, and Price, *The Religions of Rome*, vol. 2, 254.

33 See Beard, North, and Price, *The Religions of Rome*, vol. 1, 348–61.

CHAPTER 4

1 Adolf Harnack, *The Expansion of Christianity in the First Three Centuries*, vol. 2, trans. James Moffatt (New York: G. P. Putnam's Sons, 1908), 248. As Harold Drake indicates: "Almost everyone is willing to admit that this number feels about right." H. A. Drake, "Models of Christian Expansion," in W. V. Harris, ed., *The Spread of Christianity in the First Four Centuries: Essays in Explanation* (Leiden, Netherlands: Brill, 2005), 2.

2 I am using "Christian" as a broad umbrella term here to encompass all the varieties of Christianity that existed at the time, an issue I explore more fully at the conclusion of this chapter.

3 Kenneth Scott Latourette, *A History of the Expansion of Christianity*, vol. 1, The First Five Centuries (New York: Harper & Brothers, 1937), 11.

4 E. R. Dodds, *Pagans and Christians in an Age of Anxiety: Some Aspects of Religious Experience from Marcus Aurelius to Constantine* (New York: W. W. Norton and Company, 1965), 132.

5 Edward Gibbon, *The History of the Decline and Fall of the Roman Empire*, J. B. Bury, ed. 6 vols. (London: Methuen, 1909; original 1776–89).

6 Ibid., vol. 2, chapter 15, 60.

7 Ibid., 2.

8 Ibid., 2–3.

9 This is the view taken, for example, by Arthur Darby Nock in his classic work, *Conversion: The Old and the New in Religion from Alexander the Great to Augustine of Hippo* (London: Oxford University Press, 1933). See William James, *Varieties of Religious Experience* (New York: Longmans, Green, 1902), republished innumerable times.

10 As I will point out later, this appears to be the view not only of the triumphant "orthodox" Christianity but also of many of the variant forms of the religion competing for dominance in the early centuries. See note 40 for this chapter.

11 Nock, *Conversion*, 9.

12 For authors who prefer to use the term "monotheism" for this phenomenon, see, for example, Stephen Mitchell and Peter Van Nuffelen, *One God: Pagan Monotheism in the Roman Empire* (Cambridge, UK: Cambridge University Press, 2010).

13 Translation by Stephen Mitchell, as cited in A. D. Lee, "Traditional Religions," in Lenski, ed., *The Age of Constantine*, 165–66.

14 See Angelos Chaniotis, "Megatheism: The Search for the Almighty God and the Competition of Cults," in Mitchell and Nuffelen, *One God*, 112–40.

15 Ibid., 128.

16 On the inscriptions, see Stephen Mitchell, "Further Thoughts on the Cult of Theos Hypsistos," in Mitchell and Nuffelen, *One God*, 167–208.

17 Augustine, Epistle 16.1; translation by G. Clark; slightly modified; quoted by Stephen Mitchell and Peter van Nuffelen, *Monotheism Between Pagans and Christians in Late Antiquity* (Leuven, Belgium: Peeters, 2010), 2.

18 Athenagoras, "Embassy" 7.1; translation by Joseph Hugh Crehan, *Athenagoras: Embassy for the Christians, The Resurrection of the Dead* (New York: Newman Press, 1955).

19 This is one of the truly great insights argued forcefully by Ramsay MacMullen, *Christianizing the Roman Empire* (New Haven, CT: Yale University Press, 1984).

20 Ramsay MacMullen, *Paganism in the Roman Empire* (New Haven, CT: Yale University Press, 1981), 98–99.

21 Roger Beck, "On Becoming a Mithraist: New Evidence for the Propagation of the Mysteries," in *Religious Rivalries in the Early Roman Empire and the Rise of Christianity*, ed. Leif E. Vaage (Waterloo, ON: Wilfrid Laurier University Press, 2006), 175–94.

22 Martin Goodman, *Mission and Conversion: Proselytizing in the Religious History of the Roman Empire* (Oxford, UK: Clarendon, 1994), 105.

23 Ibid., 160.

24 Ibid., 106.

25 MacMullen, *Christianizing*, 34.

26 A couple of others are named—Pantaenus in Alexandria, Ulfilus among the Goths, and Frumentius in Ethiopia—but not a single thing is said in any of our sources about their actual work. For Gregory the Wonderworker and Martin of Tours, see the discussion of chapter 5.

27 This is a thesis of Rodney Stark, *The Rise of Christianity: How the Obscure, Marginal Jesus Movement Became the Dominant Religious Force in the Western World in a Few Centuries* (San Francisco: HarperSanFrancisco, 1996).

28 I do not mean that pagans never talked with one another about their religious festivals and practices, and the benefits they derived from them (from, for example, divine intervention in their lives). Obviously this was a matter of widespread discussion. But

in none of the other religious cults was there any sustained effort to convert others, let alone the inclination to insist that only one set of cultic practices was acceptable to the gods.

29 Again, no one has expressed this view more forcefully or convincingly than Ramsay MacMullen, *Christianizing*.

30 An idea pursued especially by a number of scholars, including John North. A particularly insightful discussion of these issues can be found in James B. Rives, "Religious Choice and Religious Change in Classical and Late Antiquity: Models and Questions," *Antigüedad, Religiones y Sociedades* 9 (2011), 265–80.

31 I have borrowed this idea (with a modified illustration) directly from Rives, "Religious Choice."

32 A possible exception, in rare instances, may have involved the most fervent followers of some of the mystery religions. See my discussion of Apuleius on pp. 122–25.

33 See note 9 for this chapter.

34 I am using the translation by Jack Lindsay, *The Golden Ass* (Bloomington: Indiana University Press, 1960).

35 MacMullen, *Christianizing*.

36 For the following insights, I am indebted to James B. Rives, "Religious Choice."

37 Rives, "Religious Choice."

38 See James B. Rives, "Christian Expansion and Christian Ideology," in W. V. Harris, ed., *The Spread of Christianity in the First Four Centuries: Essays in Explanation* (Leiden, Netherland: Brill, 2005), 15–41.

39 For starters, see my book *Lost Christianities: The Battles for Scripture and the Faiths We Never Knew* (New York: Oxford University Press, 2003). See also note 40 for this chapter.

40 I would hold that to be true of Marcionites, for example. Jewish Christian groups such as the Ebionites were also exclusivist, whether or not they were aggressively evangelistic. On the other hand, some forms of Christian Gnosticism, such as Valentinianism, appear to have drawn most of their members not directly from paganism but from fellow Christians who had already left pagan traditions.

CHAPTER 5

1 See the discussions of the book of Acts and the claims of Tertullian on pp. 162–63.

2 We will be considering a much shorter account—the very first from a pagan pen, that of the Roman governor Pliny—in chapter 6.

3 I will be citing the book from *Celsus: On the True Doctrine: A Discourse Against the Christians*, trans. R. Joseph Hoffmann (New York: Oxford University Press, 1987).

4 For example, Wayne A. Meeks, *The First Urban Christians: The Social World of the Apostle Paul*, 2nd ed. (New Haven, CT: Yale University Press, 2003).

5 Robin Lane Fox, *Pagans and Christians* (New York: Knopf, 1987), 310.

6 E. R. Dodds, *Pagans and Christians in an Age of Anxiety: Some Aspects of Religious Experience from Marcus Aurelius to Constantine* (New York: W. W. Norton and Company, 1965), 137–38.

7 Adolf Harnack, *The Expansion of Christianity in the First Three Centuries*, vol. 2, trans. James Moffatt (New York: G. P. Putnam's Sons, 1908), 480.

8 Rodney Stark, *The Rise of Christianity: How the Obscure, Marginal Jesus Movement Became the Dominant Religious Force in the Western World in a Few Centuries* (San Francisco: HarperSanFrancisco, 1996), chapter 4; Hector Avalos, *Health Care and the Rise of Christianity* (Grand Rapids, MI: Baker Academic, 1999).

9 Stark's uncritical use of sources is probably the most criticized aspect of his work among scholars in the field of early Christian studies. For a particularly trenchant critique, see Elizabeth A. Castelli, "Gender, Theory, and *The Rise of Christianity*: A Response to Rodney Stark," *Journal of Early Christian Studies* 6 (1998), 227–57.

10 Eusebius, *Church History*: see Eusebius, *The History of the Church from Christ to Constantine*, trans. G. A. Williamson, revised and edited by Andrew Louth (London: Penguin, 1965), 7.22.

11 No scholar has argued this case more forcefully than Ramsay MacMullen, *Christianizing the Roman Empire* (New Haven, CT: Yale University Press, 1984).

12 For a translation of the letter and fuller introduction, see Bart D. Ehrman and Zlatko Pleše, *The Other Gospels: Accounts of Jesus from Outside the New Testament* (New York: Oxford University Press, 2014), 214–16.

13 Eusebius, *Church History* 1.13.

14 Eusebius, *Church History* 2.1.

15 Translations of these narratives can be found in J. K. Elliott, *The Apocryphal New Testament* (Oxford, UK: Clarendon Press, 1993).

16 Acts of John 60–61.

17 Acts of John 42.

18 Acts of John 44–47.

19 Acts of Peter 12–13.

20 Acts of Peter 25–26.

21 One exception to the rule that miracles convert appears to be the conversion of Thecla in the famous Acts of Paul and Thecla. She is a young woman who overhears Paul preaching a sermon about the virtues of celibacy in the house next door, and she converts on the spot.

22 Gregory of Nyssa, "On the Life and Wonders of Our Father Among the Saints, Gregory the Wonderworker." I have used the translation by Michael Slusser, *Fathers of the Church: St. Gregory Thaumaturgus Life and Works* (Washington, DC: Catholic University of America Press, 1998).

23 "Life of St. Martin" 13.8–9. I have used the translation by Richard J. Goodrich in *Sulpicius Severus: The Complete Works* (New York: Newman Press, 2015).

24 Augustine of Hippo, *The City of God*, trans. Marcus Dods (New York: Random House, 1950), 22.8.

25 Cyprian, "Letter to Demetrius," chapter 24. Translation by Ernest Wallis, in Alexander Roberts and James Donaldson, eds., *Ante-Nicene Fathers*, reprint ed. (Peabody, MA: Hendrickson, 1994).

26 Ramsay MacMullen, "What Difference Did Christianity Make?" *Historia: Zeitschrift für Alte Geschichte* 35 (1986), 335.

27 Translation by T. R. Glover, *Tertullian: Apology; De Spetaculis*, Loeb Classical Library 250 (Cambridge, MA: Harvard University Press, 1931).

28 Hoffman, *Celsus*, 70.

29 Augustine, "On Catechizing the Uninstructed" 5.9; translation by Robin Lane Fox, *Pagans and Christians*, 263.

30 Arthur Darby Nock, *Conversion: The Old and the New in Religion from Alexander the Great to Augustine of Hippo* (London: Oxford University Press, 1933), 9.

31 Ramsay MacMullen, "Two Types of Conversion to Early Christianity," *Vigiliae Christianae* 37 (1983), 181, 185.

32 Herbert Musurillo, "The Martyrdom of Perpetua and Felicitas," in *The Acts of the Christian Martyrs* (Oxford, UK: Oxford University Press, 1972), 106–31.

33 *Martyrdom of Polycarp*, 11; translation by Bart D. Ehrman, *The Apostolic Fathers*, Loeb Classical Library 24 (Cambridge, MA: Harvard University, 2003).

34 Saint Justin Martyr, *The Second Apology*, trans. Thomas B. Falls (Washington, DC: Catholic University of America Press, 1948).

35 Saint Justin Martyr, *Dialogue with Trypho*, trans. Thomas B. Falls (Washington, DC: Catholic University of America Press, 1948).

36 Apology 50, translation by Gerald Rendall, modified slightly, *Tertullian: Apology; De Spetaculis*, Loeb Classical Library 250 (Cambridge, MA: Harvard University Press, 1931).

37 *Octavius* 27.6. Translation by C. W. Clarke, *The Octavius of Minucius Felix* (New York: Newman Press, 1974).

38 Marcus Aurelius, *The Meditations*, trans. G.M.A. Grube (Indianapolis: Hackett Publishing Company, 1983), 11.3.

39 See Candida Moss, *The Myth of Persecution: How Early Christians Invented a Story of Martyrdom* (San Francisco: HarperOne, 2014).

40 *Against Celsus* 8; translation by Henry Chadwick, *Origen: Contra Celsum* (Cambridge, UK: Cambridge University Press, 1953).

CHAPTER 6

1 Pliny 10.96; translation by P. G. Walsh, in *Pliny the Younger: Complete Letters* (Oxford, UK: Oxford University Press, 2006).

2 Translation by S. Thelwall, in Alexander Roberts and James

Donaldson, eds., *The Ante-Nicene Fathers*, vol. 3, reprint ed. (Grand Rapids, MI: Eerdmans, 1989).

3 Robin Lane Fox, *Pagans and Christians* (New York: Knopf, 1987), 201.

4 Lane Fox illustrates the point by pointing to the oracle and temple of Apollo at Claros on the coast of Ionia, where at the time we find more than three hundred pagan dedications.

5 Adolf Harnack, *The Expansion of Christianity in the First Three Centuries*, vol. 2, trans. James Moffatt (New York: G. P. Putnam's Sons, 1908), 248.

6 As already observed. See note 1 for chapter 4.

7 Ramsay MacMullen, *The Second Church: Popular Christianity, A.D. 200–400* (Atlanta: Society of Biblical Literature, 2009).

8 Ibid., 101.

9 Ramsay MacMullen, *Roman Social Relations, 50 B.C. to A.D. 284* (New Haven, CT: Yale University Press, 1974), 63.

10 Roger Bagnall, "Religious Conversion and Onomastic Change in Early Byzantine Egypt," *Bulletin of the American Society of Papyrologists* 19 (1982), 105–124.

11 Bagnall's findings were disputed by other scholars making different calculations; in his reply he stressed that, even based on other calculations, "we may reasonably suppose that Christians were well more than a majority before the end of the century; but it is hard to be more precise than that" (p. 249). Roger Bagnall, "Conversion and Onomastics: A Reply," *ZPE* 69 (1987), 243–50.

12 Harnack, *Expansion of Christianity*, 2.324–37.

13 Frank Trombley, "Overview: The Geographical Spread of Christianity," in Margaret Mitchell and Frances Young, eds., *The Cambridge History of Christianity: Origins to Constantine* (Cambridge, UK: Cambridge University, 2006), 302–13.

14 Rodney Stark, *The Rise of Christianity: How the Obscure, Marginal Jesus Movement Became the Dominant Religious Force in the Western World in a Few Centuries* (San Francisco: HarperSanFrancisco, 1996).

15 Keith Hopkins, "Christian Number and Its Implications," *Journal of Early Christian Studies* 6 (1998), 185–226.

16 An effort to update Harnack in light of new evidence can be found in Roderic Mullen, *The Expansion of Christianity: A Gazetteer of Its First Three Centuries* (Leiden, Netherlands: Brill, 2004).

CHAPTER 7

1 The book was almost certainly not actually written by Jesus's disciple Peter. On the question of authorship, see Bart D. Ehrman, *Forged: Writing in the Name of God—Why the Bible's Authors Are Not Who We Think They Are* (San Francisco: HarperOne, 2012), 65–77.

2 Translation in Alexander Roberts and James Donaldson, eds., *The Ante-Nicene Fathers*, vol. 5, reprint ed. (Grand Rapids, MI: Eerdmans, 1989).

3 Translation by Herbert Musurillo, *Acts of the Christian Martyrs* (Oxford, UK: Clarendon Press, 1972).

4 I have taken quotations from the translation by C. W. Clarke, *The Octavius of Minucius Felix* (New York: Newman Press, 1974). The Introduction to the volume is an excellent guide to both the book and its author.

5 See, for example, Stephen Benko, *Pagan Rome and the Early Christians* (Bloomington: University of Indiana Press, 1984).

6 Andrew McGowan, "Eating People: Accusations of Cannibalism Against Christians in the Second Century," *Journal of Early Christian Studies* 2 (1994), 413–42.

7 Candida Moss, *The Myth of Persecution: How Early Christians Invented a Story of Martyrdom* (San Francisco: HarperOne, 2013).

8 For translations of the early-martyrdom accounts, see Musurillo, *Acts of the Christian Martyrs*.

9 See Bart D. Ehrman, *Forgery and Counterforgery: The Use of Literary Deceit in Early Christian Polemics* (New York: Oxford University Press, 2012), 493–508; Moss, *The Myth of Persecution*, 94–104.

10 My own translation. See Bart D. Ehrman, ed., *The Apostolic Fathers*, vol.1, Loeb Classical Library 24 (Cambridge, MA: Harvard University, 2003).

11 Translation by Musurillo, *Acts of the Christian Martyrs*.

12 Translation by Michael Grant, *Tacitus: The Annals of Imperial Rome*, revised reprint ed. (London: Penguin, 1996).

13 Over the years some readers have wondered if the Christians, in fact, were guilty of setting the fire. The logic is that if they were heavily influenced by apocalyptic thought and assumed that God was soon to judge the world through a major conflagration, possibly they decided to initiate the proceeding themselves. It is an intriguing thesis, but in the end is probably not convincing. Tacitus himself thought the fire was either set by Nero or was a pure accident.

14 Quoted in Eusebius, *Church History*: see Eusebius, *The History of the Church from Christ to Constantine*, trans. G. A. Williamson, revised and edited by Andrew Louth (London: Penguin, 1965), 10.9.

15 The letter occupies the first part of book 5 of Eusebius's *Church History*, which is our only surviving account.

16 The best study of the incident is James B. Rives, "The Decree of Decius and the Religion of Empire," *Journal of Roman Studies* 89 (1999), 135–54, on which I am dependent for many of the points I make here.

17 Rives, "Decree of Decius."

18 Ibid., 53.

19 See Moss, *The Myth of Persecution*, 151–53; Eusebius's account can be found in *Church History* 7.10–12.

20 For a brief history of Valerian's persecution, see Bernard Green, *Christianity in Ancient Rome: The First Three Centuries* (London: T&T Clark, 2010), 161–66.

21 See Elizabeth DePalma Digeser, *The Making of a Christian Empire: Lactantius and Rome* (Ithaca, NY: Cornell University Press, 2000), Prologue.

22 For the course of the persecution, see Moss, *The Myth of Persecution*, 154–49; Green, *Christianity in Ancient Rome*, 211–13; Eusebius's account can be found in *Church History* 8.

23 Quoted in R. Joseph Hoffmann, trans., *Celsus: On the True Doctrine: A Discourse Against the Christians* (New York: Oxford University Press, 1987), 118.

24 See Arthur Droge, *Homer or Moses? Early Christian Interpretations of the History of Culture* (Tübingen, Germany: Mohr Siebeck, 1989).

CHAPTER 8

1 In a letter he wrote to the inhabitants of the eastern provinces of the empire, as quoted in Eusebius, *Life of Constantine*, trans. Averil Cameron and Stuart G. Hall (Oxford, UK: Clarendon Press, 1999), 2.51.

2 The letter is cited by Eusebius in *Church History*: see Eusebius, *The History of the Church from Christ to Constantine*, trans. G. A. Williamson, revised and edited by Andrew Louth (London: Penguin, 1965), 10.5. Eusebius claims, probably wrongly, that Licinius was a Christian at the time of the conference in Milan but fell to the dark side later.

3 Harold A. Drake, *Constantine and the Bishops: The Politics of Intolerance* (Baltimore: Johns Hopkins, 2000), 194.

4 As emphasized especially by Drake, *Constantine and the Bishops*, and "Constantine and Consensus," *Church History* 64 (1995), 1–15.

5 Every decent book on Constantine discusses the Donatist controversy (see note 1 for chapter 1). For a good, brief summary see H. A. Drake, "The Impact of Constantine on Christianity," in Noel Lenski, ed., *The Cambridge Companion to the Age of Constantine* (New York: Cambridge University Press, 2006), 111–36.

6 Drake, "The Impact of Constantine on Christianity," 119.

7 Eusebius, *Life of Constantine* 2.60.

8 The letter is cited in Eusebius, *Life of Constantine* 1.64–72.

9 For a fuller discussion of the council, the events leading up to it, the theological issues involved, and the eventual outcome, see my book *How Jesus Became God: The Exaltation of a Jewish Preacher from Galilee* (San Francisco: HarperOne, 2014), chapter 9.

10 Some scholars, such as Paul Stephenson in *Constantine: Unconquered Emperor, Christian Victor* (London: Quercus, 2009), have expressed doubts about this. It is, however, what our few surviving sources report and is the more convincing position argued,

among others, by Timothy Barnes, *Constantine: Dynasty, Religion and Power in the Later Roman Empire* (Chichester, UK: Wiley Blackwell, 2014), 126–31.

11 See chapter 1, pp. 32–38.

12 A. D. Lee, "Traditional Religions," in Lenski, ed., *The Age of Constantine*, 174.

13 Eusebius, *Life of Constantine* 3.42.

14 This has long been the thesis in particular of Timothy Barnes. See Timothy D. Barnes, *Constantine and Eusebius* (Cambridge, MA: Harvard University, 1981), and Barnes, *Constantine: Dynasty, Religion and Power*.

15 He did, however, take a different line with Christian heretics, legislating harshly against them, disallowing their meetings, destroying their houses of worship, and generally making their lives miserable. See his letter to the Christian groups called Novatians, Valentinians, Marcionites, Paulians, and Cataphrygians (Montanists) in Eusebius, *Life of Constantine* 3.64–65.

16 For different views see Barnes, *Constantine: Dynasty, Religion, and Power*, 108–109; Drake, *Constantine and the Bishops*, 465; as well as Timothy D. Barnes, "Constantine's Prohibition of Pagan Sacrifice," *American Journal of Philology* 105 (1984), 69–72; R. Malcolm Errington, "Constantine and the Pagans," *Greek, Roman and Byzantine Studies* 29 (1988), 309–18; and Scott Bradbury, "Constantine and the Problem of Anti-Pagan Legislation in the Fourth Century," *Classical Philology* 89 (1994), 120–39.

17 Translation by Clyde Pharr, *The Theodosian Code* (Princeton, NJ: Princeton University Press, 1952).

18 Translation by A. F. Norman, *Libanius: Selected Works*, vol. 2, Loeb Classical Library 452 (Cambridge, MA: Harvard University Press, 1977).

19 For example, it has been argued that he originally passed such a law but then almost immediately rescinded it in a letter; or that it was a "law" only loosely defined, in that it could be found not in actual legislation but only in correspondence sent to an administrative underling. See the articles by Bradbury and Errington in note 16 for this chapter.

20 Ramsay MacMullen, "What Difference Did Christianity Make?" *Historia: Zeitschrift für Alte Geschichte* 35 (1986), 322–43.

21 See pp. 152–56.

22 MacMullen, "What Difference Did Christianity Make?" 336.

23 Ibid.

24 There are a number of intriguing discussions. See, for example, David Woods, "On the Death of the Empress Fausta," *Greece and Rome* 45 (1998), 70–86, and Barnes, *Constantine: Dynasty, Religion, and Power*, 144–50.

25 Noel Lenski, "The Reign of Constantine," in Noel Lenski, ed., *The Cambridge Companion to the Age of Constantine* (New York: Cambridge University Press, 2006), 79.

26 See Woods, "The Death of the Empress Fausta."

27 Even if he did not as a rule apply force to implement his specifically Christian views, there were exceptions: his confiscation of bronze statues and gold plate for the New Rome he constructed and the destruction of five pagan sites he viewed as particularly problematic either because they were located on sites sacred to the Christians or because they entailed sacred prostitution, a practice he could not countenance.

CHAPTER 9

1 These instances are cited by Clifford Ando, "Pagan Apologetics and Christian Intolerance in the Ages of Themistius and Augustine," *Journal of Early Christian Studies* 4 (1996), 171–207.

2 Peter Brown, *Power and Persuasion in Late Antiquity: Towards a Christian Empire* (Madison: University of Wisconsin Press, 1992), 129.

3 For a good summary of the imperial history after Constantine that I lay out here, see Robert M. Frakes, "The Dynasty of Constantine Down to 363," in Noel Lenski, ed., *The Cambridge Companion to the Age of Constantine* (New York: Cambridge University Press, 2006), 91–107.

4 One very readable recent account of Julian's life is Adrian Murdoch, *The Last Pagan: Julian the Apostate and the Death of the Ancient World* (Stroud: Sutton, 2003). Never surpassed, however,

is G. W. Bowersock, *Julian the Apostate* (Cambridge, MA: Harvard University, 1978).

5 See pp. 76–78.

6 Letter 26, quoted in Bowersock, *Julian*, 61.

7 The best account of these policies, again, is Bowersock, *Julian*.

8 Letter 60, quoted in Bowersock, *Julian*, 80–81.

9 Bowersock, *Julian*, 84.

10 Letter 84, quoted in Bowersock, *Julian*, 87.

11 *Divine Institutes* 5.19–20. Translation by Mary Francis McDonald, *Lactantius: The Divine Institutes* (Washington, DC: Catholic University of America Press, 1964).

12 For the contrast between Lactantius and Firmicus Maternus, see Maijastina Kahlos, "The Rhetoric of Tolerance and Intolerance: From Lactantius to Firmicus Maternus" in Jörg Ulrich, Anders-Christian Jacobsen, and Maijastina Kahlos, *Continuity and Discontinuity in Early Christian Apologetics* (Frankfurt: Peter Lang, 2009), 79–96.

13 *On the Error of the Pagan Religions* 29.2. Translation by Clarence A. Forbes in *Firmicus Maternus: The Error of Pagan Religions* (New York: Newman Press, 1970).

14 *De Vita* 1293–1302. Quoted in Harold A. Drake, *Constantine and the Bishops: The Politics of Intolerance* (Baltimore: Johns Hopkins Press, 2000), 406.

15 Troels Myrup Kristensen, *Making and Breaking the Gods: Christian Responses to Pagan Sculpture in Late Antiquity* (Aarhus, Denmark: Aarhus University Press, 2013).

16 Ibid., 9.

17 Ibid., 15.

18 Ibid., 14.

19 *Prudentius* 2.481–84, trans. M. Clement Eagan; quoted by Kristensen, *Making and Breaking the Gods*, 21.

20 Amelia Robertson Brown, "Hellenic Heritage and Christian Challenge: Conflict over Panhellenic Sanctuaries in Late Antiquity," in *Violence in Late Antiquity: Perceptions and Practices*, H. A. Drake, ed. (Burlington, VT: Ashgate, 2006), 309.

21 Mark the Deacon, *Life of Porphyry* 76, quoted by Brown, "Hellenic Heritage and Christian Challenge," 319.

22 Among many fine discussions, see Christopher Haas, *Alexandria in Late Antiquity: Topography and Social Conflict* (Baltimore: Johns Hopkins Press, 1997), 159–72, 307–316.

23 The first quotation is from Aphthonius, a student of Libanius. Both quotations come from the important study by Judith McKenzie, Sheila Gibson, and A. T. Reyes, "Reconstructing the Serapeum in Alexandria from the Archaeological Evidence," *Journal of Roman Studies* 94 (2004), 73–121.

24 Translation by Philip Amidon, *The Church History of Rufinus of Aquileia: Books 10 and 11* (New York: Oxford University Press, 1997).

25 The events are recounted in Rufinus, *Church History* 11.

26 Quoted by MacKenzie et al., "Reconstructing the Serapeum," 166.

27 Theodoret, *Church History* 5.22; quoted in Christopher Haas, *Alexandria in Late Antiquity: Topography and Social Conflict* (Baltimore: Johns Hopkins Press, 1997), 167.

28 Haas, *Alexandria in Late Antiquity*, 168–69.

29 Garth Fowden, "Bishops and Temples in the Eastern Roman Empire A.D. 320–435," *Journal of Theological Studies* 29 (1978), 77.

30 The episode is recounted in the definitive study, Maria Dzielska, *Hypatia of Alexandria*, trans. F. Lyra (Cambridge, MA: Harvard University Press, 1995), 50. See also Michael A. B. Deakin, *Hypatia of Alexandria: Mathematician and Martyr* (New York: Prometheus, 2007).

31 In addition to Dzielsak, *Hypatia*, see especially Edward Watts, "The Murder of Hypatia: Acceptable or Unacceptable Violence?" in *Violence in Late Antiquity: Perceptions and Practices*, H. A. Drake, ed. (Burlington, VT: Ashgate, 2006), 333–42.

32 For a discussion of this view, and a strong rejection of it, see Christoph Markschies, "The Price of Monotheism: Some New Observations on a Current Debate About Late Antiquity," in *One God: Pagan Monotheism in the Roman Empire*, Stephen Mitchell and Peter Van Nuffelen, eds. (Cambridge, UK: Cambridge University Press, 2010), chapter 6.

33 See, for example, Harold A. Drake, "Lambs into Lions: Explaining Early Christian Intolerance," *Past and Present* 153 (1996), 3–36; and "Intolerance, Religious Violence, and Political Legitimacy in Late Antiquity," *Journal of the American Academy of Religion* 79 (2011), 193–235.

34 For these and other anti-Jewish laws, see James Carroll, *Constantine's Sword: The Church and the Jews; A History* (Boston: Houghton Mifflin, 2001).

35 With respect to pagan objects of worship (though, in this case, not their worshipers), a similar view is propounded by the great theologian Augustine: "God who speaks truth has both predicted that the images of the many, the false gods, are to be overthrown and commands that it be done." Elsewhere he insists that this "is what God wants, God commands, God proclaims." See Augustine, Epistle 91 and Sermon 14.6, quoted in Ramsay MacMullen, *Christianity and Paganism in the Fourth to Eighth Centuries* (New Haven, CT: Yale University Press, 1997), 169.

36 Drake, "Lambs into Lions," 35.

37 Themistius, Oration 5, translation from Peter Heather and David Mondur, eds., *Politics, Philosophy and Empire in the Fourth Century: Select Orations of Themistius* (Liverpool: Liverpool University Press, 2001).

38 Translation by H. de Romestin, "Memorial of Symmachus," in *Nicene and Post-Nicene Fathers*, second series, vol. 10, Ambrose: Select Works and Letters, Philip Schaff and Henry Wace, eds., reprint ed. (Peabody, MA: Hendrickson Publishers, 1994).

39 See Ramsay MacMullen, *Christianizing the Roman Empire* (New Haven, CT: Yale University Press, 1984).

40 Michele Renee Salzman, "Rethinking Pagan-Christian Violence," in *Violence in Late Antiquity: Perceptions and Practices*, H. A. Drake, ed. (Burlington, VT: Ashgate, 2006), 285.

41 Peter Brown, *Authority and the Sacred: Aspects of the Christianization of the Roman World* (Cambridge, UK: Cambridge University Press, 1995), 39.

AFTERWORD

1 On how Christian bishops came to replace pagan intellectuals as the Roman aristocrats who held real power—seen, for example, in personal access to and influence over the emperor—see Peter Brown, *Power and Persuasion in Late Antiquity: Towards a Christian Empire* (Madison: University of Wisconsin Press, 1992).

2 As quoted in Raymond van Dam, *Remembering Constantine at the Milvian Bridge* (New York: Cambridge University Press, 2011), 22.

3 I have taken these quotations from Van Dam's insightful study, *Remembering Constantine at the Milvian Bridge*.

4 For a discussion of the role of Theodosius I in the loss of freedom and the rise of intolerance, see the readable account of Charles Freeman, *A.D. 381: Heretics, Pagans, and the Dawn of the Monotheistic State* (New York: Overlook Press, 2008). On the specific question of Christian opposition to Jews and Judaism, see James Carroll, *Constantine's Sword: The Church and the Jews; A History* (Boston: Houghton Mifflin, 2001).

APPENDIX

1 Rodney Stark. *The Rise of Christianity: How the Obscure, Marginal Jesus Movement Became the Dominant Religious Force in the Western World in a Few Centuries* (San Francisco: HarperSanFrancisco, 1996).

2 See the articles published as a collection in the *Journal of Early Christian Studies* 6 (1998), especially Elizabeth A. Castelli, "Gender, Theory, and *The Rise of Christianity*: A Response to Rodney Stark," 227–57.

3 See Castelli, "Gender, Theory, and *The Rise of Christianity*."

4 Candida Moss, *The Myth of Persecution: How Early Christians Invented a Story of Martyrdom* (San Francisco: HarperOne, 2014).

5 I am exceedingly grateful to James Bell for constructing a population growth calculator for me and for his interesting reflections on the rates of Christian growth.

Index

About the Author

BART D. EHRMAN is the author or editor of more than thirty books, including the *New York Times* bestsellers *Misquoting Jesus* and *How Jesus Became God*. Ehrman is a professor of religious studies at the University of North Carolina, Chapel Hill, and a leading authority on the New Testament and the history of early Christianity. He has been featured in *Time*, the *New Yorker*, and the *Washington Post*, and has appeared on NBC, CNN, the *Daily Show* with Jon Stewart, the History channel, the National Geographic channel, BBC, major NPR shows, and other top print and broadcast media outlets.